Richard Haskell holds a Ph.D. from Rensselaer Polytechnic Institute and is an engineering professor at Oakland University in Michigan. In addition, he has designed numerous microprocessor-based systems for industrial applications and written two other books in the Prentice-Hall computer series entitled *PET/CBM BASIC* and *TRS-80 Extended Color BASIC*.

BASIC

APPLE BASIC

RICHARD HASKELL

A SPECTRUM BOOK

PRENTICE-HALL, INC.
Englewood Cliffs, NJ 07632

Library of Congress Cataloging in Publication Data

Haskell, Richard E.
  Apple basic.

  "A Spectrum Book."
  Includes index.
    1. Apple II (Computer)—Programming.   2. Basic
(Computer program language)   I. Title.
QA76.8.A662H28   001.64'2   82-362
ISBN 0-13-039107-7   AACR2
ISBN 0-13-039099-2 (pbk.)

This Spectrum Book is available to business and organizations at a special discount when ordered in large quantities. For information, contact Prentice-Hall, Inc., General Publishing Division, Special Sales, Englewood Cliffs, N.J. 07632.

10 9 8 7 6 5 4 3 2 1

Editorial/production supervision by Kimberly Mazur
Interior design by Frank Moorman
Page layout by Fred Dahl
Manufacturing buyer: Cathie Lenard

Table 10.2 is based on the March 10, 1980 issue of *Time* Magazine

ISBN 0-13-039107-7

ISBN 0-13-039099-2 {PBK.}

Prentice-Hall International, Inc., *London*
Prentice-Hall of Australia Pty. Limited, *Sydney*
Prentice-Hall of Canada Inc., *Toronto*
Prentice-Hall of India Private Limited, *New Delhi*
Prentice-Hall of Japan, Inc., *Tokyo*
Prentice-Hall of Southeast Asia Pte. Ltd., *Singapore*
Whitehall Books Limited, *Wellington, New Zealand*

CONTENTS

PREFACE

Anyone planning to teach a BASIC programming course using Apple II personal computers is faced with a problem in selecting an appropriate text. The programming manuals provided by the manufacturer are generally more suitable for reference than for teaching, and standard textbooks on BASIC programming describe a BASIC language enough at variance with APPLESOFT BASIC to lead to considerable frustration on the part of the student. In addition, such texts are no help in learning to use the graphics capability of the Apple II, which is considerable and offers many interesting programs.

This book is designed to be used as a text for learning to program in BASIC using the Apple II computer. Like its companion texts, *PET BASIC* and *TRS-80 COLOR BASIC,* it is suitable for introductory programming courses at the high school, junior college, or university levels, as well as for independent study.

The strategy of this book is learning by doing. Step by step the student is led through all aspects of BASIC programming on an Apple II. All examples are illustrated with photographs taken from the screen of the computer. Many of the fundamental programming ideas are developed with examples involving graphics, which has the advantage of providing a direct visual picture of what the program is doing. It also provides examples that will be useful for anyone wish-ing to write Apple II programs in a specific applications area.

Chapter 1 introduces the Apple II keyboard and the idea of string variables. The use of low-resolution graphics follows in Chapter 2, while Chapter 3 talks about the general nature of BASIC programs and the operation of the cassette tape recorder and floppy-disk drive.

Chapter 4 covers numerical variables, arithmetic expressions, the Apple's built-in functions, and more graphics. The INPUT and GET statements are presented in Chapter 5 with examples, including the drawing of variable size boxes. Chapter 6 contains the IF . . . THEN statement and relational and logical operators.

The important topic of loops begins in Chapter 7 and continues in Chapter 8, where loops are used to display the American flag on the screen. Chapter 9, is devoted to the use of subroutines which enable the student to draw multiple figures of varying size.

The READ . . . DATA statement is delineated in Chapter 10, with a discussion of drawing bar graphs. Chapter 11 takes up the topic of arrays and the ON . . . GOSUB statement, and Chapter 12 describes string functions in detail, with examples for dealing a hand of cards. Chapter 13 deals with high-resolution graphics, including the use of shape tables, while

Chapter 14 explains the use of the PEEK and POKE statements, with reference to reading the keyboard, animated graphics, and making sounds with the Apple II. Chapter 15 describes the development of two complete programs: the Hangman word game and an Apple organ that plays three octaves of music on the keyboard. This chapter also includes a detailed example of how to use sequential disk files.

Students who complete this text will have a solid foundation in fundamental programming techniques and will have acquired the particular skills needed to program the Apple II computer with BASIC.

It is a pleasure to acknowledge my students of years past, who were the test subjects for many of the ideas in this book, and had to learn to program on a large computer with none of the graphics capability of the Apple II. Special thanks go to Carol Ashmore, who typed the manuscript with skill, patience, and good humor.

1

LEARNING TO USE
THE APPLE II KEYBOARD

There is only one way to learn to program a computer. You must write programs and run them. It is not possible to learn by reading about it because programming is an *action* activity. You must *do it!* This book is designed to help you learn to program in the BASIC programming language by actually using an Apple II Computer.

The Apple II computer is one of several popular personal computers (like the PET, the TRS-80, and the Atari) that are finding their way into an increasing number of homes and schools. All these personal computers will run programs written in the BASIC programming language. However, the BASIC programming language is implemented somewhat differently on each one, and this is particularly true with respect to graphics programming. This means that a BASIC program written for a PET computer will not, in general, run on an Apple II without some modification. It also means that if you are learning BASIC for the first time, you will find it easier if you use a book written specifically for the kind of computer you are using because you will not become frustrated by all of the little "exceptions" that apply only to your computer.

This book is written with the assumption that you have an Apple II computer available for use. Your computer may have a cassette recorder or a floppy disk drive attached to it. The cover on the computer may contain the words *Apple II* or *Apple II Plus* as shown in Figure 1.1.

Figure 1.1 (a) (top) An Apple II computer with an attached cassette recorder. (b) (bottom) An Apple II plus computer with an attached floppy disk drive.

(a)

(b)

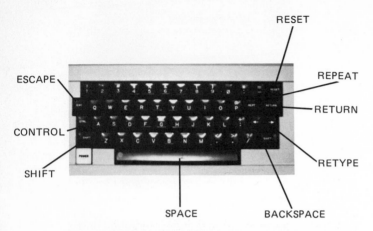

FIGURE 1.2 Special keys discussed in this chapter.

In this chapter you will become familiar with the use of the Apple II keyboard. In particular you will learn the meaning of the special keys shown in Figure 1.2.

You will also learn the following:

1. How to use the PRINT statement

2. What strings and string variables are

3. The difference between the immediate and deferred mode of execution

4. How to use the LIST and RUN commands

5. How to edit a statement using the backspace and retype keys.

Begin by turning on your Apple II. This is done with the switch on the left rear of the computer shown in Figure 1.3. Depending upon the specific computer configuration you have, the TV screen may look like any of the displays shown in Figure 1.4.

FIGURE 1.3 Turning on the Apple II.

If your screen display is like (a) in Figure 1.4, you have an Apple II Plus with a 3.2 Disk Operating System, Autostart ROM, and Applesoft BASIC in ROM. If (b) is displayed on your screen, you have an Apple II Plus with a 3.3 Disk Operating System; Autostart ROM, and Applesoft BASIC in ROM. If display (c) came up on your screen, you have an Apple II with Applesoft and no disk.

Your Apple II computer contains a *Read Only Memory* (called a ROM) that contains the BASIC interpreter and other systems programs. Older versions of the Apple II contain a *Monitor ROM* that puts you into the Apple II monitor program when you press the RESET key. (This is the only way to get these computers started after you turn the power switch on). An asterisk will appear on the lower left-hand side of the screen, indicating that you are in the monitor program. To get into BASIC you must type

CTRL B

RETURN

This means press key B while holding down the CTRL (Control) key, and then press the RETURN key.

If you are using a newer Apple II, it may contain an Autostat ROM. In this case when you turn on the Apple II, something will happen automatically without your having to press the RESET key. Exactly what happens will depend on whether you are using a disk drive and what language your Apple II has in its ROM.

Your Apple II may contain INTEGER BASIC in its ROM, or its ROM may contain the floating point APPLESOFT BASIC. (All Apple II Plus computers contain APPLESOFT.) An Apple II computer that has INTEGER BASIC in its ROM may be adapted to run APPLESOFT BASIC by inserting a special *firmware* card in one of the peripheral slots inside the computer. INTEGER BASIC is primarily a subset of the more powerful APPLESOFT BASIC. This book is based on the assumption that you are using APPLESOFT BASIC. However, many of the programs will also run using INTEGER BASIC. We will point out the statements not available in INTEGER BASIC as we go along.

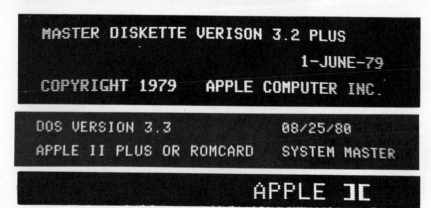

FIGURE 1.4 Possible initial screen displays using an Apple II.

To find out whether your Apple II is running IN-TEGER BASIC or APPLESOFT BASIC, look at the prompt character that precedes the blinking cursor. If the prompt character is a *greater than* sign (>), you are running INTEGER BASIC. If the prompt character is a *right bracket,* (]) you are running APPLESOFT BASIC. (See Figure 1.4 and the list of Apple II Computer configurations on page 2.)

In addition to the Read Only Memory (ROM), your Apple II computer contains some read/write memory called RAM (for *Random Access Memory*). The difference between ROM and RAM is that you can change the contents of a RAM location, but the contents of a ROM location are fixed and cannot be changed. Also when you turn off the power to your Apple II, the contents of the RAM locations are lost, but the contents of the ROM locations are retained. This is why the BASIC interpreter, located in ROM, is always there every time you turn on your Apple II. On the other hand, every program you write in RAM is lost whenever you turn off the power to your Apple II. This is why you must save your programs on a cassette tape or diskette if you wish to run them at a later time without having to type in the entire program again.

The amount of RAM that you have in your Apple II depends on the number of memory chips installed in the sockets shown in Figure 1.5. The more RAM you have, the larger the programs you can run, and the more data you can store in the computer. If you have *16K* of RAM, your Apple II contains 16,384 bytes of RAM (1K equals 1,024 bytes). A byte is 8 bits, whereas a bit is a 1 or a 0. Thus, for example, 10101101 in bit notation is a byte. It takes one byte to store a character in the Apple II.

If your Apple II contains 32K of RAM (two rows of chips in Figure 1.5), you actually have 32,768 bytes of

RAM. If all three rows of RAM sockets in Figure 1.5 are filled with chips, your Apple II contains 48K, or 49,152 bytes of RAM.

When the TV screen shows the prompt character (> or]) followed by a blinking cursor, the computer is ready and waiting for you to type in something. Try typing your name and pressing the **RETURN** key. If your name is JOHN, you should see something like that shown in Figure 1.6.

FIGURE 1.6   A SYNTAX ERROR occurs when you type an invalid BASIC command.

Note that the message **?SYNTAX ERROR** appears on the screen and that you heard a beep sound when you pressed the RETURN key. This is because JOHN is not a valid BASIC command, and the computer can respond only to BASIC commands that it understands. You will learn all these valid BASIC commands in this book. However, any time you type a command that is invalid for any reason, such as misspelling, the Apple II will respond with a beep and a ?SYNTAX ERROR message. You cannot hurt the Apple II by pressing the wrong key. If it doesn't like what you typed, it will just beep and display ?SYNTAX ERROR on the screen.

FIGURE 1.5   Each row of RAM chips in the Apple II contains 16K bytes of memory.

STRINGS AND THE PRINT STATEMENT

Type the word **HOME**, and then press the RETURN key. This will clear the screen and move the cursor to the upper left-hand corner of the screen. (The statement HOME will not work in INTEGER BASIC. Instead type **CALL -936.** This will also work in APPLESOFT BASIC.) Now type **PRINT "THIS IS A STRING"**, followed by RETURN. The result should be like Figure 1.7. Note that the computer immediately printed the words **THIS IS A STRING.** Any sequence of characters enclosed between quotation marks ('' '') is called a *string*. If you type the word PRINT followed by a string, the computer will immediately print this string (with-out the quotation marks) on the screen. This is called the *immediate mode* of execution.

Any characters can be included in a string. For example, if you type **PRINT "***** ***** *****"**, the computer will print this line of asterisks just as you typed it in the string, as shown in Figure 1.8.

Note that you must press RETURN at the end of each statement (such as PRINT) or command (such as RUN). The Apple II does not look at what you have typed on a line until you press RETURN. When you press RE-TURN, the Apple II then deciphers what you typed on the line and decides what to do.

FIGURE 1.7   Using the PRINT statement in the immediate mode of execution.

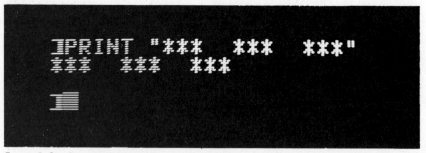

FIGURE 1.8   Strings can contain any characters.

DEFERRED MODE OF EXECUTION

If a BASIC statement like PRINT is preceded by a line number (such as 10), the statement is *not* executed immediately; its execution is deferred until the command RUN is typed. For example, Figure 1.9 shows how to print a line of asterisks using the deferred mode of execution. When BASIC statements have line numbers, these statements are *stored* in the computer. They can be RUN at any time. If you type **RUN** again, the computer will again display the line of asterisks. Try it.

FIGURE 1.9   PRINT statement using the deferred mode of execution.

You can always look to see what BASIC statements you currently have stored in the Apple II by typing **LIST**. Try it. You should have listed the single PRINT statement number 10 shown in Figure 1.10.

FIGURE 1.10 The LIST command will list all BASIC statements stored in memory.

The question mark (?) can be used as an abbreviation for the word PRINT. (This will not work in INTEGER BASIC.) Try typing **? "THIS WILL STILL PRINT"**. In the deferred mode, if you type

10 ? "HELLO"

RUN

the word **HELLO** will be printed. Note that if you now type **LIST**, the word **PRINT** has been substituted for the question mark (see Figure 1.11).

```
]? "THIS WILL STILL PRINT"
THIS WILL STILL PRINT

]10 ? "HELLO"

]RUN
HELLO

]LIST

10  PRINT "HELLO"
```

FIGURE 1.11 The question mark (?) can be used as a substitute for the word PRINT.

If more than one PRINT statement is stored in the Apple II, all of the PRINT statements will be executed in ascending numerical order by line number when the program is RUN. For example, if you type

10 PRINT "******"

20 PRINT "******"

30 PRINT "**   **"

40 PRINT "**   **"

50 PRINT "******"

60 PRINT "******"

RUN

you should obtain the result shown in Figure 1.12.

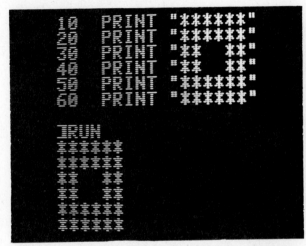

FIGURE 1.12 Simple figures can be drawn by printing a string for each row in the figure.

As a second example, Figure 1.13 shows how to make the Apple II print the name JEFF in block letters.

FIGURE 1.13 Example of using PRINT statements to print your name in block letters.

```
]LIST

10  PRINT "        JJ  EEEEEE  FFFFFF
            FFFFFF"
20  PRINT "        JJ  EEEEEE  FFFFFF
            FFFFFF"
30  PRINT "        JJ  EE      FF
            FF      "
40  PRINT "        JJ  EEEEE   FFFFF
            FFFFF  "
50  PRINT "        JJ  EEEEE   FFFFF
            FFFFF  "
60  PRINT "JJ  JJ  EE      FF
            FF      "
70  PRINT "JJJJJJ  EEEEEE  FF
            FF      "
80  PRINT "JJJJJJ  EEEEEE  FF
            FF      "
```

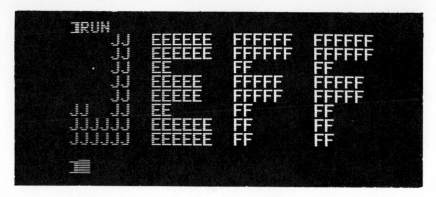

FIGURE 1.3 (continued).

EXERCISE 1-1

Make the Apple II print your name in block letters, using the technique shown in Figure 1.13.

EDITING WITH THE BACKSPACE AND RETYPE KEYS

The two keys shown in Figure 1.14 can be used to make corrections or change a line after you have typed it. When you press the BACKSPACE key, the cursor moves one space to the left. When you press the RE-TYPE key, the cursor moves one space to the right. However, these are *not* pure cursor moves.

The BACKSPACE key effectively erases any character that it backspaces over. Although the character is not erased from the screen until the RETURN key is pressed, the BACKSPACE causes the computer to forget the character. For example, type **10 PRINT "ABCDEF"**, but *do not* press the RETURN key. Now press the BACKSPACE key 4 times so that the cursor is over the **D**. This will cause the computer to forget the characters **DEF"**. To verify this, press RETURN. The line you just typed should change to **10 PRINT "ABC**.

FIGURE 1.14 The backspace and retype keys are used for editing a line.

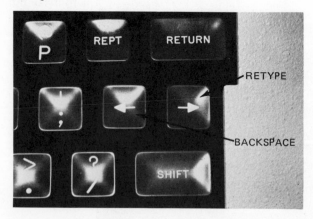

The RETYPE key causes the character under the cursor to be retyped. For example, suppose you type **10 PRUNT**, and you realize that you typed a **U** instead of an **I** in the word PRINT. The cursor is positioned just to the right of the **T**. Press the BACKSPACE key 3 times so the cursor is over the **U**. Now press key **I**. This changes the **U** to an **I**. However, you have effectively erased the characters **NT** by backspacing over them. You can retype easily by just pressing the RETYPE key twice. Try it.

Suppose you pressed the RETURN key before you noticed the mistake. There are a couple of things you can do. You can just type the entire line over again. Any time you type a BASIC statement beginning with a particular line number, the new statement will replace any previous statement having the same line number. However, there is an easier way to erase an entire line in a BASIC program: if you type the number **50** and press the RETURN key immediately (no spaces), line 50 will be completely erased from the program.

Another way to edit a line that has already been stored in the computer is to use the ESC (ESCAPE) key with the I, J, K, M keys, which produce the pure cursor moves shown in Figure 1.15.* Once you press the ESC key, pressing keys, I, J, K, or M will cause the cursor to

---

*The ESC I, J, K, M pure cursor movement keys may not work in INTEGER BASIC. In this case you may have to use ESC A, ESC B, ESC C, and ESC D to achieve the same effects. The difference is that in the ESC A series, both the ESC key and the directional key must be pressed for every cursor movement, and in the ESC I series, ESCAPE must be pushed only once to move the cursor in any direction any number of times.

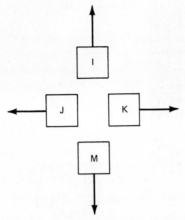

Figure 1.15 After pressing the ESC key the keys I,J,K, and M will cause pure cursor movements in the directions shown.

move up, left, right, or down, as shown in Figure 1.15. This ESC mode will stay in effect until some other key is pressed.*

Suppose you want to correct the spelling in the line **40 PRUNT "HELLO"**, which is already stored in the computer, so the cursor is below this line on the screen. You can do this by performing the following steps:

1. Press the ESC key

2. Press key I until the cursor is on the line to be edited

3. If necessary, press key J until the cursor is over the first character on the line (the **4**)

4. Press the RETYPE key 5 times until the cursor is over the **U** (this will retype the characters **40 PR**)

5. Type I to correct the misselling

6. Press the RETYPE key 10 times to retype the rest of the line

7. Press the RETURN key. The correction has now been made.

You should try using the BACKSPACE, RETYPE and ESC I, J, K, M keys to become familiar with them, as they will save you a lot of work when you are making corrections in your programs. Another way to speed up the retyping of a long string of characters is to use the REPT (REPEAT) key. If you press the RETYPE key and hold down the REPT key, the cursor will move rapidly to the right, just as if you were pressing the RETYPE key repeatedly. In fact the REPT key can be used with any key to repeat a character. Try it.

STRING VARIABLES

As you have seen, any sequence of characters enclosed between quotation marks is called a string. Thus, for example, the following are strings:

"HELLO"

"**"**

"THIS IS A STRING"

Any character can be included in a string. To the Apple II a blank space is just another character when included in a string.

A string can be given a special name, sometimes called a *string variable,* which is then used to refer to it. The name of a string must start with a letter and end with a dollar sign ($). It can contain one or two characters, the second of which can be either a letter or a number. Thus, the following are valid string names:

A$
B3$

AX$
MA$
Z7$

Actually, APPLESOFT will allow you to use longer names, like HOUSE$ and BOOT$. However, it only uses the *first two* letters to identify the string. Thus, APPLESOFT would consider the two names BALL$ and BAD$ to be the same, since it looks at only the first two letters, BA.†

The reason for using longer names is to make the name more meaningful to the programmer, not to APPLESOFT. However, there are other reasons for keeping your names short. Shorter names will use less memory, and, in addition to the necessity for names with two unique first characters, there is another problem with long names. The Apple II has a number of *reserved* words that it is constantly looking for like RUN and LIST. A complete list of reserved words is given in Appendix A. If *any* of these occur *anywhere* within a name that you make up, your program will not run properly.

*ESC F and ESC E produce special results: Pressing ESC F will clear the screen from the current cursor position to the bottom of the screen. Pressing ESC E will clear the current line from the cursor to the right margin.

†INTEGER BASIC uses all characters in a name.

The equal sign (=) can be used in BASIC to *assign* a particular string to a particular string variable, or name.* Thus, for example, you could type **10 A$="THIS IS A STRING"**. From now on the name A$ is considered to be the same thing as the string **"THIS IS A STRING"**. You can, for example, print it with the PRINT statement **20 PRINT A$**. Try this. You should get the result shown in Figure 1.16.

FIGURE 1.16   Using string variables in a PRINT statement.

The box that we drew in Figure 1.12 could be drawn by defining the two strings

10 A$="*****"

20 B$="**   **"

and then printing strings in the following order

30 PRINT A$

40 PRINT A$

50 PRINT B$

60 PRINT B$

70 PRINT A$

80 PRINT A$

This is illustrated in Figure 1.17.

FIGURE 1.17   Drawing a box using string variables.

*Some versions of BASIC require you to use the word LET in an assignment statement. Thus, you should write **10 LET A$="THIS IS A STRING."** The use of the word LET is optional in APPLESOFT BASIC. We will not use it.

Each line on the Apple II screen contains 40 character positions. However, the Apple II is able to process up to about 240 characters per statement in APPLESOFT (about 120 in INTEGER BASIC). This means that you can use a maximum of about six screen lines for any APPLESOFT BASIC statement (about three lines for INTEGER BASIC). Thus, for example, if you are defining a string using a statement such as **10 A$=" ------** and you get to the end of the line on the screen, you just keep on typing. DO NOT PRESS RETURN. The Apple II will automatically continue the statement on the next line. When you finish the statement you must then press RETURN.

EXERCISE 1-2

Write and run a BASIC program that will print the figures from Figure 1.18 on the screen.

FIGURE 1.18.

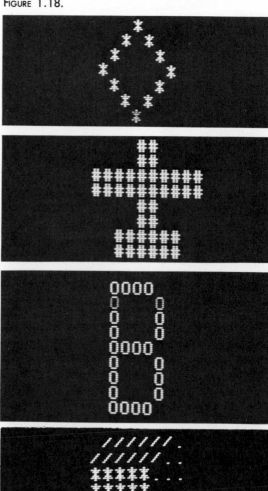

LEARNING TO USE
LOW-RESOLUTION GRAPHICS

In Chapter 1 you learned to make simple block letters using the PRINT statement by printing a series of letters or other special characters. In this chapter you will learn how to draw block letters using the low-resolution graphics capability of the Apple II. A separate high-resolution graphics feature available on the Apple II will be described in Chapter 13.

In this chapter you will learn how to

1. get in and out of the low-resolution graphics mode by using the statements GR and TEXT
2. plot various colored dots by using the statements COLOR and PLOT
3. use the statements HLIN and VLIN to draw horizontal and vertical lines
4. draw your name in large, colored block letters.

THE LOW-RESOLUTION GRAPHICS MODE

To enter the low-resolution graphics mode, type **GR**. When you do this, the screen will clear, and the cursor will move to the lower left-hand corner of the screen.

In the low-resolution graphics mode the screen is considered to be divided into a 40 × 40 grid with four lines of text at the bottom of the screen as shown in Figure 2.1.* The column positions of the grid are numbered 0 through 39 from left to right. This is called the X position or X coordinate. The row positions of the grid

are numbered 0 through 39 from top to bottom. This is called the Y position or Y coordinate. Any one of the 1,600 (40 × 40 = 1,600) small squares or blocks on the grid can be identified by giving its X and Y coordinates. For example, in Figure 2.1 the shaded block is located at the coordinates X=25, Y=15.

You can plot a colored spot at any of the 1,600 grid positions on the screen. These spots can be one of the 16 different colors shown in Figure 2.2. To set a particular color, type **COLOR = C** where C can be any number from 0–15. For example, the statement **COLOR = 13** will set the color to yellow, according to Figure 2.2. All subsequent spots plotted will be yellow until a new COLOR statement is executed.

*The four lines of text at the bottom of the screen can be replaced by 8 more rows of low-resolution graphics spots making a 48 × 40 grid on the screen. The method of doing this will be described in Chapter 14.

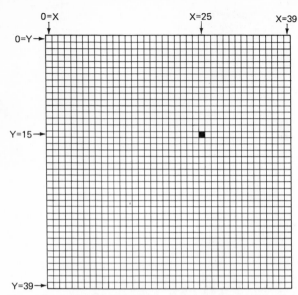

FIGURE 2.1 The low resolution graphics mode divides the screen into a 40 x 40 grid with four text lines at bottom.

When you type the statement **GR** to enter the low-resolution graphics mode, the value of COLOR is automatically set to zero (black). Therefore, to plot any spots on the screen you must first change the value of COLOR to a number corresponding to another color.

Once you have set the color, you can plot a spot located at coordinates, X,Y by typing **PLOT, X,Y**. For example, typing

    GR
    COLOR = 15: PLOT 25, 15

will plot a white spot at coordinates X = 25, Y = 15, as shown in Figure 2.3.

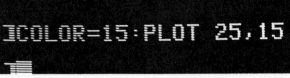

FIGURE 2.3 PLOT 25,15 will plot a spot at location X = 25, Y = 15.

In order to get out of the low-resolution graphics mode, type **TEXT**. This will cause the Apple II to return to the full screen text mode (24 lines of 40 characters each) with the cursor on the last line of the screen. However, the portion of the screen that was associated with the 40 × 40 grid in the low-resolution graphics mode will now display the strange-looking ''garbage'' shown in Figure 2.4. The screen can be cleared by typing **HOME**.

Return to the low-resolution graphics mode by typing **GR** again. Now type **COLOR=15: PLOT 20,20: PLOT 21,21: PLOT 22,22**. The screen should display 3 white spots located along a diagonal line as shown in Figure 2.5.

The low-resolution graphics commands can be used in the deferred mode of execution by including them in a BASIC program. For example, return to the text mode by typing

    TEXT
    HOME

FIGURE 2.2 Sixteen colors numbered 0-15 can be plotted using low resolution graphics.

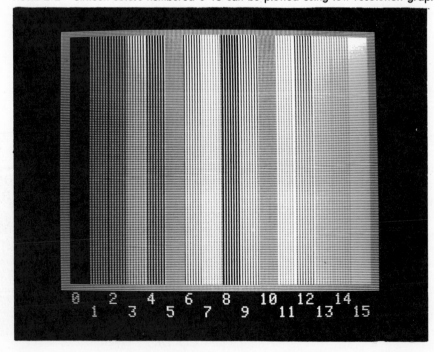

0 Black
1 Magenta
2 Dark Blue
3 Purple
4 Dark Green
5 Grey
6 Medium Blue
7 Light Blue
8 Brown
9 Orange
10 Grey
11 Pink
12 Green
13 Yellow
14 Aqua
15 White

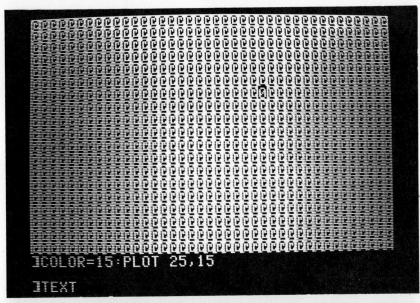

```
]COLOR=15:PLOT 25,15

]TEXT
```

FIGURE 2.4 The statement TEXT from the low-resolution graphics mode returns to the text mode, leaving the screen filled with "garbage."

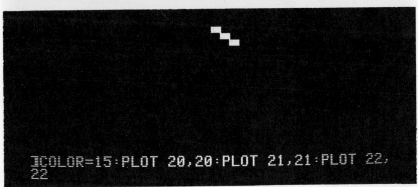

```
]COLOR=15:PLOT 20,20:PLOT 21,21:PLOT 22,
22
```

FIGURE 2.5 Multiple spots can be plotted with multiple PLOT statements.

and then type in the following program.

```
10 GR
20 COLOR = 15
30 PLOT 15,30: PLOT 16,31: PLOT 17,32
40 PLOT 18,33
50 PLOT 19,32: PLOT 20,31: PLOT 21,30
```

This program should plot the V-shaped figure shown in Figure 2.6. The listing of this program and the result of its execution are shown in Figure 2.7. Note that after this program is run, you are still in the low-resolution graphics mode. The only way to get out is to type TEXT.

FIGURE 2.6 Plotting seven spots can produce a V-shaped figure.

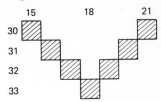

FIGURE 2.7 (a) Listing of program to plot V-shaped figure and (b) result of running the program shown in (a).

```
LIST
10   GR
20   COLOR= 15
30   PLOT 15,30: PLOT 16,31: PLOT
     17,32
40   PLOT 18,33
50   PLOT 19,32: PLOT 20,31: PLOT
     21,30
]
```

(a)

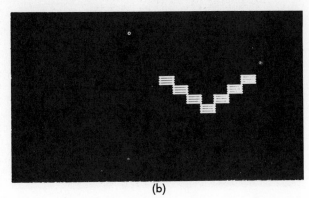

(b)

DRAWING HORIZONTAL AND VERTICAL LINES

The BASIC statements HLIN and VLIN can be used to draw horizontal and vertical lines in low-resolution graphics.

HLIN

Enter the low-resolution graphics mode by typing **GR**, and set the color to white by typing **COLOR = 15**. Then type **HLIN 5,30 AT 15**. This will cause a horizontal line to be drawn from X = 5 to X = 30 at row Y = 15 as shown in Figure 2.8.

In general, the statement **HLIN X1, X2, AT Y** will plot a horizontal line from X = X1 to X = X2 at row Y. The values of X1 and X2 must be in the range 0–39, and the value of Y must be in the range 0–47; otherwise, the error message **?ILLEGAL QUANTITY ERROR** will be displayed on the screen when the computer tries to execute the HLIN statement.

Remember that the color of a line is determined by the last number used in the COLOR statement **COLOR = number**. Thus, for example, if you type the statement

```
COLOR = 13
HLIN 20, 30 AT 5
COLOR = 6
HLIN 0,39 AT 20
```

the computer will plot a short yellow line in row 5 and a long blue line in row 20. Try it.

EXERCISE 2-1.

Plot the following horizontal lines on the screen:

a. a blue line from X = 10 to X = 35 at Y = 3

b. a yellow line 8 spots long starting at column number 10 on row number 12

c. a pink line all the way across the top of the screen

VLIN

Clear the screen by typing

TEXT

HOME

and then reenter the low-resolution graphics mode by typing **GR**. Set the color to white by typing **COLOR = 15**. Then type **VLIN 5,30 AT 15**. This will cause a vertical line to be drawn from row Y = 5 to row Y = 30 at column X = 15 as shown in Figure 2.9.

FIGURE 2.9   VLIN 5,30 AT 15 will plot a vertical line from Y = 5 to Y = 30 at column X = 15.

FIGURE 2.8   HLIN 5,30 at 15 will plot a horizontal line from X = 5 to X = 30 at row Y = 15.

In general, the statement **VLIN Y1, Y2 AT X** will plot a vertical line from Y = Y1 to Y = Y2 at column X. The values of Y1 and Y2 must be in the range 0– 47, and the value of X must be in the range 0–39; otherwise, the error message **?ILLEGAL QUANTITY ERROR** will be displayed on the screen when the computer tries to execute the VLIN statement.

The value of Y2 may be less than the value of Y1, in which case the vertical line will be drawn from bottom to top on the screen. To see how this works, try typing **VLIN 39,0 AT 20.**

EXERCISE 2-2

Plot the following vertical lines on the screen:

a. a green line from Y = 3 to Y = 15 at X = 2

b. a purple line 15 blocks high with the top at row 10, located in column 18

c. a magenta line along the entire right edge of the screen

DRAWING YOUR NAME

Suppose you want to draw your name in large block letters on the screen. The first step is to draw your name on quadrille paper the way you want it to appear on the 40 × 40 grid on the screen. For example, Figure 2.10 shows the name JEFF sketched on a 40 × 40 grid. Some of the column and row numbers are written next to each letter.

From Figure 2.10 you can see that to plot the letter J the computer must execute the statements

PLOT 2,19

HLIN 2,8, AT 20

VLIN 10,19 AT 8

Similarly, to plot the letter E the statements

VLIN 10,20 AT 11

HLIN 12,17 AT 10

HLIN 12,15 AT 15

HLIN 12,17 AT 20

must be executed. The statements

VLIN 10,20 AT 20

HLIN 21,26 AT 10

HLIN 21,24 AT 14

FIGURE 2.10   Sketch your name on a 40 x 40 grid in order to define the coordinates of all letter segments.

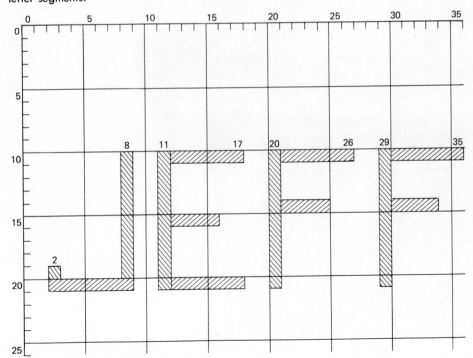

will plot the first F, and the second F can be plotted with the statements

VLIN 10,20 AT 29

HLIN 30,35 AT 10

HLIN 30,33 AT 14.

You can type these statements in the immediate mode and watch each letter being plotted one segment at a time. Alternatively, you can return to the TEXT mode and type in the entire program using line numbers. Then you can execute the program by typing RUN.

A listing of this program as it would be run in the deferred mode is shown in Figure 2.11. Line 20 enters the low-resolution graphics mode. Each letter is plotted in a different color. Lines 30–60 plot a green J. Lines 70–110 plot a yellow E. Lines 120–150 plot a pink F, and lines 160–190 plot a blue F. The result of running this program is shown in Figure 2.12.

```
]LIST
20    GR
30    COLOR= 12
40    PLOT 2,19
50    HLIN 2,8 AT 20
60    VLIN 10,19 AT 8
70    COLOR= 13
80    VLIN 10,20 AT 11
90    HLIN 12,17 AT 10
100   HLIN 12,15 AT 15
110   HLIN 12,17 AT 20
120   COLOR= 11
130   VLIN 10,20 AT 20
140   HLIN 21,26 AT 10
150   HLIN 21,24 AT 14
160   COLOR= 6
170   VLIN 10,20 AT 29
180   HLIN 30,35 AT 10
190   HLIN 30,33 AT 14
```

FIGURE 2.11   Listing of program to plot the name JEFF in block letters.

EXERCISE 2-3

Write a program that will plot your name in block letters on the screen. Make each letter a different color.

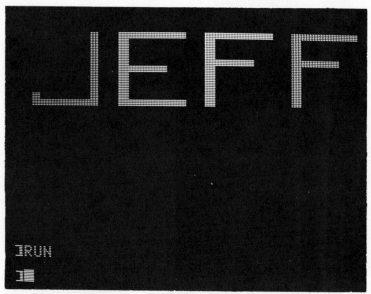

FIGURE 2.12   Result of running the program shown in Figure 2.11.

LEARNING TO PROGRAM
IN BASIC

In Chapter 2 you learned how to use low-resolution graphics to draw simple block figures on the Apple II. Graphics can be used to advantage in almost all types of computer programs to make them more interesting and appealing, and you will continue to learn more about incorporating them to enhance your programs throughout this book. However, in this chapter we will begin to look at some of the ideas associated with writing BASIC programs.

In this chapter you will learn

1. to use the cassette tape recorder or floppy-disk drive to preserve your program
2. the commands NEW, SAVE, LOAD, and CONT
3. what happens when you press CTRL C
4. the general structure of a BASIC program
5. the statements GOTO, STOP, END, and REM.

BASIC PROGRAMMING LANGUAGE

The programming language BASIC was developed at Dartmouth College in 1963. The word BASIC stands for Beginners All-purpose Symbolic Instruction Code, and the language was designed to be easy to learn and easy to use. Over the years the BASIC language has been extended and modified by various manufacturers. APPLESOFT BASIC is similar to the BASIC that is found on most microcomputers today.

The benefits of BASIC are that it is readily intelligible and available: it is built into your Apple II. For all its simplicity you will find that APPLESOFT BASIC is quite powerful and will allow you to write high performance programs fairly easily.

There are, however, certain drawbacks to APPLE-SOFT BASIC. First of all, it is slow. You probably will not notice this until you try to draw a large picture quickly. The reason it is slow is that the Apple II contains a BASIC *interpreter* in its ROM. This means that each time you RUN your program the Apple II decodes and executes each of your BASIC statements one by one. This takes time.

Assembly Language

To speed up the execution time of a program considerably, you must write the program in *assembly language* rather than in BASIC. This is a lower-level language that the Apple II can execute directly. The "brain" of the Apple II is a 40-pin chip called a 6502 microprocessor, which is shown in Figure 3.1. This chip enables the Apple II—and any other microcomputer that has it—to decode and execute a 6502 assembly language program. The PET microcomputer also uses the 6502 microprocessor, but the Radio Shack TRS-80 uses the Z80 microprocessor, which executes a completely different assembly language. The Radio Shack TRS-80 Color Computer uses a 6809 microprocessor, which executes still a different assembly language.

FIGURE 3.1   The 6502 microprocessor is the "brain" of the Apple II computer.

A short assembly language program must be used to produce musical tones on the Apple II speaker. We will show you how to store such a program in the Apple II memory in Chapter 14.

Structured Programming

You may hear that BASIC is not a very "well-structured" language and that other languages, such as PASCAL, are "better" in some sense. While it is true that PASCAL almost forces you to write well-structured programs, it is also true that well-structured programs can be written in any language, including BASIC. In this book we will try to minimize any bad pro-

gramming habits that BASIC might encourage and show you how to write good programs in BASIC.

Learning the Language

There are two aspects to learning computer programming. The first is learning a programming language. This is the easy part. The second is learning how to write programs to accomplish a particular task. This is the hard part. Learning a computer language consists of learning the *syntax* and *semantics* of the various statements that make up the language. *Syntax* refers to the rules for forming the various statements: For example, the PRINT statement must be spelled PRINT, and a string must be enclosed between quotation marks. We will look at more details of the PRINT statement in the next chapter. *Semantics* refers to what a particular statement does. For example, the statement PRINT followed by a string will print the string on the screen.

Learning How to Write Programs

Learning how to write a program to accomplish a particular task is the hard part of computer programming. You must determine what you have to tell the computer to get it to do what you want. You will find that the computer *always* does exactly what you tell it to do. However, what you tell it is often not what you think you are telling it. This will lead to errors that are sometimes hard to find. The best way to avoid many of these errors is to think through the problem carefully before you start to write any BASIC statements. Understanding exactly what you want to do is a major step in solving a problem.

It turns out that there are only a few basic rules for telling a computer what to do. Computers like to do the same thing over and over again. This is accomplished in a computer program by means of a *loop*. We will look at a simple loop later in this chapter. More detailed discussions of loops are given in Chapters 7 and 8. The other thing that computers like to do is to make a simple choice between two alternatives. This process of making choices will be described in Chapter 6. Any computer program can be constructed by combining loops with the process of making simple choices.

SAVING YOUR PROGRAMS

Your Apple II may have either a cassette tape recorder or a floppy-disk drive connected to it. These devices store your programs on a cassette tape or a floppy disk respectively. A floppy disk drive is more expensive than a cassette tape recorder, but it is much more convenient because you can store many programs on a disk and retrieve any one quickly by name. In this section we will show you how to save a program on either a cassette tape or a floppy disk.

NEW. Type **NEW** followed by RETURN. This will clear any BASIC program that you have stored in the computer. You should always type NEW before you begin typing in a new program. Failure to do this may cause parts of old programs to be combined with your new program.

Now type in the following program.

```
10 A$="333"
20 B$="666666"
30 C$="999999999"
40 PRINT A$
50 PRINT B$
60 PRINT C$
```

This program listing and its execution are shown in Figure 3.2.

FIGURE 3.2 This program prints three strips of numbers.

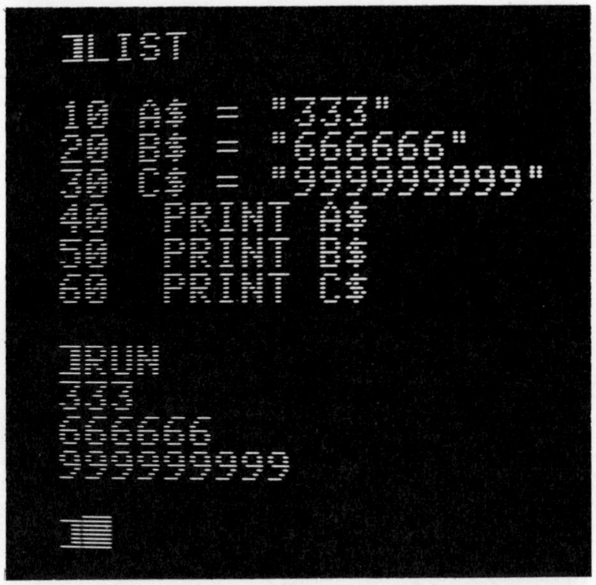

Cassette Tape Recorder. Suppose you wish to save the program shown in Figure 3.2 on a cassette tape. First make sure that the tape recorder is properly connected to the back of the Apple II and that the volume control is set near the maximum volume. Rewind the tape if necessary, and then put the recorder into the RECORD mode. The tape should now be moving. Wait for any leader to pass, then type **SAVE** followed by RETURN. The blinking cursor should disappear.

After a few seconds you should hear a beep. This means that the Apple II has started to store your program on the cassette tape. When it has finished writing your program on the tape (usually less than a minute), you will hear a second beep, and the blinking cursor will return to the sceen.

Your program is now stored on the cassette tape. To verify this, type **NEW**, which will clear your BASIC program in the Apple II. For example, if you now type **LIST**, you will find that nothing gets listed. To retrieve your program, you must load it back in from the cassette tape.

Rewind the tape and press the PLAY key on the tape recorder. Now type **LOAD** followed by RETURN. The cursor should disappear, and after a few seconds you should hear a beep. Your program is now being loaded into the Apple II. When you hear a second beep and the blinking cursor returns to the screen, your program has been completely loaded. You can see the program listing now by typing **LIST**, and you can execute the program by typing **RUN**.

Floppy-Disk Drive. If your Apple II has a floppy-disk drive connected to it, you can save your program on a floppy disk by typing **SAVE THREE STRINGS** if THREE STRINGS is the name of the program. You can make up any names you want for your programs. The red light on the disk drive will light up, and the disk drive will make a whirring sound for a few seconds while your program is being written on the disk.

After the red light on the disk drive goes out, type **CATALOG**. This will list all of the programs that are stored on the disk, and it should now contain the name **THREE STRINGS**. To confirm that your program is really on the disk, type **NEW**, which will clear your BASIC program in the Apple II. If you now type **LIST**, you will find that nothing gets listed. To retrieve your program from the disk, type **LOAD THREE STRINGS**. The red light on the disk drive will come on, and you will hear the whirring sound again as your program is loaded into the Apple II memory from the disk. When the red light goes out, your program will be completely loaded. You can see the program listing by typing **LIST**, and you can execute the program by typing **RUN**.

It is possible to both LOAD and RUN a program with a single command. Typing **RUN THREE STRINGS** will make the Apple II LOAD the program **THREE STRINGS** from the floppy disk and then execute the program as soon as it is completely loaded into the Apple II memory.

Add the statement **70 GOTO 40** to the program shown in Figure 3.2. If the program in Figure 3.2 is in the Apple II memory, you can add the above statement simply by typing it as shown. Type **LIST** in order to see the entire program. It should look like Figure 3.3.

FIGURE 3.3   Program to display a continuous sequence of three number strings.

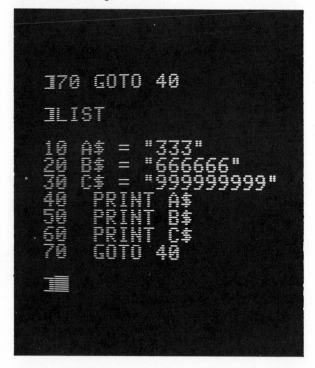

The statement **70 GOTO 40** means exactly what it says. When statement number 70 is executed, it simply branches back and executes statement number 40 again. This is a *loop* that continues indefinitely as shown in Figure 3.4

FIGURE 3.4   An indefinite loop that prints figures until you press CTRL C.

40 PRINT A$	prints three 3s
50 PRINT B$	prints six 6s
60 PRINT C$	prints nine 9s
70 GOTO 40	

Now RUN this program. As you can see, the three strings A$, B$, and C$ are being printed endlessly. To stop this program, press CTRL C (hold the CTRL key down and then press key C). Note that you can get a **BREAK** message, as shown in Figure 3.5.

FIGURE 3.5   Stop a program by pressing CTRL C.

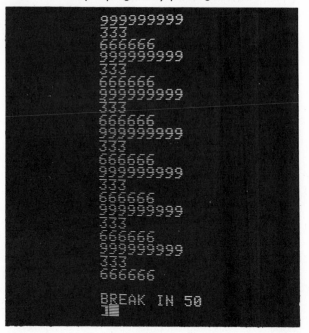

CONT

The program shown in Figure 3.3 displays three 3s, six 6s, and nine 9s over and over again. Every time the program is RUN, it will start with the three 3s. This can be seen in Figure 3.6, where the program was stopped by pressing CTRL C just after displaying the six 6s. Note

FIGURE 3.6   RUN causes the program to start at the beginning.

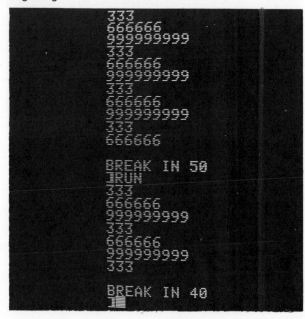

that when the program starts again, it displays the three 3s.

If a program has been stopped, the statement CONT can be used to continue the program where it left off.* This is illustrated in Figure 3.7 where the program was again stopped just after displaying the six 6s. Note that after typing **CONT** the program restarts at the point of displaying the nine 9s.

STOP†

The statement **STOP** can be included in a BASIC program. This will have the same effect as pressing **CTRL C**. This can be very useful in debugging (i.e. finding the errors in) a program that doesn't work properly. You can just insert a STOP statement and then check what the program has done up to that point. You can then resume execution of the program by typing **CONT**.

END

The END statement is traditionally used to stop a BASIC program at the end of the program. It does not cause a BREAK message as the STOP statement does. in APPLESOFT BASIC the END statement is optional.‡ As you have seen we have not been using the END statement in our programs. A BASIC program in the Apple II will automatically stop if there are no more statements to execute.

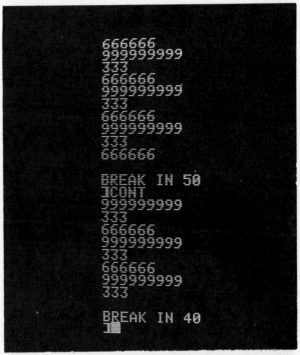

FIGURE **3.7** CONT causes the program to start where it left off.

THE STRUCTURE OF A BASIC PROGRAM

Sequence Numbers

A BASIC program consists of a sequence of BASIC statements. Each line of a BASIC program must begin with a *sequence number*. When the program is executed, the statement with the lowest sequence number is executed first. Additional statements are then executed in the order of increasing sequence number.

When you write a BASIC program you should increment your sequence numbers by 10. That is, your program should look like this.

```
10 first statement
20 second statement
30 third statement
        •
        •
        •
      etc.
```

The reason for doing this is that if you later want to insert a new statement between the second and third statement you can just type

```
25 new statement
```

---

*Use CON in INTEGER BASIC.

†Not available in INTEGER BASIC.

‡The END statement is required in INTEGER BASIC.

This new statement will be inserted between statement number 20 and statement number 30. If you had not left any room between the second and third statements, you would have had to renumber all of your statements!

If you think that you may want to add some new statements at the beginning of your program, it would be a good idea to start your program with a sequence number of 100 and then continue with 110, 120, 130, and so on.

REM

A good statement to include at the beginning of your program is a REMark statement. This statement consists of the three letters REM. The remainder of the line can then be used for any kind of remark. These remarks are ignored by the Apple II when the program is executed. Their only purpose is to make the program easier to understand. For example, in the program shown in Figure 2.11, you may want to add the statement **5 REM PROGRAM TO PRINT THE NAME JEFF USING LOW-RESOLUTION GRAPHICS** shown in Figure 3.8. Note that in the figure, the remark takes up three lines on the screen.

As mentioned earlier, any BASIC statement can use more than one screen line. When you type the remark

in Figure 3.8, you must keep on typing when you get to the end of the first line. *Do not type* RETURN at the end of the first line or you will terminate the statement at that point and have to start the next line with a new sequence number and another REM statement.

Multiple Statements Per line

APPLESOFT BASIC allows you to write more than one BASIC statement per line by separating the statements with a colon (:). By a *line* we mean the characters from the line (or sequence) number to the RETURN, which may consist of several screen lines. This can be an advantage for a number of reasons: 1) It allows you to group a number of short related statements together; 2) it allows you to include remarks on the same line as a BASIC statement; and 3) it saves some memory by reducing the number of sequence numbers in the program. Only the *first* BASIC statement on a line has a sequence number. The remaining BASIC statements on the line are simply separated by a colon.

There are, however, some disadvantages to writing more than one statement per line. Used indiscriminately, it can result in a program that is very difficult to read and understand. You will not be able to branch (for example, by using a GOTO statement) to a statement that starts in the middle of a line, since it will not have a sequence number. Finally, it is more difficult to insert a new statement between existing multiple

FIGURE 3.8   Use of the REM statement to make *remarks* in a program.

```
]LIST
10   REM    PROGRAM TO PRINT THE NA
     ME JEFF USING LOW RESOLUTION
     GRAPHICS
20   GR
30   COLOR= 12
40   PLOT 2,19
50   HLIN 2,8 AT 20
60   VLIN 10,19 AT 8
70   COLOR= 13
80   VLIN 10,20 AT 11
90   HLIN 12,17 AT 10
100   HLIN 12,15 AT 15
110   HLIN 12,17 AT 20
120   COLOR= 11
130   VLIN 10,20 AT 20
140   HLIN 21,26 AT 10
150   HLIN 21,24 AT 14
160   COLOR= 6
170   VLIN 10,20 AT 29
180   HLIN 30,35 AT 10
190   HLIN 30,33 AT 14
```

FIGURE 3.9   Multiple statements on a single line are separated by a colon (:).

```
LIST
10   REM    PROGRAM TO PRINT THE NA
     ME JEFF USING LOW RESOLUTION
     GRAPHICS
20   GR
30   COLOR= 12: REM   PLOT GREEN J
40   PLOT 2,19
50   HLIN 2,8 AT 20
60   VLIN 10,19 AT 8
70   COLOR= 13: REM   PLOT YELLOW E

80   VLIN 10,20 AT 11
90   HLIN 12,17 AT 10
100   HLIN 12,15 AT 15
110   HLIN 12,17 AT 20
120   COLOR= 11: REM   PLOT PINK F
130   VLIN 10,20 AT 20
140   HLIN 21,26 AT 10
150   HLIN 21,24 AT 14
160   COLOR= 6: REM   PLOT BLUE F
170   VLIN 10,20 AT 29
180   HLIN 30,35 AT 10
190   HLIN 30,33 AT 14
```

statements because you will have to rewrite some of the existing ones, and there may not be enough room left on the line for the insertion. You should, therefore, be careful when writing multiple statements on a single line.

One good use of the multiple statement capability is to include remarks that tell what is going on in the program. For example, in Figure 3.9 we have added three remarks that tell what letter is being displayed by various groups of HLIN and VLIN statements. You can see how the remarks in Figure 3.9 make the program easier to understand. Note the use of the colon (:) to separate multiple statements on a single line.

More About LIST

We have seen that the command LIST will list the entire BASIC program that is stored in memory. You can stop the listing process at any time by pressing

CTRL S.* This is particularly useful when listing long programs.

It is also possible to list only selected parts of a program. For example, if **LIST 30** is typed, only the line with the sequence number 30 will be printed on the screen. This is useful if you want to edit line 30 using the ESC I, J, K, M, BACKSPACE and RETYPE keys.

You can also list lines 20 through lines 40 by typing** **LIST 20–40.** Typing **LIST -30** will list all of the lines from the beginning of the program through line 30. Typing **LIST 30-** will list all of the lines from line 30 to the end of the program. These examples are shown in Figure 3.10.

*May not work in INTEGER BASIC.
**These features are not available in INTEGER BASIC. *List* 20,40 is valid in both versions of BASIC and behaves the same as LIST 20–40.

FIGURE 3.10 Examples of using the LIST statement.

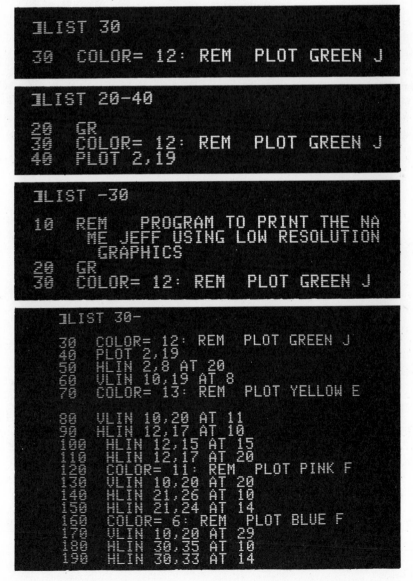

DEL

The command DEL can be used to delete a block of consecutive statements in a BASIC program. For example, if you type **DEL 40,60** statements 40 through 60 will be deleted. If you want to delete only a single line, such as line 50, then it is easiest to type **50** followed by RETURN. You could accomplish the same result by typing **DEL 50,50** but this is more work.

If you were to type **DEL 150,370** lines 150–370 would be deleted. If there were no line 150, the Apple II would start deleting lines with the next *higher* line number. If there were no line 370, the Apple II would stop deleting lines after deleting the line with the next *smaller* line number.

Memory Locations and Computer Programs

A computer program is like a train going on a trip. The seats in the train are like the memory locations or memory cells in the computer. Each seat has an "address," or name that identifies the seat and corresponds to the *variable* names in a BASIC program. For example, three different seat names could be A$, B$, and C$, each representing a separate seat.

Whoever or whatever is in a particular seat corresponds to the *contents* of a particular memory location in the computer. For example, if "JOHN" is sitting in seat A$, then the BASIC statement **A$="JOHN"** can be interpreted as meaning 'put "JOHN" in seat A$'. It is very important to distinguish clearly between the name of the memory location or seat on the train (A$) and the contents of that memory location or seat ("JOHN"). See Figure 3.11.

Up to now all of our memory locations have contained strings and have had names that end with a dollar sign. If a memory cell name does *not* end with a dollar sign, the computer will assume that the memory cell contains a number. The use of memory cells containing numbers will be discussed in the next chapter.

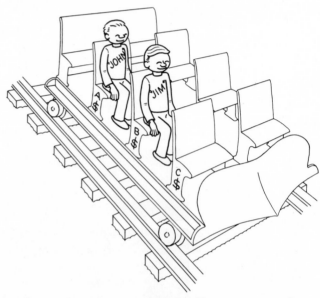

FIGURE 3.11   Memory locations are like seats on a train.

LEARNING MORE ABOUT PRINT

In the first three chapters of this book you have written short programs that print strings and draw various graphic figures. In this chapter you will see how the Apple II can work with *numbers* as well as strings. You will find that the Apple II can serve as a very good calculator.

In this chapter you will learn to

1. use the Apple II as a calculator
2. write arithmetic expressions involving addition,

subtraction, multiplication, division, and exponentiation
3. use the comma and semicolon in a PRINT statement
4. use the BASIC functions SPC and TAB, and the statements VTAB and HTAB
5. use the PRINT statement in the low-resolution graphics mode
6. display characters in *reverse video*
7. use some of the built-in functions of the Apple II.

THE APPLE II AS A CALCULATOR

By using the PRINT statement in the immediate mode of execution, you can use your Apple II as a calculator. You can add, subtract, multiply, divide, and raise a number to a power.

Addition

If you type **PRINT 5 + 3** the Apple II will respond with **8**. You can use the question mark as an abbreviation for PRINT. Thus if you type **? 5 + 3** the Apple II will also respond with **8** as shown in Figure 4.1. Try it.

Subtraction

If you type **? 12−5** the Apple II will respond with **7** as shown in Figure 4.1., Try it.

Multiplication

The symbol for multiplication in BASIC is the *asterisk* (*). Thus, if you type **? 3*4** the Apple II will respond with **12** as shown in Figure 4.1. Try it.

23

Division

The symbol for division in BASIC is the *slash /*. Thus, if you type **? 15/3** the Apple II will respond with **5** as shown in Figure 4.1. Try it.

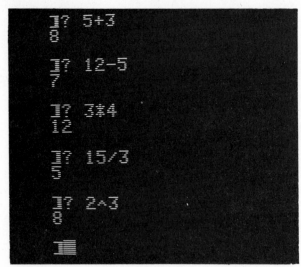

FIGURE 4.1   Using the Apple II in the calculator mode.

Exponentiation

The symbol for exponentiation in BASIC is the *upward arrow* ∧ (the symbol over the N). Thus, if you want to raise 2 to the power of 3 (2 cubed) you would type **? 2∧ 3** and the Apple II would respond with **8** as shown in Figure 4.1. Try it. Note that if the exponent is an integer, exponentiation is equivalent to repeated multiplication. Thus, **2 ∧ 3 = 2*2*2.**

Arithmetic Expressions

The arithmetic operators, $+,-,*,/,$ and ∧ can be combined in a single arithmetic expression. For example, if you type **? 5 + 3 − 2** the Apple II will respond with **6.** Now type the expression **? 6+ 12/2+ 4.** Did the Apple II display what you thought it would?

You should have found that the computer gave the answer **16.** This is because the Apple II does division before addition. All computer languages do not work this way. For example, the language APL evaluates all expressions right to left, so it would evaluate the above expression as a value of 8. (Do you see why?)

In BASIC, arithmetic expressions are evaluated according to the following *order of precedence:*

1. all exponentiations, ∧ , first
2. all multiplications, *, and divisions, /, next
3. all additions, +, and substractions, −, last.

Within each level of precedence, the expression is evaluated *left to right.* Parentheses can always be used to change the above order of precedence. In this case expressions within the innermost parentheses are evaluated first.

Try to evaluate each of the following arithmetic expressions, and then type them on the Apple II to check your results. The answers are shown in Figure 4.2.

$$? 8-3+4/2$$
$$? 3*2-5+8/4$$
$$? 8+1/3$$
$$? 5+3*4/6$$
$$? (3+4)*(6-3)$$
$$? 20/2/5$$

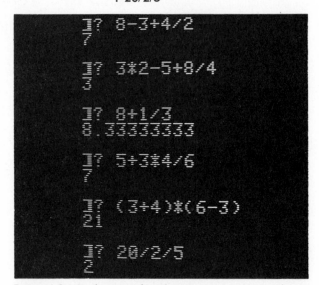

FIGURE 4.2   Evaluation of arithmetic expressions on the Apple II.

Did you guess the correct answer for the last one? Remember that the two divisions are evaluated left to right, so the correct result is

$$\frac{20/2}{5} = \frac{10}{5} = 2$$

and not

$$\frac{20}{2/5} = \frac{20*5}{2} = 50$$

If you want the second result, you can type **? 20/(2/5).** Try it.

Note that in the next to last example in Figure 4.2, it is necessary to use the multiplication symbol *. Although (3+4)(6−3) is used to imply multiplication in ordinary algebra, it does *not* imply multiplication to the Apple II. Any time you want to multiply anything on the Apple II, you *must* use the multiplication symbol *.

We have seen that strings such as "JOHN" can be stored in memory cells with names such as S3$. If a memory cell name does *not* end with a dollar sign, the Apple II will assume that the memory cell contains a numerical value. For example, if you type

$$A = 3$$
$$? A$$

the Apple II will respond with **3** as shown in Figure 4.3a. Similarly, if you type

$$A = 5$$
$$B = 3$$
$$? A*B$$

the Apple II will respond with **15** as shown in Figure 4.3b.

(a)

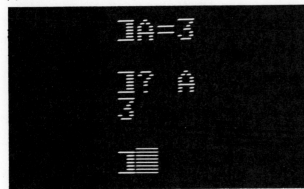

(b)

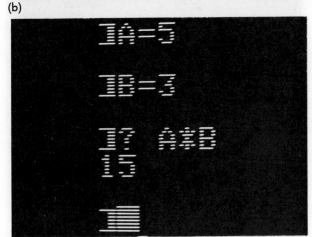

FIGURE 4.3 Numerical variables can be used in (a) the immediate mode of execution, and (b) in arithmetic expressions.

Note that the above examples used the immediate mode of execution. The deferred mode of execution can also be used, as shown in Figure 4.4

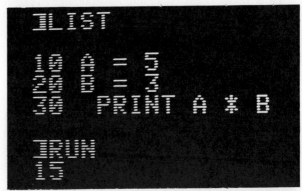

FIGURE 4.4 Use of numerical variables in the deferred mode of execution.

The rules for naming numerical variables are the same as for naming string variables except that there is no dollar sign at the end. That is, each name can contain one or two characters; the first character must be a letter while the second one can be a letter or a numeral. Thus, for example, the following are valid names for numerical variables.

$$Q$$
$$A3$$
$$XX$$
$$C2$$

Like string variables, numerical variables can have more than two characters in their names, but again the Apple II looks only at the first two characters. To verify this, try typing

$$BOX = 7$$
$$? BOB$$

as shown in Figure 4.5. This will serve as a reminder to be careful if you use memory cell names containing more than two characters.

FIGURE 4.5 The Apple II uses only the first two characters of a memory cell name.

How many digits of a number does the Apple II display?* Try typing **? 1/3** and **? 2/3** as shown in Figure 4.6. Note that nine digits are displayed, and the last 6 in 2/3 is rounded to **7**.

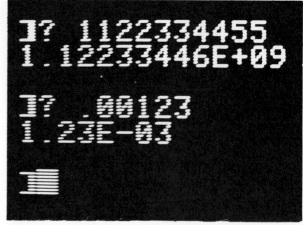

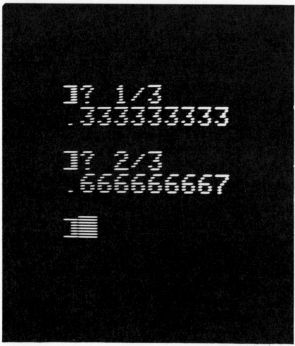

FIGURE 4.6   The Apple II displays 9 digits and rounds the last digit.

Scientific Notation†

What happens if you type in a number containing 10 or more digits? Try typing **? 1122334455** as shown in Figure 4.7. Note that the Apple II has rewritten the number in a form that contains an **E**. This is called *scientific notation*. The number after the E is the number of places you must move the decimal point in order to obtain the correct number. If the number after the E is positive, move the decimal point to the right. If the number after the E is negative, move the decimal point to the left. Try typing **? .00123** as shown in Figure 4.7.

FIGURE 4.7   Scientific notation is used by the Apple II for numbers greater than 999999999 and less than 0.01.

The Apple II uses scientific notation for numbers greater than 999999999 and less than 0.01. You can use scientific notation if you want, and the Apple II will convert back to standard notation if your number is between 0.01 and 999999999. Some examples are shown in Figure 4.8. Note that the Apple II printed **?OVERFLOW ERROR** when we tried to print **1.8E38**. It turns out that the *largest number* (magnitude) that the Apple II can store is $\pm 1.70141183E+38$. If you try to store a larger number, you will get an overflow error. Also, any number with a magnitude smaller than $\pm 2.93875388E-39$ will be stored in the Apple II as zero.

FIGURE 4.8   You can use scientific notation in your programs.

---

*INTEGER BASIC will not display decimals.
†INTEGER BASIC does not use scientific notation.

When you use the PRINT statement, you can control the location of the output printed on the screen by using commas, semicolons, and the functions SPC and TAB.

Comma

The comma has a special meaning in BASIC. It can *not* be used in the customary way to separate every three digits in a large number. For example, in BASIC the number 3,526,489 must be written without commas as 3526489.

Try printing the number 3,526,489 with the commas by typing **? 3,526,489** as shown in Figure 4.9. Note that instead of printing one number, the Apple II thought you wanted to print the three numbers 3, 526, 489. In a PRINT statement the comma is used to move to the next fixed *tab* position. These fixed tab positions are located in columns 1, 17, and 33, where the screen columns are numbered 1–40. If you try to PRINT

more than three numbers on a line, separated by commas, the extra numbers will be printed on the next line as shown in the first example in Figure 4.10. Note in the second example of Figure 4.10 that the negative sign in a negative number is printed at the tab position. If the number contains more than nine digits, it will be converted to scientific notation, as shown by the third example in the figure. One or more commas can precede a number in order to skip tab positions, as shown in the last two examples of Figure 4.10.

The comma can also be used with strings, as in Figure 4.11. Note that up to 15 characters can be included in a string before a tab position is skipped prior to printing a second string. Also note that strings begin printing in column number 1 and at the start of all other tab positions (17, 33).

The comma can be used in PRINT statements to separate strings from numerical variables as in Figure 4.12. Note that after the string "A=" is printed, the

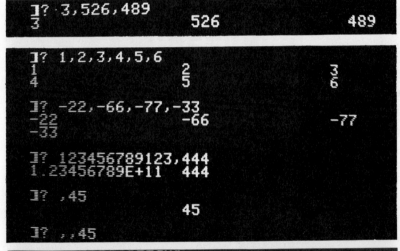

FIGURE 4.9   The comma acts like a tab in a PRINT statement.

FIGURE 4.10   Examples of using the comma as a tab.

FIGURE 4.11   Using the comma tab with strings.

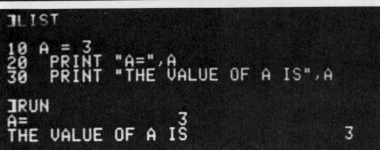

FIGURE 4.12   Using the comma to separate strings and numerical variables.

comma causes a tab to column number 17 before the value of A (3) is printed. This looks a little awkward. This gap can be eliminated by using a semicolon instead of a comma.

Semicolon

If numerical values are separated by semicolons instead of commas, no space is inserted after each value, as shown in Figure 4.13. Note that commas and semicolons can be mixed in a single PRINT statement.

Used with *strings,* the semicolon leaves *no* blank spaces in between, as shown in Figure 4.14. In combining strings and numerical variables, the semicolon can be used to eliminate unsightly gaps, as shown in Figure 4.15. Note that you may need to include a blank space at the end of the string in line 30 of Figure 4.15b in order to leave a space before the number.

SPC*

The function SPC(X) can be used in a PRINT statement to move the cursor X spaces to the right. The value of X must be between 0 and 255. If the cursor reaches the end of a line, it will continue at the beginning of the next line.

---

*Not available in INTEGER BASIC.

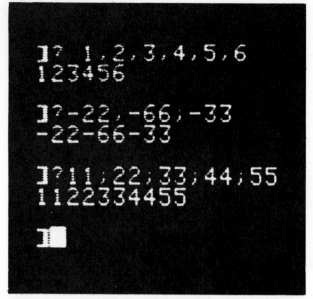

FIGURE 4.13   Using the semicolon to separate numerical values.

FIGURE 4.14   The semicolon leaves no blank spaces between strings.

```
]LIST

10 A = 3
20  PRINT "A=";A
30  PRINT "THE VALUE OF A IS";A

]RUN
A=3
THE VALUE OF A IS3
```

```
]LIST

10 A = 3
20  PRINT "A=";A
30  PRINT "THE VALUE OF A IS ";A

]RUN
A=3
THE VALUE OF A IS 3
```

FIGURE 4.15   Using the semicolon to separate strings and numerical variables.

As an example, suppose you want to print the word HELLO near the top center of the screen. The program shown in Figure 4.16 will do this. The first statement, **HOME,** will clear the screen. The PRINT statement in line 20 skips 15 spaces using the function SPC(15) and then prints **HELLO.** Note that the semicolon must be used between SPC(15) and "HELLO" in the PRINT statement in order to keep the cursor at its present location after skipping 15 spaces.

TAB*

While the comma can be used to tab to the next *fixed* tab position on a line (1, 17, 33), the TAB function can be used to tab to *any* position on a line. For example, TAB(15) will move the cursor to column number 15 on the line. Thus, if SPC(15) in Figure 4.16 is replaced

---

*TAB in INTEGER BASIC is like HTAB (described later) in APPLESOFT.

with TAB(16), the program will produce the same result. The difference between SPC and TAB can be seen in Figure 4.17. The function SPC(10) skips 10 spaces after the string "1979". On the other hand the function TAB(10) moves the cursor to column number 10.

If the function TAB(X) is to be used, the value of X must be between 0 and 255. (A value of 0 will actually tab to position 256.) If the value of X is less than the current position of the cursor on the line, the TAB function is ignored.

VTAB

It is possible to tab vertically down the screen using the statement **VTAB Y** if Y is a number between 1 and 24. The top line on the screen is number 1, and the bottom line is number 24. Note that VTAB is *not* used in a PRINT statement.

FIGURE 4.16   The function SPC(15) will skip 15 spaces.

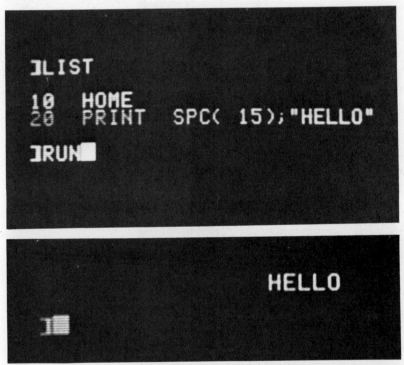

FIGURE 4.17   SPC and TAB will, in general, produce different results.

For example, if you wanted to print the word HELLO near the center of the screen, you could type

```
10 HOME
20 VTAB 10
30 PRINT SPC(15); "HELLO"
```

as shown in Figure 4.18.

The statement VTAB will always tab to an absolute line number, regardless of the current cursor location. For example, if you add the statements

```
40 VTAB 5
50 PRINT "APPLE II"
```

the result of executing this new program is shown in Figure 4.19.

If the value of the argument in the VTAB statement is outside of the range 1–24, then the error message

?ILLEGAL QUANTITY ERROR will be displayed on the screen.

HTAB*

The HTAB statement is similar to VTAB but tabs horizontally instead of vertically. It differs from TAB in that it is *not* used in a PRINT statement. The statement **HTAB X** will tab to position X on the current line whenever X is between 0 and 255. (A value of 0 will actually tab to position 256.) The statement **HTAB 1** will position the cursor at the left-most position on the current line. The statement **HTAB 40** will position the cursor at the right-most position on the current line. If the value of X in the statement **HTAB X** is greater than 40, the tab position will continue on the next line. For example, **HTAB 49** will tab to position 9 on the line following the current cursor location. The use of the statement HTAB is illustrated in Figure 4.20.

---

*TAB performs this function in INTEGER BASIC.

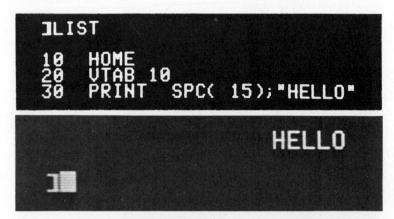

FIGURE 4.18   The statement VTAB 10 will tab vertically to line number 10.

FIGURE 4.19   The statement VTAB will tab to lines above the current cursor position.

```
]LIST

10  HTAB 20
20  PRINT "APPLE II"

]RUN
                    APPLE II

]LIST

10  HTAB 44
20  PRINT "APPLE II"

]RUN

        APPLE II
```

FIGURE 4.20   Illustrating the use of the HTAB statement.

MIXING TEXT AND LOW-RESOLUTION
GRAPHICS

Recall from Chapter 2 that in the low-resolution graphics mode the screen is divided into a 40 × 40 grid with four lines of text at the bottom of the screen. The PRINT statement can be used to write text into these four bottom lines. It is *not* possible to PRINT characters in the 40 × 40 grid portion of the screen using the PRINT statement. Only the statements PLOT, HLIN, and VLIN will produce any drawing in the 40 × 40 grid region.

As an example, suppose you want to plot a color chart that will show the colors associated with the color numbers 6, 9, 12, and 13. Figure 4.21 shows a layout sketch of the chart. Four vertical lines are drawn in the four different colors, and the corresponding color numbers are printed under each color bar.

Figure 4.22 shows the listing of a program that will produce this color chart. Lines 20–100 plot the four colored vertical bars. Note that sketching the desired pictures on quadrille paper as shown in Figure 4.21 makes it an easy matter to translate this picture into the BASIC statements in Figure 4.22.

FIGURE 4.21   Layout of a COLOR CHART sketched on quadrille paper.

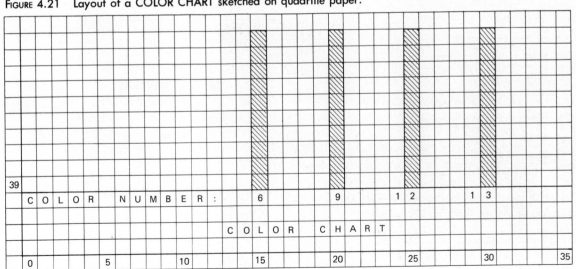

```
]LIST
10   REM    COLOR CHART
20   GR
30   COLOR= 6
40   VLIN 39,0 AT 15
50   COLOR= 9
60   VLIN 39,0 AT 20
70   COLOR= 12
80   VLIN 39,0 AT 25
90   COLOR= 13
100  VLIN 39,0 AT 30
110  HOME
120  PRINT "COLOR NUMBER:   6     9
        12    13"
130  PRINT : HTAB 14
140  PRINT "COLOR CHART";
150  GOTO 150
```

FIGURE 4.22   Listing of a BASIC program to draw the color chart.

Line 110 moves the cursor to the home position. This is the upper left-hand corner of the 4-line text area at the bottom of the screen. It does not move the cursor to the upper left-hand corner of the entire screen.

Line 120 prints the color numbers on the first line of the 4-line text area. Note again that Figure 4.21 is used to determine the exact spacing needed to make the numbers end up directly under the colored bars. Since there is no punctuation at the end of line 120, the cursor will move to the beginning of the next line (line 2 of the 4-line text area) after line 120 is executed. The PRINT statement in line 130 simply moves the cursor to the beginning of the next line (line 3 of the 4-line text area), and the statement HTAB 14 moves the cursor to

position 14 (column number 13) on that line. Line 140 then prints the title "COLOR CHART" near the center of the third line of the 4-line text area.

The last statement in the program, **150 GOTO 150**, is an "infinite" loop that just keeps branching to itself. The purpose of this statement is to prevent the cursor from returning to the screen. To stop the program, you can type **CTRL C**. Type in and run the program shown in Figure 4.22. The result of running this program appears in Figure 4.23.

EXERCISE 4-1

Delete line 150 in the program in Figure 4.22. Run the resulting program. What is the difference? Delete the semicolon at the end of line 140. Run the program again. Explain what you observe.

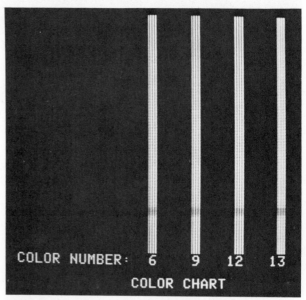

FIGURE 4.23   Result of running the program shown in Fig. 4.22.

REVERSE VIDEO

Add the statements*

115 INVERSE
125 NORMAL

to the program shown in Figure 4.22 and rerun the program. You should get the result shown in Figure 4.24. Note that the string printed in line 120 is printed in *reverse video,* that is, black characters on a white background, rather than white on black.

---

*In INTEGER BASIC, type **POKE 50, 127** instead of INVERSE and **POKE 50, 255** instead of NORMAL.

The statement **INVERSE** sets the reverse video mode, and the statement **NORMAL** reverts back to the normal white on black video mode.

Delete statements 115 and 125 (by typing **115 RE-TURN** and **125** RETURN), then add the two statements

135 INVERSE
145 NORMAL

and rerun the program. What do you see?

Now add the statement† **137 FLASH**. This will cause

---

†FLASH is not available in INTEGER BASIC.

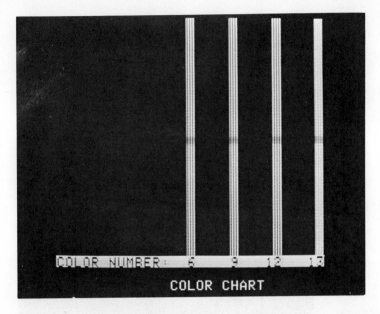

COLOR CHART

FIGURE 4.24 The INVERSE statement sets the reverse video mode.

the words **COLOR CHART** to flash alternately between the reverse video and normal mode. The FLASH mode remains in effect until NORMAL is executed. Delete line 137, add the line **115 FLASH** and rerun the program. What do you see?

EXERCISE 4-2

Modify the program shown in Figure 4.22 so that

1. Both lines of text are displayed in reverse video.
2. Both lines of text flash.

SOME BUILT-IN FUNCTIONS

The Apple II has a number of built-in arithmetic functions that simplify many calculations. If you have never learned some of these concepts, don't worry. You will only want to use the ones whose meaning you understand.

SQUARE ROOT*

The square root of a number can be found by using the BASIC function **SQR(X)** where X is a positive number. For example, to find the square root of 16, type **?** **SQR(16)** as shown in Figure 4.25a. To find the hypotenuse, R, of the right triangle shown in Figure 4.26, you could use the program shown in Figure 4.25b.

*Not available in INTEGER BASIC.

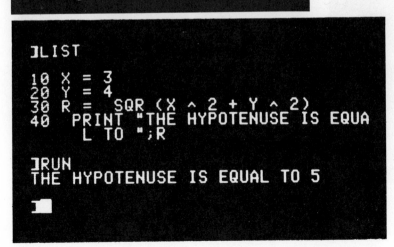

FIGURE 4.25 Use of the square root function, SQR.

33

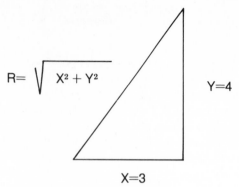

$$R = \sqrt{X^2 + Y^2}$$

Y=4

X=3

FIGURE 4.26 Finding the hypotenuse of a right triangle.

The Functions ABS, INT, and SGN

The *absolute value* of a number is the magnitude of a number without regard to its sign, and it can be found by using the built-in function ABS(X). Thus, for example, if X = −7, the value of ABS(X) will be 7.

The value of the function INT(X) is equal to the *integer part* of X. Thus, if X = 3.25, INT(X) is equal to 3. When computing INT(X), the Apple II will round to the next lower *signed number*. Thus, if X = −3.25, the value of INT(X) will be −4.

The function SGN(X) can be used to determine the *sign of a number*. It can have the following three values:

$$SGN(X) = \begin{cases} +1 \text{ if } X>0 \\ 0 \text{ if } X=0 \\ -1 \text{ if } X<0 \end{cases}$$

Examples of using ABS, INT, and SGN are shown in Figure 4.27.

FIGURE 4.27 Examples of finding the absolute value, ABS, the integer part, INT, and the sign, SGN, of a number.

```
]? ABS(-3.2)
3.2
]? INT(3.2)
3
]? INT(-3.2)
-4
]? SGN(3.2)
1
]? SGN(-3.2)
-1
]? SGN(0)
0
```

The Paddle Functions

The Paddle Functions PDL(0) and PDL(1) can be used to incorporate game paddles into a BASIC program. Make sure that the game paddles are plugged into the game I/O socket on the main board of the Apple II. Turn one of the paddle knobs completely counterclockwise and the other one completely clockwise. Then type **? PDL(0)** and **? PDL(1)** as shown in Figure 4.28.

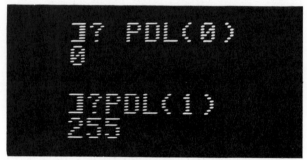

FIGURE 4.28 The Paddle Functions return a value between 0 and 255 depending upon the position of the paddle knobs.

The result of typing **? PDL(0)** will be either 0 or 255. If it is zero, then paddle #0 is the one whose knob is completely counterclockwise. (This is the case in Figure 4.28. Your results may be reversed.) If the value of PDL(0) is 255, paddle #0 is the one whose knob is completely clockwise.

The value of the function PDL(0) will vary from 0 to 255 as the knob on paddle #0 is rotated from the completely counterclockwise position to the completely clockwise position. The function PDL(1) behaves the same for paddle #1. Turn the knob of each game paddle to some middle position and type **? PDL(0)** and **? PDL(1)** again. In each case you should get some value between 0 and 255.

Now type in the program shown in Figure 4.29. Line 20 sets the low resolution graphics mode with a white color. Line 30 assigns X a value between 0 and 255 depending upon the position of the knob on paddle #0. Similarly, line 40 assigns Y a value between 0 and

FIGURE 4.29 Program to draw figures using the game paddles.

```
]LIST
10   REM   USING THE PADDLES
15   HOME
20   GR : COLOR= 15
30  X =   PDL (0)
40  Y =   PDL (1)
50  X =   INT (X / 7)
60  Y =   INT (Y / 7)
70   PLOT X,Y
80   GOTO 30
```

255 depending upon the position of the knob on paddle #1. Lines 50 and 60 convert these numbers to integer values between 0 and 36 by dividing the original number by 7 and then taking the integer part. This is done so that in the PLOT statement in line 70 the maximum value of either X or Y will be 36 (corresponding to the knob turned completely clockwise). Remember that a value of X or Y greater than 39 will cause an error when the statement **PLOT X,Y** is executed.

The PLOT statement in line 70 causes a white dot to be plotted on the screen. The exact position of the dot will depend on the position of the two paddle knobs. Line 80 branches back to line 30, and the two paddles are read again. Thus, this program should continually display new spots on the screen as the paddle knobs are turned.

A sample run of this program is shown in Figure 4.30. You should try running this program.

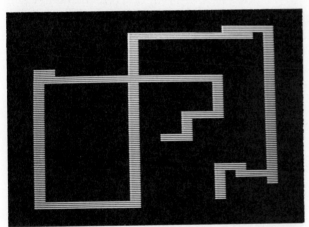

FIGURE 4.30 Sample run of program shown in Fig. 4.29.

Random Numbers

In many programs, particularly game programs, it is useful to be able to generate random numbers. These can be used to simulate dealing cards, rolling dice, or creating other unpredictable results. BASIC has a built-in function called RND that makes generating random numbers easy.

Type and run the following program twice, as shown in Figure 4.31.

> 10 ? RND(1)
> 20 ? RND(1)
> 30 ? RND(1)

The function RND(X)* will return a pseudo-random number between 0 and 1 if the argument X is a positive

---

*In INTEGER BASIC, RND(X) is a pseudo-random integer less than X.

number. (It does not matter what the positive value is. We will use 1.) It looks as if this is happening in Figure 4.31. Each time RND(1) is called, it produces a different number between 0 and 1. Actually, you will find that if you turn your Apple II off and then back on and rerun the program in Figure 4.31, you will obtain the same set of "random" numbers. This is because the function RND uses a *seed* that determines the initial random number that is subsequently generated. This seed is set to the same value each time the Apple II is turned on. Therefore, the first time you call RND(1) after the Apple II is turned on, you will always get the same random number.

This is not a good state of affairs unless you want to

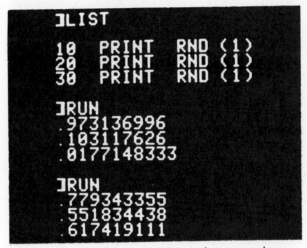

FIGURE 4.31 The function RND(1) produces a random number between 0 and 1.

deal the same bridge hand every time you turn the Apple II on. You need some way to change the seed. You can do this by calling the RND function with a *negative* argument. For example, if you add the statement **5 X=RND(−1)** to the above program, you will generate a different sequence of random numbers. However, you will always generate the same sequence following the execution of statement number 5, as demonstrated in Figure 4.32.

A different negative argument will produce a different seed and therefore a different random sequence, as shown in Figure 4.33.

Thus, if you know what negative number is used in RND(−X) you will, in principle, know what sequence of random numbers will follow. It would be useful if you could introduce some "randomness" into the selection of a seed so you could get different random numbers every time. One way to do this will be described in Chapter 14.

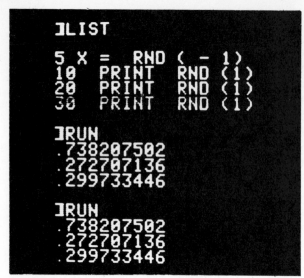

FIGURE 4.32 The function RND(−1) produces a particular seed.

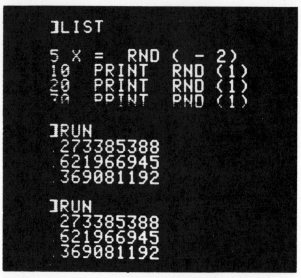

FIGURE 4.33 The function RND(−2) produces a different seed.

Trigonometric Functions*

The Apple II contains the following built-in trigonometric functions:

APPLE II FUNCTION	VALUE OF FUNCTION
SIN(X)	sine of X
COS(X)	cosine of X
TAN(X)	tangent of X
ATN(Y)	arctangent of Y

In the above expressions, X is a numeric constant, variable, or expression that represents the value of an angle in *radians*. The value of ATN(Y) is expressed in radians in the range ±1.57, and Y is a numeric constant, variable, or expression.

The definition of a radian is shown in Figure 4.34. To convert degrees to radians, multiply by $\pi/180$. Examples of using the trigonometric functions are shown in Figure 4.35.

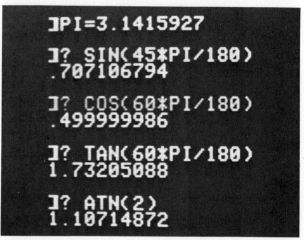

FIGURE 4.35 Examples of using the trigonometric functions SIN, COS, TAN, and ATN.

FIGURE 4.34 Definitions of a *radian*.

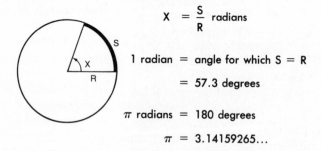

$$X = \frac{S}{R} \text{ radians}$$

$$1 \text{ radian} = \text{angle for which } S = R$$
$$= 57.3 \text{ degrees}$$

$$\pi \text{ radians} = 180 \text{ degrees}$$

$$\pi = 3.14159265\ldots$$

Natural Logarithms and the Exponential Function†

Consider the equation

$$y = b^x$$

In this expression x is called the logarithm of y to the base b and is written

$$x = \log_b y$$

If the base b is equal to e = 2.718281 . . . , we say that y is the exponential function $y = e^x$ and x is the natural logarithm of y:

$$x = \ln y$$

---

*Not available in INTEGER BASIC.

†Not available in INTEGER BASIC.

In BASIC e^x can be computed using the function EXP(X), and ln x can be computed using the function LOG(X).

The following properties of logarithms are illustrated in the examples shown in Figure 4.36:

$$LOG(A*B) = LOG(A) + LOG(B)$$
$$LOG(A/B) = LOG(A) - LOG(B)$$
$$LOG(A \wedge K) = K*LOG(A)$$

```
]? LOG(3*4)
2.48490665

]? LOG(3)+LOG(4)
2.48490665

]? LOG(9/2)
1.5040774

]? LOG(9)-LOG(2)
1.5040774

]? LOG(2.5^3)
2.7488722

]? 3*LOG(2.5)
2.7488722
```

FIGURE 4.36   Illustrating properties of logarithms.

When the rate at which a quantity grows is proportional to the amount of the quantity, we have *exponential growth*. The amount of money in a savings account that is compounded *continuously* grows exponentially. Thus D dollars invested at P percent annual interest compounded continuously will yield X dollars after T years where:

$$X = De^{PT/100}$$

For example, to find the amount of money you would have in 7 years by investing $3,000 at 9.5% interest compounded continuously, type **? 3000*EXP(9.5*7/100)** as shown in Figure 4.37.

Note that the answer is more than $5,833, or almost double your original investment. A characteristic of exponential growth is a constant doubling time T_d. From the above equation for X, we see that X will be equal to 2D in the time T_d where

$$2D = De^{PT_d/100}$$

or

$$2 = e^{PT_d/100}$$

Taking the natural logarithm of both sides of this equation and using the third property of logarithms illustrated in Figure 4.36 we obtain

$$\ln(2) = (PT_d/100)\ln(e)$$
$$= PT_d/100$$

or

$$T_d = \frac{100\ln(2)}{P}$$

Note that $\ln(e) = 1$. (Try typing **? LOG(2.718281)**).

To see how long this doubling time is, type **? 100*LOG(2)** as shown in Figure 4.37. We see that the doubling time is approximately 70 divided by the percentage growth rate, or

$$T_d \approx 70/P$$

Thus, for example, a 10% inflation rate will double prices every 7 years.

FIGURE 4.37   Examples related to the exponential function.

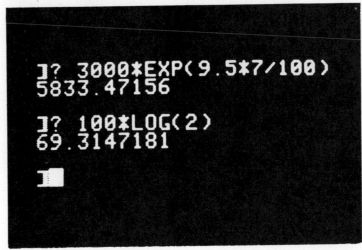

```
]? 3000*EXP(9.5*7/100)
5833.47156

]? 100*LOG(2)
69.3147181
```

USER-DEFINED FUNCTIONS*

Sometimes it is convenient if you can define your own BASIC function. For example, suppose you want to calculate the area of a circle for different values of the circle radius. You can define a function FNA(R) that is equal to the area of a circle of radius R using the DEF FN statement as follows:

$$5 \text{ PI} = 3.1415926$$
$$10 \text{ DEF FNA(R)} = \text{PI*R} \wedge 2$$

Later in the program any reference to the function FNA(R) will cause the expression PI*R ∧ 2 to be calculated. For example, the statement **20 PRINT FNA(3), FNA(5)** will print the areas of circles of radius 3 and 5. This example is shown in Figure 4.38.

FIGURE **4.38** The defined function FNA(R) computes the area of a circle of radius R.

*Not available in INTEGER BASIC.

The general form of the *define function* statement is **DEF FN name (arg) = expression.** The *name* can be any valid variable name (one or two characters), and the *expression* can be any arithmetic expression containing numeric constants and variables. Only one argument, *arg,* can be passed to the user-defined function. The defining expression may, however, contain previously defined functions.

EXERCISE 4-3

Let the variables A,B,C, and D have the following values:

$$A = 2, B = 3, C = 4, D = 5$$

Use the Apple II to evaluate the following expressions:

a. $X = (A - \dfrac{C}{D})^{0.5}$

b. $Z = \dfrac{A(B-C)}{D(B^A - 1)}$

c. $Y = \dfrac{(A+B)}{C(D-A)}$

d. $R = \sqrt{(A+B)/(D-A)}$

e. $S = \dfrac{e^A - e^{-A}}{2}$

ENTERING DATA FROM THE KEYBOARD: LEARNING ABOUT INPUT AND GET

In earlier chapters of this book you have learned to use the PRINT statement to make the Apple II output various forms of data on the screen. In this chapter you will learn how to make the Apple II accept various forms of data that you type on the keyboard. You do this by using the INPUT statement in a BASIC program. You will learn to use this INPUT statement by studying the following sample programs:

1. add two numbers
2. compute the area of a rectangle
3. compute the area of a circle
4. calculate gas mileage
5. display your name and address
6. draw various graphic figures.

THE INPUT STATEMENT

The INPUT statement can only be used in the deferred mode of execution. The following are valid forms of the INPUT statement:

    10 INPUT R
    10 INPUT A,B
    10 INPUT "ENTER 3 VALUES"; X,Y,Z*
    10 INPUT A$

When the first INPUT statement above is executed, the Apple II will print a question mark and wait for you to enter some numerical value from the keyboard.

---

*The semicolon must be a comma in INTERGER BASIC.

When you press the RETURN key, the value that you typed on the screen will be stored in the memory cell R. The next statement in the BASIC program will then be executed.

When the second INPUT statement above is executed, the Apple II will expect you to enter *two* numerical values, separated by a comma. If you press RETURN after entering only one value, the Apple II will print a double question mark and wait for you to enter the second value. These two values will then be stored in the two memory cells A and B.

The third form of the INPUT statement shown above will print the message **ENTER 3 VALUES**, followed by the blinking cursor. The Apple II will then wait for you to enter three values separated by commas. These three values will then be stored in the three memory cells X, Y, and Z. If someone else will be entering data, the program should always be set up to prompt the user so that he or she will know when to enter data. This can be done either as shown in the third example above, or

by using a PRINT statement just before the INPUT statement.

The fourth form of the INPUT statement shown above will store whatever you type on the screen in the string variable A$. You do not need to type the quotation marks when entering a string with the INPUT statement.

The use of the INPUT statement will be illustrated in the following sample programs.

SUM OF TWO NUMBERS

Figure 5.1 shows a listing and sample run of a program that will add two numbers entered from the keyboard and display the sum. You should type in this program and run it.

Line 20 prints the message **ENTER 2 NUMBERS SEPARATED BY A COMMA.** Line 30 prints a question mark on the next line, and then the computer waits for you to enter two numbers. In the first example after RUN, the two numbers **5** and **9** were entered from the keyboard. Line 40 then prints the value stored in A **(5)** followed by a plus sign, followed by the value stored in B **(9)**, followed by an equal sign, followed by the sum A+B **(14)**. Line 50 is a PRINT statement with nothing following the word PRINT. The only purpose of this statement is to skip a line on the screen. Line 60 causes

the program to branch back to line 20, which asks for another 2 numbers to be entered.

In the second example following RUN, the value **8** is entered for the first number. But then the RETURN key was pressed. Note that the Apple II responds with a double question mark, asking you to please enter the second number. In this example −**3** was then entered.

This program will continue to ask you for two more numbers. How can you stop the program? If you press CTRL C followed by RETURN before entering any data, the program will be terminated.

You should try experimenting with this program to see how it behaves. Study the program carefully, and make sure you understand what every statement does.

FIGURE 5.1   Sample program to add two numbers.

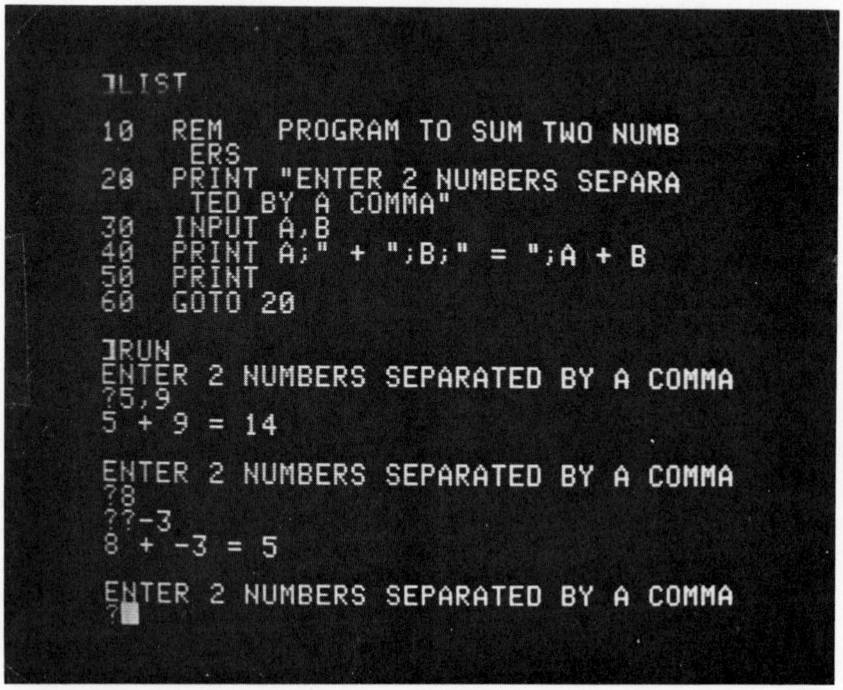

```
]LIST

10   REM    PROGRAM TO SUM TWO NUMB
     ERS
20   PRINT "ENTER 2 NUMBERS SEPARA
     TED BY A COMMA"
30   INPUT A,B
40   PRINT A;" + ";B;" = ";A + B
50   PRINT
60   GOTO 20

]RUN
ENTER 2 NUMBERS SEPARATED BY A COMMA
?5,9
5 + 9 = 14

ENTER 2 NUMBERS SEPARATED BY A COMMA
?8
??-3
8 + -3 = 5

ENTER 2 NUMBERS SEPARATED BY A COMMA
?
```

Figure 5.2 shows the listing and a sample run of a program that computes the area of a rectangle when the lengths of the two sides are entered from the keyboard. You should type in this program and run it.

The main difference between this program and the previous one is that the prompt message is included in the INPUT statement in line 30. Note that when you do this, no question mark follows the prompt message and

the blinking cursor remains on the *same line* as the message. Thus, you enter the data on the same line as the prompting message.

Note that in the second example after RUN, the RETURN key was pressed after the comma had been typed. The Apple II will then assign a value of zero to the numerical variable Y.

```
]LIST

10   REM      PROGRAM TO COMPUTE THE

20   REM      AREA OF A RECTANGLE
30   INPUT "ENTER THE 2 SIDES OF A
        RECTANGLE ";X,Y
40   PRINT "THE AREA OF A RECTANGL
        E WITH SIDES"
50   PRINT X;" AND ";Y;" IS EQUAL
        TO ";X * Y
60   PRINT
70   GOTO 30

]RUN
ENTER THE 2 SIDES OF A RECTANGLE 4,5
THE AREA OF A RECTANGLE WITH SIDES
4 AND 5 IS EQUAL TO 20

ENTER THE 2 SIDES OF A RECTANGLE 6,
THE AREA OF A RECTANGLE WITH SIDES
6 AND 0 IS EQUAL TO 0

ENTER THE 2 SIDES OF A RECTANGLE ■
```

FIGURE 5.2   Sample program to calculate the area of a rectangle.

DRAWING THE RECTANGLE

Modify the program shown in Figure 5.2 by adding the following statements:

```
25 GR: COLOR=15
60 HLIN 0,X-1 AT 0
70 VLIN 0,Y-1 AT X-1
80 HLIN X-1,0 AT Y-1
90 VLIN Y-1,0 AT 0
```

A listing of the resulting program is shown in Figure 5.3. A sample run of the program is shown in Figure 5.4. Note that this program calculates the area of a rectangle and then draws the rectangle in the upper left-hand corner of the screen. The program only calculates the area of one rectangle. You must RUN the program again to draw a different rectangle.

FIGURE 5.3   Sample program to draw a rectangle and calculate its area.

```
]LIST
10   REM      PROGRAM TO COMPUTE THE

20   REM      AREA OF A RECTANGLE
25   GR : COLOR= 15
30   INPUT "ENTER THE 2 SIDES OF A
        RECTANGLE ";X,Y
40   PRINT "THE AREA OF A RECTANGL
        E WITH SIDES"
50   PRINT X;" AND ";Y;" IS EQUAL
        TO ";X * Y
60   HLIN 0,X - 1 AT 0
70   VLIN 0,Y - 1 AT X - 1
80   HLIN X - 1,0 AT Y - 1
90   VLIN Y - 1,0 AT 0
```

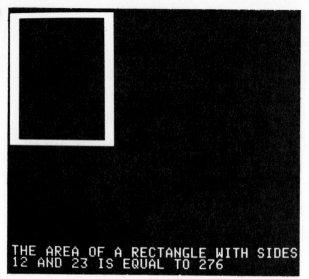

THE AREA OF A RECTANGLE WITH SIDES
12 AND 23 IS EQUAL TO 276

FIGURE 5.4   Sample run of program shown in Fig. 5.3.

Lines 60–90 in Figure 5.3 draw the rectangle illustrated in Figure 5.5. Try running this program.

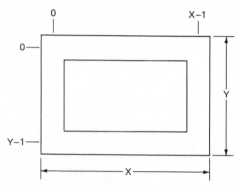

FIGURE 5.5   Lines 60-90 in Fig. 5.3 draw the rectangle in a clockwise fashion, starting with the top side.

AREA OF A CIRCLE

The area of a circle of radius r is given by

$$area = \pi r^2$$

where π(pi) is approximately equal to 3.14159265. Figure 5.6 shows the listing and a sample run of a program that computes the area of a circle whose radius is entered from the keyboard. You should type in this program and run it.

This program shows that the PRINT statement in line 20 and the INPUT statement in line 30 behave the same way as the single statement **30 INPUT "ENTER THE RADIUS OF A CIRCLE"; R** except that a question mark is included after the prompt message. The blinking cursor is displayed on the same line as the message. This is because the PRINT statement in line 20 ends with the *semicolon,* which always leaves the cursor at its present position. When a PRINT statement does not end with any punctuation, the equivalent of a RETURN is inserted at the end of the PRINT statement.

Line 35 calculates the area of the circle. The value of pi has been defined in line 15.

FIGURE 5.6   Sample program to calculate the area of a circle.

```
10  REM    PROGRAM TO COMPUTE THE
           AREA OF A CIRCLE
15 PI = 3.14159265
20    PRINT "ENTER THE RADIUS OF A
           CIRCLE ";
30    INPUT R
35 A = PI * R ^ 2
40    PRINT "THE AREA OF THE CIRCLE
           IS ";A
50    PRINT
60    GOTO 20

]RUN
ENTER THE RADIUS OF A CIRCLE ?35.2
THE AREA OF THE CIRCLE IS 3892.55896

ENTER THE RADIUS OF A CIRCLE ?6,3
?EXTRA IGNORED
THE AREA OF THE CIRCLE IS 113.097335

ENTER THE RADIUS OF A CIRCLE ?2.5E19

?OVERFLOW ERROR IN 35
```

Note that in the second example after RUN, two values, **6** and **3**, were entered. But the Apple II was expecting only one value. It therefore used only the first value (6) and printed the warning message **?EXTRA IGNORED.**

In the third example after RUN, a value of **2.5E19** was entered. But this results in a value of the area A that

is larger than 1.7E38 and therefore the message **?OVERFLOW ERROR IN 35** is printed, indicating that the overflow occurred in the calculation of the area A. (See Figure 4.9 for example of overflow error).

GAS MILEAGE

The program shown in Figure 5.7 computes gas mileage in miles/gallon. The reading on the dashboard odometer (the device that displays the mileage) at the last fill-up is stored in memory cell M1 in line 25. The

FIGURE 5.7   Program for computing gas mileage.

```
]LIST
10   REM    GAS MILAGE PROGRAM
20   PRINT "ENTER PREVIOUS ODOMETE
     R READING"
25   INPUT M1
30   PRINT "ENTER NEW ODOMETER REA
     DING"
35   INPUT M2
40   PRINT "ENTER GALLONS SINCE LA
     ST FILLUP"
45   INPUT G
50   MPG = (M2 - M1) / G
60   PRINT "GAS MILAGE: "MPG;" MIL
     ES/GAL."
```

odometer reading at the present fill-up is stored in memory cell M2 in line 35. The number of gallons it takes to fill the tank is stored in memory cell G in line 45. The total number of miles traveled since the last fill-up is equal to M2–M1. Therefore the number of miles per gallon is given by (M2–M1)/G. This is calculated in line 50 and stored in the memory cell MPG. It is printed on the screen in line 60. Line 70 skips a line and line 80 branches back to line 20 to run the program again.

A sample run is shown in Figure 5.8a. The answer is printed as **19.556962 MILES/GAL.** This answer contains many more digits after the decimal point than are meaningful. Because of variations in fill-ups, it probably makes sense to compute the miles per gallon only to the nearest tenth. How can we have the Apple II display the miles per gallon to the nearest tenth? The following steps will do it:

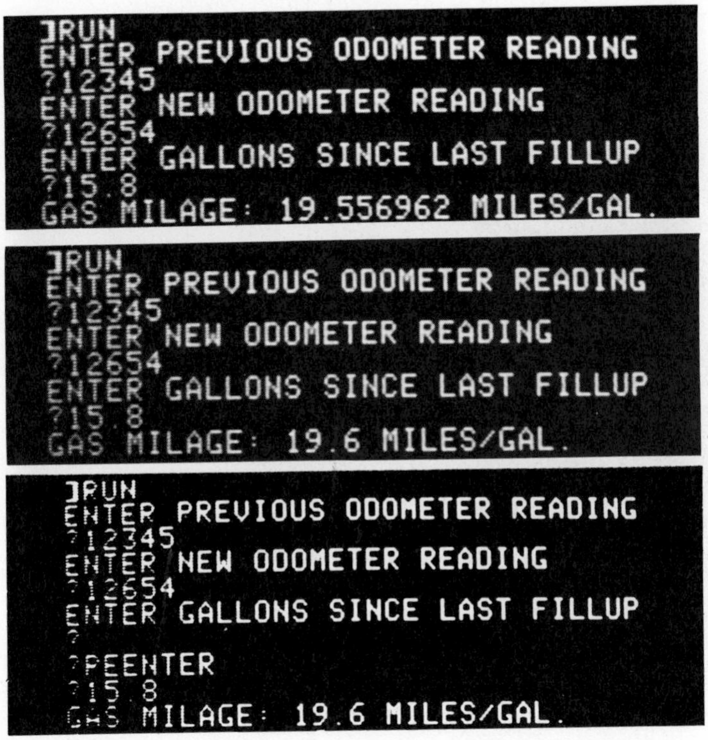

FIGURE 5.8   Sample runs of gas mileage program.

1. Multiply the present value by 10
$19.556962 \times 10 = 195.56962$

2. Add 0.5
$195.56962 + 0.5 = 196.06962$

3. Take the *integer part* of the result
$INT(196.06962) = 196$

4. Divide by 10
$196/10 = 19.6$

Although this may look complicated, it can all be done with the following *single* BASIC statement, **55 MPG = INT(MPG*10+0.5)/10**. Note that the result is stored back in memory cell MPG. Therefore, if you add this statement to the program shown in Figure 5.7 and run the program with the same values used in Figure 5.8a, the result will be as shown in Figure 5.8b.

The example shown in Figure 5.8c shows that if you mistakenly press RETURN when the INPUT statement is waiting for a value, the Apple II will ask you to **?REENTER** the value (or values) required by the INPUT statement.

NAME AND ADDRESS

The INPUT statement can be used to enter *string* data into the computer, as well as numerical data. The statement **INPUT A$** will assign whatever characters you type to the string variable A$. As an example, consider the program shown in Figure 5.9. Line 15 clears the screen. Line 30 will assign whatever you type for your name to the string variable N$. Line 50 will assign whatever you type for your street address to the string variable S$. Line 70 will assign whatever you type for your city, state, and zip code to the string variable C$. Lines 80–100 will then print these three strings on three separate lines.

A sample run of this program is shown in Figure 5.10a. Note that only the city, ROCHESTER, was included in the string C$, and the message **?EXTRA IG-NORED** is printed on the screen. This is because the

```
]LIST
10    REM    NAME AND ADDRESS
15    HOME
20    PRINT "ENTER YOUR NAME"
30    INPUT N$
40    PRINT "ENTER YOUR STREET ADDR
      ESS"
50    INPUT S$
60    PRINT "ENTER YOUR CITY, STATE
      , AND ZIP CODE"
70    INPUT C$
80    PRINT N$
90    PRINT S$
100   PRINT C$
```

FIGURE 5.9 Program to display your name and address.

FIGURE 5.10 Sample runs of program shown in Fig. 5.9.

comma typed after ROCHESTER was interpreted as a separator between different input data*, and only one data item C$ was specified in the INPUT on line 70. Therefore, only the name ROCHESTER was assigned to C$, and the "extra" data following the comma was ignored. To include a comma as part of a string, it is necessary to put quotation marks around the string, as illustrated in the sample run in Figure 5.10b. Note that

the closing quotation mark was omitted following the zip code. This is allowed if a string appears at the end of a line.

Type in and run the program shown in Figure 5.9, entering your own name and address.

DRAWING GRAPHIC FIGURES

The INPUT statement can be used to enter the color, size, and location of a graphic figure to be plotted on the screen. For example, Figure 5.11 shows a square box with a side of length S, centered at the coordinates X,Y. From this figure you can see that the top line of the box can be plotted using the statement **HLIN X−S/2, X+S/2 AT Y−S/2**. The right side of the box can be plotted (from top to bottom) using the statement **VLIN Y−S/2, Y+S/2 AT X+S/2**. The bottom line of the box can be plotted (from right to left) using the statement **HLIN X+S/2, X−S/2 AT Y+S/2**. Finally, the left side of the box can be plotted (from bottom to top) using the statement **VLIN Y+S/2, Y−S/2 AT X−S/2**.

```
JLIST
10      REM     PLOTTING BOXES
20      HOME
30      GR
40      INPUT "ENTER A COLOR, 1-15 ";
        C
45      COLOR= C
50      INPUT "ENTER A SIZE, 2-20 ";S
60      INPUT "ENTER CENTER X,Y (10-2
        9) ";X,Y
70      HLIN X - S / 2,X + S / 2 AT Y
        - S / 2
80      VLIN Y - S / 2,Y + S / 2 AT X
        + S / 2
90      HLIN X + S / 2,X - S / 2 AT Y
        + S / 2
100     VLIN Y + S / 2,Y - S / 2 AT
        X - S / 2
110     INPUT "PRESS C FOLLOWED BY R
        ETURN TO CONTINUE ";A$
120     TEXT
130     GOTO 20
```

FIGURE 5.12 Program to plot boxes of different colors, sizes, and locations.

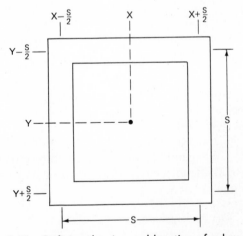

FIGURE 5.11 Defining the size and location of a box.

A program that will plot boxes of different colors, sizes, and locations is shown in Figure 5.12. Line 40 waits for a color number between 1 and 15 to be entered from the keyboard. Line 50 stores a number (between 2 and 20) entered from the keyboard in

memory cell S. This will be the length of the sides of the box. Keeping this number between 2 and 20 will insure that the box fits on the screen if the X and Y coordinates of the center of the box are in the range 10–29. These center coordinates are entered through the keyboard in line 60.

The sides of the box are drawn in lines 70–100. Line 110 is used to wait until a key is pressed before rerunning the program. Line 120 returns to the text mode, and line 130 branches to line 20, which clears the screen, and then the program is run again.

A sample run of this program is shown in Figure 5.13. Type in this program, and try some other examples.

*INTEGER BASIC allows commas in string variables in an INPUT statement, but each string must be entered on a separate line.

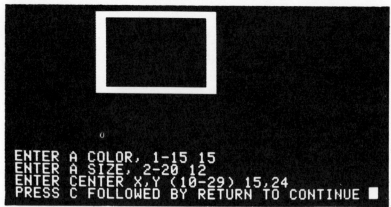

ENTER A COLOR, 1-15 15
ENTER A SIZE, 2-20 12
ENTER CENTER X,Y (10-29) 15,24
PRESS C FOLLOWED BY RETURN TO CONTINUE ■

FIGURE 5.13   Sample run of program shown in Fig. 5.12.

THE GET STATEMENT

Up to this point the only method you know for entering data from the keyboard is the INPUT statement. One potential disadvantage of using the INPUT statement is that the data is not accepted by the Apple II until you press the RETURN key. Sometimes you would like the Apple II to input a single character from the keyboard as soon as the key is pressed. The GET statement will do this.

The GET statement is used to store a single character typed on the keyboard in a string variable such as A$. The form of the GET statement is **GET A$**, where A$ can be any string variable. When a BASIC program encounters the statement **GET A$**, it waits for a key to be pressed. When a key is pressed, the character corresponding to the key is stored in A$.

Type in the program

```
10 GET A$
20 PRINT A$: GOTO 10
```

If you run this two-line program, the Apple II should print on the screen any key that you press, as shown in Figure 5.14.

Run this program, and try a variety of keys. Note that you can print any character plus the RETURN key.

EXERCISE 5-1
The temperature in degrees Celsius (°C) is related to the temperature in degrees Fahrenheit (°F) by the formula

$$°C = \frac{5}{9}(°F - 32)$$

Write a program that will input a temperature in °F and print on the screen the temperature in both °F and °C.

EXERCISE 5-2
Write a program that will ask the user to enter a color C, a length L, and a center coordinate pair X,Y and will then plot a cross with height and width equal to L centered at X,Y.

FIGURE 5.14   This program GETs a character from the keyboard and displays it at the next screen location.

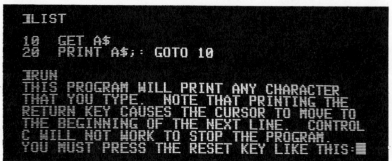

```
]LIST

10  GET A$
20  PRINT A$;: GOTO 10

]RUN
THIS PROGRAM WILL PRINT ANY CHARACTER
THAT YOU TYPE.  NOTE THAT PRINTING THE
RETURN KEY CAUSES THE CURSOR TO MOVE TO
THE BEGINNING OF THE NEXT LINE.  CONTROL
C WILL NOT WORK TO STOP THE PROGRAM.
YOU MUST PRESS THE RESET KEY LIKE THIS:■
```

MAKING CHOICES: LEARNING ABOUT IF . . . THEN

All of the programs we have written up to this point have consisted of a simple sequence of instructions. The Apple II simply does what it is told and executes one statement after another. However, the thing that makes computers appear to be smart is the ability to make a decision based on the current state of affairs. The primary decision-making statement in APPLE-SOFT BASIC is the IF . . . THEN statement. This statement allows the Apple II to branch to one of two possible statements, depending upon the truth or falsity of a particular logical expression. A *logical expression* is an expression that can be either *true* or *false*.

In this chapter you will learn

1. the use of the IF . . . THEN statement to make simple choices
2. the meaning of the Apple II's relational operators
3. the meaning of the Apple II's logical operators
4. about the *if . . . then . . . else* statement, flowcharts, and structured flowcharts.

THE IF . . . THEN STATEMENT

The IF . . . THEN statement in APPLESOFT BASIC allows your program to execute some statements conditionally or to branch conditionally to some statement. The following are three different forms of the IF . . . THEN statement:

50 IF logical expression THEN statement
50 IF logical expression THEN statement 1: statement 2: . . .
50 IF logical expression THEN line number

In each of these forms the logical expression is some BASIC expression that is either true or false. These expressions will normally contain relational operators (such as <) and/or logical operators (such as OR) which will be defined and discussed in detail below.

In the first form of the IF . . . THEN statement shown above, if the logical expression is *true*, the statement following the word THEN is executed. This can be any BASIC statement that can be executed conditionally. If the logical expression is *false*, the statement with the *next* line number is executed.

The second form of the IF . . . THEN statement shown above behaves in a similar way. However, if the logical expression is *true,* then all of the statements following the word THEN are executed.* Remember that if the logical expression is *false,* the statement with the *next* line number is executed.

In the third form of the IF . . . THEN statement shown above, if the logical expression is *true,* the program will branch to "line number." This form is equivalent to the first form when the statement is a GOTO statement. Thus, for example, the following two statements are equivalent.

50 IF A<0 THEN 90

50 IF A<0 THEN GOTO 90

In fact, the word THEN can be omitted in the second form and you can write **50 IF A<0 GOTO 90.**

We will illustrate the use of the IF . . . THEN statement by adding some conditional statements to the programs we wrote in the last chapter.

Gas Mileage Program

In the gas mileage program shown in Figure 5.4 of the last chapter, M1 is the old odometer reading, and M2 is the new odometer reading. To make sense, M2 must be greater than M1, (that is, M2>M1). It is always a good idea when writing computer programs to check the data entered through the keyboard to try to detect any typing errors. For example, if after entering the value of M2 in line 35, M1 is greater than M2, a typing error has probably been made. In any event M2 is too small to make sense. Thus, we could add the statements **37 IF M1>M2 THEN PRINT "READING TOO SMALL": GOTO 20** to the program in Figure 5.4 as shown in Figure 6.1.

```
]LIST
10  REM    GAS MILAGE PROGRAM
20  PRINT "ENTER PREVIOUS ODOMETE
     R READING"
25  INPUT M1
30  PRINT "ENTER NEW ODOMETER REA
     DING"
35  INPUT M2
37  IF M1 > M2 THEN  PRINT "READI
     NG TOO SMALL": GOTO 20
40  PRINT "ENTER GALLONS SINCE LA
     ST FILLUP"
45  INPUT G
50 MPG = (M2 - M1) / G
60  PRINT "GAS MILAGE: "MPG;" MIL
     ES/GAL."
```

FIGURE 6.1 Gas mileage program containing an IF . . . THEN statement.

A sample run of this new program is shown in Figure 6.2. Note that during the first execution the last digit of the new odometer reading was omitted. This made M2<M1, and statement number 37 caught it, printed the message **READING TOO SMALL,** and then branched back to statement number 20 where the program started over again.

In statement number 37 you might have branched back to statement number 30 and asked to enter only the new odometer reading. However, the error may have occurred when entering M1 (you may have typed an extra digit), and therefore it is better to reenter both odometer readings.

*INTEGER BASIC will execute only the first statement following THEN.

FIGURE 6.2 Program will check to make sure that M2 is greater than M1.

```
]RUN
ENTER PREVIOUS ODOMETER READING
?12345
ENTER NEW ODOMETER READING
?1265
READING TOO SMALL
ENTER PREVIOUS ODOMETER READING
?12345
ENTER NEW ODOMETER READING
?12654
ENTER GALLONS SINCE LAST FILLUP
?15.8
GAS MILAGE: 19.556962 MILES/GAL.
]
```

Circle Program

In the circle program shown in Figure 5.3 the radius should obviously be positive. Actually, if you want to calculate only the area of the circle given by πr^2, a negative radius will give the same answer as the same positive radius. On the other hand, if you also calculate the circumference of the circle given by $2\pi r$, the radius must be positive. We can calculate the circumference by adding the two statements

    45 C = 2*PI*R
    47 PRINT "CIRCUMFERENCE="; C

to the program in Figure 5.3. We can then test to see if the radius is negative by adding the statement **32 IF R<0 THEN PRINT "RADIUS MUST BE POSITIVE": GOTO 20.** If the value of R entered in the INPUT statement on line 30 is less than 0, then the message **RADIUS MUST BE POSITIVE** will be printed, and the program will branch back to line 20 and ask for another radius to be entered.

We saw in Figure 5.3 that if the radius is too large, an overflow error will occur when the area is computed in line 35. Inasmuch as the value of the area A can not be greater than 1.7E38, the largest radius R that will not result in an overflow can be found as follows:

$$A = \pi r^2 < 1.7E38$$
$$r^2 < 1.7E38/\pi$$
$$r < \sqrt{1.7E38/\pi}$$

Thus, if R >SQR(1.7E38/PI), the area will be greater than 1.7E38 and cause an overflow . We can test this by adding the following statement to the program: **33 IF R>SQR(1.7E38/PI) THEN PRINT "RADIUS TOO LARGE": GOTO 20.**

The complete revised program is shown in Figure 6.3, and a sample run is shown in Figure 6.4. Note the use of the two IF . . . THEN statements in lines 32 and 33. The first IF . . . THEN statement checks to see if R is less than 0. If this is *false* (that is, if R is positive), the next IF . . . THEN statement on line 33 is executed. If R is not greater than SQR(1.7E38/PI), the program will continue on line 35.

FIGURE 6.3 Modified circle program that checks the value of the radius R.

```
]LIST
10   REM    PROGRAM TO COMPUTE THE
           AREA OF A CIRCLE
15   PI = 3.14159265
20   PRINT "ENTER THE RADIUS OF A
           CIRCLE ";
30   INPUT R
32   IF R < 0 THEN  PRINT "RADIUS
           MUST BE POSITIVE": GOTO 20
33   IF R >  SQR (1.7E38 / PI) THEN
           PRINT "RADIUS TOO LARGE": GOTO
           20
35 A = PI * R ^ 2
40   PRINT "THE AREA OF THE CIRCLE
           IS ";A
45 C = 2 * PI * R
47   PRINT "CIRCUMFERENCE=";C
50   PRINT
60   GOTO 20
```

FIGURE 6.4 Sample run of program in Fig. 6.3.

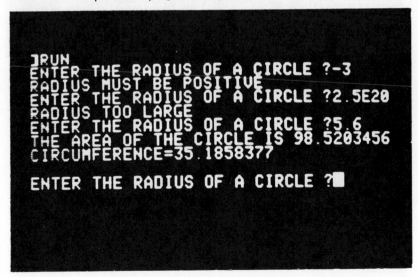

Rectangle Program

As another example of using the IF . . . THEN statement to check data entered with the INPUT statement, consider the program shown in Figure 5.2 that computes the area of a rectangle. It is clear that *both* sides of a rectangle must be positive. Thus, if *either* of the two values entered in the INPUT statement on line 30 is negative, then the program should print an error message and ask for new inputs. We can do this by adding the following single IF . . . THEN statement:

35 IF X<0 OR Y<0 THEN PRINT "VALUES MUST BE POSITIVE": GO TO 30.

The resulting program is shown in Figure 6.5, and a sample run is shown in Figure 6.6. Note from this sample run that the Apple II will not allow the program to continue if either value entered is negative or if both are negative. Thus, the meaning of the logical expression X<0 OR Y<0 is that it is *true* if either X<0 *or* Y <0 is true, or if both are true.

In the above logical expression the symbol < is one of the *relational operators*. The word OR is one of the *logical operators*. Relational operators and logical operators will be discussed in more detail in the following two sections.

FIGURE 6.5 The IF . . . THEN statement in line 35 contains a compound logical expression.

```
]LIST
10   REM      PROGRAM TO COMPUTE THE

20   REM      AREA OF A RECTANGLE
30   INPUT "ENTER THE 2 SIDES OF A
        RECTANGLE ";X,Y
35   IF X < 0 OR Y < 0 THEN  PRINT
        "VALUES MUST BE POSITIVE": GOTO
        30
40   PRINT "THE AREA OF A RECTANGL
        E WITH SIDES"
50   PRINT X;" AND ";Y;" IS EQUAL
        TO ";X * Y
60   PRINT
70   GOTO 30
```

FIGURE 6.6 Sample run of program in Fig. 6.5.

RELATIONAL OPERATORS

A *relational operator* is used to form a logical expression by comparing two arithmetic expressions. (An arithmetic expression can be a numerical constant, variable, or expression.) Thus, for example, A<0 is a logical expression (either true or false) formed using the relational operator < (meaning *less than*). If the contents of memory cell A is less than zero, this logical expression is true; otherwise, it is false.

The Apple II stores the logical value "false" as a zero (0). It stores the logical value "true" as 1. You can see this by typing

$$A=3$$
$$? A <0$$

and

$$A = -3$$
$$? A < 0$$

as shown in Figure 6.7. Note that you can print the value of logical expressions such as A<0.

The relational expressions used in the Apple II are given in Table 6.1. Figure 6.8 shows some examples of using these relational operators. You should try some examples of your own.

TABLE 6.1   Relational Operators

Operator	Meaning
=	equal to
<> or ><	not equal to
<	less than
>	greater than
<= or =<	less than or equal to
>= or =>	greater than or equal to

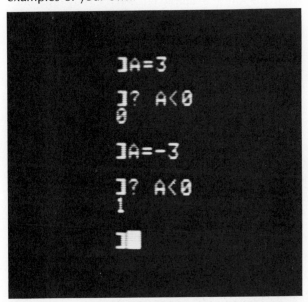

FIGURE 6.7   The Apple II stores "true" as 1 and "false" as 0.

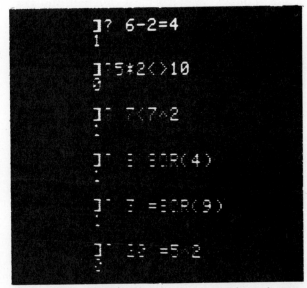

FIGURE 6.8   Examples of logical expressions formed using the relational operators.

LOGICAL OPERATORS

In addition to the relational operators (=,<>, <,>,<=,>=), the Apple II uses the three logical operators NOT, AND, and OR. The meanings of these operators are shown in Table 6.2.

TABLE 6.2   Logical operators
(A and B are logical expressions)

A		NOT A	
true		false	
false		true	

A	B	A AND B	A OR B
false	false	false	false
false	true	false	true
true	false	false	true
true	true	true	true

NOT

The logical operator NOT is a unary operator; that is, it operates on a single logical expression, A. If A is *true*, NOT A is *false*. If A is *false*, NOT A is *true*.

Examples of using the logical operator NOT are shown in Figure 6.9. When using NOT you should use parentheses because the NOT operation is performed before a relational operator. For example, in the last example in Figure 6.9, NOT 1 is equal to 0, and 0 is less than 2.

FIGURE 6.9   Examples of using the logical operator NOT.

```
]? NOT(3=3)
0

]? NOT(5<2)
1

]? NOT(10<>5*2)
1

]? NOT(1<2)
0

]? NOT 1<2
1
```

51

AND

The logical operator AND is a *binary* operator that operates on *two* logical expressions. Note in Table 6.2 that A AND B is *true* only if *both* A and B are true. It is *false* if either A or B is false, or if both are false. Examples of using the logical operator AND are shown in Figure 6.10.

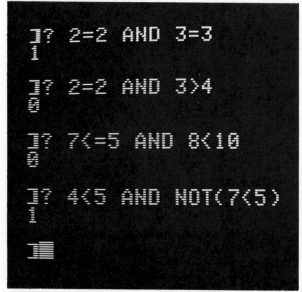

FIGURE 6.10 Examples of using the logical operator AND.

OR

The logical operator OR is, like AND, a binary operator. Note from Table 6.2 that A OR B is *false* only if *both* A and B are false. It is *true* if either A or B is true, or if both are true. Examples of using the logical operator OR are shown in Figure 6.11.

Note that the third example in Figure 6.11 is *false,* while the fourth example is *true.* The only difference between the two is the inclusion of the parentheses in the third example. The reason that the fourth example is true is that the AND operation is performed *before* the OR operation. There is thus an order or precedence for logical and relational operators as well as for arithmetic operators, (see Chapter 4). When the Apple II evaluates an expression, it uses the order of precedence shown in Table 6.3.

TABLE 6.3 Order of precedence for evaluating expressions

Operator	Meaning
()	Parenthesis
$\wedge$	Exponentiation
$-$,NOT	Unary Minus, Logical Complement
*,/	Multiplication and Division
+,$-$	Addition and Subtraction
=,<>, <, >, <=, >=	Relational Operators
AND	Logical AND
OR	Logical OR

Within each level of precedence the expression is evaluated left to right.

FIGURE 6.11 Examples of using the logical operator OR.

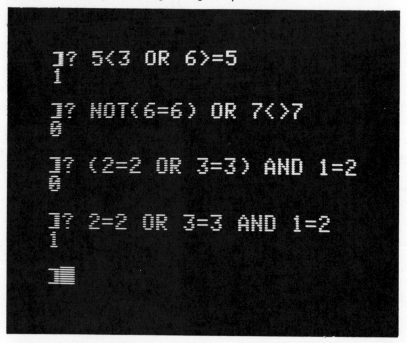

As another example of the IF . . . THEN statement, consider the problem of calculating the weekly pay of an employee whose hourly rate is $4.00 per hour and who receives time-and-a-half for overtime. Suppose that the total hours worked per week cannot exceed 60 hours. Thus, we want to write a program that will

1. ask for the number of hours worked to be entered from the keyboard

2. check to make sure that the number of hours entered is not greater than 60

3. check to make sure that the number of hours entered is not negative

4. compute the pay at $4.00 per hour for the first 40 hours and at $6.00 per hour for any hours over 40

5. print the total amount of pay.

The program to do this is shown in Figure 6.12. Lines 20 and 30 ask for the number of hours to be INPUT, and the value is stored in H. Line 40 checks to make sure that H is not greater than 60. Line 50 checks to make sure that H is not negative.

Line 60 will compute the total pay to be **M=H*4** if H is less than or equal to 40. Note that this line ends with the statement **GOTO 90** which will branch to statement 90. Line 90 rounds the value of M to two places after the decimal point (see the discussion of rounding for the gas mileage program in Chapter 5). Line 100 prints the amount of pay.

If H is greater than 40, the logical expression **H=40** in line 60 will be false, and line 70 will be executed next. Line 70 computes the number of overtime hours, OV. Line 80 computes the total pay, **M=40*4+OV*6**, consisting of the first 40 hours at $4.00 per hour, plus the remaining overtime hours at $6.00 per hour. Lines 90 and 100 will then round and print the total pay.

```
]LIST
10   REM   PROGRAM TO COMPUTE WEEK
     LY WAGES
20   PRINT "ENTER NUMBER OF HOURS
     WORKED"
30   INPUT H
40   IF H > 60 THEN  PRINT "TOO MA
     NY HOURS": GOTO 20
50   IF H < 0 THEN  PRINT "INVALID
     DATA": GOTO 20
60   IF H <  = 40 THEN M = H * 4: GOTO
     90
70   OV = H - 40
80   M = 40 * 4 + OV * 6
90   M =  INT (M * 100 + 0.5) / 100

100  PRINT "WEEKLY PAY= $ ";M
```

FIGURE 6.12 Listing of weekly pay program.

Sample runs of this program are shown in Figure 6.13. Note that trailing zeros are not printed on the screen. Thus, for example, $233.50 is printed as **$233.5**. In Chapter 12 we will see how to make the total number of cents appear on the screen.

FIGURE 6.13 Sample runs of program in Fig. 6.12.

```
]RUN
ENTER NUMBER OF HOURS WORKED
?32
WEEKLY PAY= $ 128

]RUN
ENTER NUMBER OF HOURS WORKED
?52 25
WEEKLY PAY= $ 233.5

]RUN
ENTER NUMBER OF HOURS WORKED
?47.34
WEEKLY PAY= $ 204.04
```

AREA OF A TRIANGLE

The area of the triangle shown in Figure 6.14 can be calculated from the formula

$$\text{AREA} = [S(S-A)(S-B)(S-C)]^{0.5}$$
$$= \sqrt{S(S-A)(S-B)(S-C)}$$

where A, B, and C are the sides of the triangle and

$$S = \frac{1}{2}(A+B+C)$$

is the semi-perimeter.

FIGURE 6.14 Finding the area of a triangle.

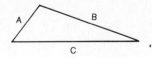

Semi-perimeter, $S = \frac{1}{2}(A+B+C)$

Area $= [S(S-A)(S-B)(S-C)]^{0.5}$

In BASIC the formula for the area can be written as **AREA = (S*(S−A)*(S−B)*(S−C)) ∧ 0.5** or **AREA = SQR (S*(S− A)*(S− B)*(S− C))**.

Remember that the multiplication symbol * must *always* be explicitly typed and every left parenthesis, (, must have an accompanying right parenthesis,).

We want to write a program than will ask the user to enter the three sides of the triangle from the keyboard and will then display the area of the triangle on the screen. It should be clear that not all combinations of three numbers can represent the sides of a triangle. For example, a triangle can not be formed from the three sides 10, 5, and 3 shown in Figure 6.15. From this figure you can see that to form a triangle, the sum of the two sides A+B must be greater than C, if C is the longest side. This is equivalent to requiring C to be less than the semi-perimeter S = (A+B+C)/2. Note that if this were not true, the above formula for the area would involve taking the square root of a negative number, which is not a real value.

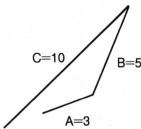

FIGURE 6.15   To form a triangle the following relations must be true:

$$A + B > C; \qquad C < S = \frac{1}{2}(A+B+C).$$

Therefore, our program should check to make sure that the three numbers entered from the keyboard can really represent the sides of a triangle. We need to check to make sure that C<S. Which side is C? It is the longest side. But the longest side may be the first, second, or third number to be entered from the keyboard. If the program uses the INPUT statement **INPUT A,B,C**, the longest side may actually be stored in memory cell A,B, or C. Therefore, the program must find the longest side, L, and then make sure that L is less than the semi-perimeter, S.

We can determine the largest number stored in memory cells A,B, and C by using the following procedure:

1. Compare A and B
   if A>B
   then set L=A
   else set L=B
2. Compare C and L
   if C>L
   then set L=C

You should convince yourself that this *algorithm,* or step-by-step procedure, will, in fact, result in the memory cell L containing the largest value. This value of L can then be compared to the semi-perimeter S to see if a triangle is possible.

The BASIC program to do all this is shown in Figure 6.16. Line 20 asks for the three sides of the triangle to be entered, and line 30 stores these three values in A,B, and C. Line 40 compares A and B, and if A>B, it stores the value of A in L, and branches to line 60. If A is not greater than B, line 50 will store the value of B in L. Thus, when line 60 is executed, L will contain the larger of A and B. Line 60 compares C and L and stores the value of C in L if C is greater than L. Therefore, by the time line 70 is executed, L will contain the largest number stored in A,B, and C.

```
]LIST
10   REM    PROGRAM TO FIND THE
15   REM    AREA OF A TRIANGLE
20   PRINT "ENTER THE THREE SIDES
     OF A TRIANGLE"
30   INPUT A,B,C
40   IF A > B THEN L = A: GOTO 60
50 L = B
60   IF C > L THEN L = C
70   S = (A + B + C) / 2
80   IF L > S THEN  PRINT "NO TRIA
     NGLE POSSIBLE": GOTO 20
90 AREA = (S * (S - A) * (S - B) *
     (S - C)) ^ 0.5
100   PRINT "THE AREA OF THE TRIAN
      GLE IS ";AREA
110   PRINT
120   GOTO 20
```

FIGURE 6.16   Program to find the area of a triangle.

Line 70 computes the semi-perimeter, S, and line 80 compares L and S to see if a triangle is possible. If L is greater than or equal to S, the message **NO TRIANGLE POSSIBLE** is printed, and the program branches back to line 20 and asks for three new sides. On the other hand, if L is less than S, line 90 is executed, which computes the area of the triangle. Line 100 prints the result. Line 110 skips a line, and line 120 branches back to line 20 to run the program again. A sample run of this program is shown in Figure 6.17.

```
]RUN
ENTER THE THREE SIDES OF A TRIANGLE
?7,12,9
THE AREA OF THE TRIANGLE IS 31.3049517

ENTER THE THREE SIDES OF A TRIANGLE
?7,12,4
NO TRIANGLE POSSIBLE
ENTER THE THREE SIDES OF A TRIANGLE
?3,5,7
THE AREA OF THE TRIANGLE IS 6.49519054

ENTER THE THREE SIDES OF A TRIANGLE
?3,5,9
NO TRIANGLE POSSIBLE
ENTER THE THREE SIDES OF A TRIANGLE
?■
```

FIGURE 6.17   Sample runs of the program in Fig. 6.16.

DRAWING CHECKERBOARD PATTERNS WITH THE GAME PADDLES

In Chapter 4 you learned how to draw figures on the screen using the game paddles (see Figure 4.29). In this section we will modify this program to allow the drawing of checkerboard patterns.

The four statements

$$X = PDL(0)$$
$$X = INT(X/7)$$
$$Y = PDL(1)$$
$$Y = INT(Y/7)$$

will determine integer values of X and Y in the range 0–36, depending on the positions of the game paddles. In Figure 6.18 note that for every shaded square in the checkerboard pattern the sum of X+Y is an *even* number.

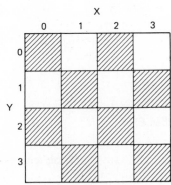

FIGURE 6.18   A checkerboard pattern results if the same color is plotted at all positions at which X+Y is even.

A number S is even if the remainder of integer division of the number by 2 is zero. This remainder is given by $R = S-INT(S/2)*2$. For example, if S = 7, then

$$R = 7-INT(7/2)*2$$
$$= 7-3*2$$
$$= 7-6$$
$$= 1$$

On the other hand, if S = 8, then

$$R = 8-INT(8/2)*2$$
$$= 8-4*2$$
$$= 8-8$$
$$= 0$$

The listing of a program that will allow you to draw checkerboard patterns is shown in Figure 6.19.

FIGURE 6.19   Program to draw checkerboard patterns.

```
]LIST
10   REM   PADDLE CHECKERBOARDS
20   GR : HOME
30   INPUT "ENTER TWO COLORS ";C1,
     C2
40   X =   PDL (0)
45   X =   INT (X / 7)
50   Y =   PDL (1)
55   Y =   INT (Y / 7)
60   S = X + Y
70   R = S -  INT (S / 2) * 2
80   IF R = 0 THEN   COLOR= C1: GOTO
     100
90   COLOR= C2
100  PLOT X,Y
110  GOTO 40
```

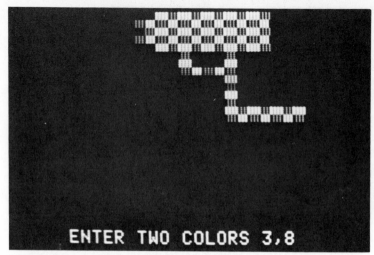

ENTER TWO COLORS 3,8

FIGURE 6.20   Sample run of the program shown in Fig. 6.19.

Line 30 asks the user to enter two color values to be used in the checkerboard pattern. Lines 60 and 70 check to see if X+Y is even. If it is, (R=0) then the color is set to C1 in line 80. Otherwise, the color is set to C2 in line 90. The resulting colored spot is plotted in line 100. The program then branches back to line 40 where the paddles are read again.

An example of running this program is shown in Figure 6.20. You should type in this program and try running it yourself.

THE IF . . . THEN . . . ELSE STATEMENT

In this chapter we have used the BASIC IF . . . THEN statement in the form of an *if . . . then . . . else* statement. For example, in the program to find the area of a triangle we used the following algorithm to find the largest value in A, B, and C and store it in L.

> *if* A>B
> *then* L=A
> *else* L=B
> *if* C>L
> *then* L=C

We coded this algorithm in BASIC as follows:

> 40 IF A>B THEN L=A: GOTO 60
> 50 L=B
> 60 IF C>L THEN L=C

The *if . . . then . . . else* statement is one of those "good" statements that is available in other programming languages, such as PASCAL, but is not directly available in BASIC. Note that after the *then* statements are executed the *else* statements are automatically skipped. However, in BASIC we must tell the computer to skip line 50 above by ending the *then* statements with **GOTO 60**.

The *else* is generally optional in an *if . . . then . . .*

else statement. In this case it reduces to the BASIC IF . . . THEN statement. If there are a number of statements in the THEN clause, you can still simulate an *if . . . then . . . else* statement in BASIC as follows:

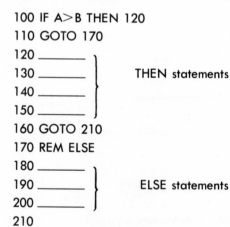

Note that line 110 is executed if A>B is *false*. This will branch to the ELSE statements. If A>B is *true*, line 120 is executed, which is the first of the THEN statements. You can use as many lines as you need for the THEN statements. However, at the end of the THEN statements you must include a GOTO statement that will skip over the ELSE statements.

In Chapter 3 we said that a computer program is like a train going on a trip. The seats in the train are like memory locations with unique names or addresses that distinguish one seat from another. The seats may contain strings (like the name of the person sitting in the seat) or numerical values (like the age of the person sitting in the seat).

As the train goes along the track it can come to a station where new people can get on, some people can get off, or others can exchange seats or add things to their seats. This is equivalent to executing BASIC statements such as PRINT, INPUT, and A=B+C.

The *if . . . then . . . else* statement is like a *switch* in the track that allows the train to go on one of two different paths as shown in Figure 6.21. These two paths lead to two different stations and then rejoin on the other side of the stations. If the logical expression following *if* is true, the train follows the track to station 1 where the *then* statements are executed. If the logical expression following *if* is false the train follows the track to station 2 where the *else* statements are executed. Note that the train can only go to station 1 *or* station 2. It *cannot* go to both stations.

FIGURE 6.21 The *if . . . then . . . else* statement takes the train to one of two possible stations.

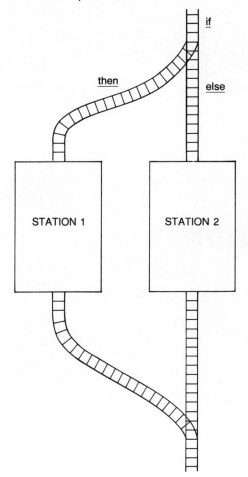

Flowcharts

Flowcharts have traditionally been used to express a computer algorithm. The *if . . . then . . . else* statement illustrated in Figure 6.21 can be represented as a flowchart as shown in Figure 6.22. The similarity to Figure 6.21 is obvious. If the logical expression in the diamond-shaped box is *true*, the path to statements A is followed. Otherwise, the path to statements B is followed.

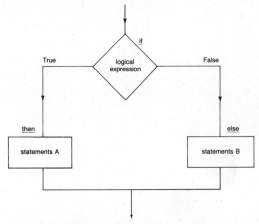

FIGURE 6.22 Flowchart representation of the *if . . . then . . . else* statement.

The algorithm given above for finding the largest value in A, B, and C is expressed as a flowchart and in *pseudocode*, (using *if . . . then . . . else*) in Figure 6.23. Many people find the pseudocode representation in Figure 6.23b to be simpler and just as easy to understand as the flowchart in Figure 6.23a. In addition, it is easy to generate flowcharts that end up looking like "bowls of spaghetti." For these reasons the use of flowcharts has declined in recent years.

FIGURE 6.23 (a) Flowchart and (b) pseudocode for algorithm to find the largest value in A, B, and C.

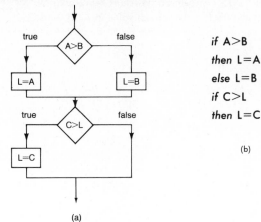

For those who still like to have some type of graphical representation of an algorithm without creating a bowl of spaghetti that is hard to understand, *structured flowcharts* are available.

Structured Flowcharts

A structured flowchart, also called a Nassi-Schneiderman chart after the people who introduced it, is an alternate representation of an alogorithm that consists of various nested "boxes" without the connecting lines shown in Figure 6.23. Two alternate representations of the *if . . . then . . . else* statement are shown in Figure 6.24. We will use the form shown in Figure 6.24a. With this structured flowchart the algorithm in Figure 6.23 can be represented as shown in Figure 6.25.

FIGURE 6.24 Two forms of a structured flowchart that represents the *if . . . then . . . else* statement.

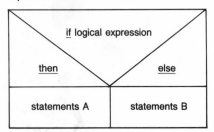

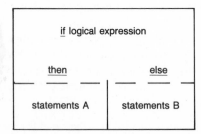

FIGURE 6.25 Structured flowchart representation of algorithm to find the largest value in A, B, and C.

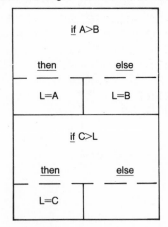

Flowcharts and pseudocode are just different ways of representing an algorithm to try to make it easier to understand. When you are developing a computer program, it is generally easier to express the program first in the form of a flowchart, structured flowchart, or pseudocode, and then convert this algorithm to BASIC.

The structured flowchart and pseudocode for the weekly pay program discussed earlier in this chapter are shown in Figure 6.26a and 6.26b. The BASIC listing of this program is shown in Figure 6.26c. You should carefully compare these three representations of the same program.

FIGURE 6.26 (a) Structured flowchart, (b) pseudocode, and (c) BASIC listing of weekly pay program.

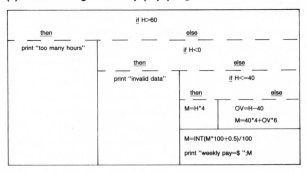

(a)

(b)

```
        if H>60
        then print "too many hours"
        else if H<0
                then print "invalid data"
                else if H<=40
                        then M=H*4
                        else OV=H-40
                            M=40*4+OV*6
                        M = INT(M*100+0.5)/100
                        print "weekly pay = $" ;M
```

(c)

```
]LIST
10   REM    PROGRAM TO COMPUTE WEEK
     LY WAGES
20   PRINT "ENTER NUMBER OF HOURS
     WORKED"
30   INPUT H
40   IF H > 60 THEN  PRINT "TOO MA
     NY HOURS": GOTO 20
50   IF H < 0 THEN  PRINT "INVALID
     DATA": GOTO 20
60   IF H < = 40 THEN M = H * 4: GOTO
     90
70 OV = H - 40
80 M = 40 * 4 + OV * 6
90 M =  INT (M * 100 + 0.5) / 100

100  PRINT "WEEKLY PAY= $ ";M
```

The advantage of the structured flowchart representation is that it clearly displays the logic of the program in a graphic form. The advantage of the pseudocode is that it describes the algorithm in a simple, straightforward manner. Note the importance of the indentation in the pseudocode description. The advantage of the BASIC representation is that it can be executed on the Apple II.

Some people have devised a variety of indentation conventions that will make a BASIC program easier to understand. Unfortunately, none of these can be used on the Apple II because the Apple II automatically changes the appearance of a program by adding and subtracting blanks when LISTing a program. You should always keep a written version of your programs on a piece of paper. This version can include indentation, pseudocode, structured flowcharts, or anything else that will help you to understand the program.

The complete structured flowchart for the program to find the area of a triangle is shown in Figure 6.27a. The BASIC listing of this program is shown in Figure 6.27b. You should compare carefully the structured flowchart with the BASIC listing. Note that the GOTO statement in line 120 is represented in the structured flowchart as an "outer loop" that continues forever (or until the program is stopped by pressing CTRL C RETURN in response to the INPUT statement).

In the next chapter we will take a closer look at loops. In particular you will learn how to stop a loop any time you want.

FIGURE 6.27
(a) Structured flowchart and

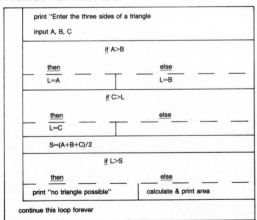

EXERCISE 6-1

For married taxpayers filing joint returns with a taxable income between $20,200 and $24,600, the Federal income tax is $3,273 plus 28% of the amount over $20,200. Write a program that will input a taxable income, check that it is between $20,200 and $24,600, and then compute and print the income tax on the screen.

EXERCISE 6-2

Write a program to compute take-home pay. The program should input an hourly wage and the number of hours worked. Assume that 6.65% of the gross pay is deducted for Social Security taxes, 14.8% of the gross pay is deducted for federal income taxes, and 4% of the gross pay is deducted for state income taxes. The program should print out the wage rate, the number of hours worked, the amount deducted for Social Security, federal and state income taxes, and the take-home pay.

EXERCISE 6-3

Write a program that will continuously input a series of test scores. When a negative score is entered, the program should print the number of scores entered, the largest score, the smallest score, and the average of the test scores.

(b) BASIC listing of program to find the area of a triangle.

```
]LIST
10    REM     PROGRAM TO FIND THE
15    REM     AREA OF A TRIANGLE
20    PRINT "ENTER THE THREE SIDES
         OF A TRIANGLE"
30    INPUT A,B,C
40    IF A > B THEN L = A: GOTO 60
50    L = B
60    IF C > L THEN L = C
70    S = (A + B + C) / 2
80    IF L > S THEN  PRINT "NO TRIA
         NGLE POSSIBLE": GOTO 20
90    AREA = (S * (S - A) * (S - B) *
         (S - C)) ^ 0.5
100   PRINT "THE AREA OF THE TRIAN
         GLE IS ";AREA
110   PRINT
120   GOTO 20
```

7 LEARNING ABOUT LOOPS: ANOTHER LOOK AT IF . . . THEN

In Chapter 6 we used the IF . . . THEN statement to make simple choices between two alternatives. We saw that this use of the IF . . . THEN statement was equivalent to using an *if . . . then . . . else* statement. In this chapter we will use the IF . . . THEN statement for a completely different purpose—that of forming loops. Inasmuch as you are using the same IF . . . THEN statement, you may think that there is no difference between the use of IF . . . THEN to form loops and its use to form an *if . . . then . . . else* construct. But this is not so. There is a fundamental difference between loops and an *if . . . then . . . else* statement. An *if . . . then . . . else* statement merely makes a decision between two different paths. A loop, on the other hand, implies repetition in which the same statements are executed over and over again until (or while) some condition is met.

In this chapter you will learn

1. to repeat a loop while an affirmative answer is given to a question
2. to use the IF . . . THEN statement to form a *repeat while* loop
3. to use nested loops
4. the difference between a *repeat while,* a *repeat until,* a *do while,* and a *do until* loop and how to implement these loops in BASIC
5. how to implement a *loop . . . exit if . . . endloop* and a *loop . . . continue if . . . endloop* construct in BASIC.

THE REPEAT WHILE LOOP

Very often you will have a sequence of BASIC statements that you will want to repeat as long as a particular logical expression is *true.* For example you may wish to do the following:

30 _____
40 _____
50 _____
60 _____
repeat lines 30–60 while A>0

You can do this with the following statement: **70 IF A>0 THEN 30.**

Lines 30–70 form a *loop* that is exited only when A>0 becomes false, that is, when A<=0. Obviously, in order to get out of the loop there must be something in lines 30–60 that will eventually cause A to become less than or equal to zero.

Later in this chapter we will look at other types of loops. For now, let's look at some examples.

TRIANGLE PROGRAM

The program to find the area of a triangle was discussed in Chapter 6 and the BASIC listing is given in Figure 6.16. Because of the GOTO statement in line 120, this program executes over and over again until CTRL C RETURN is pressed in response to the INPUT statement. A better way to end the program would be to ask the user if he or she wants to continue. This can be done by replacing the GOTO 20 statement on line 120 with the following statements:

120 INPUT "DO YOU WANT TO CONTINUE? (Y,N)";A$
130 IF A$= "Y" THEN 20
140 END

Line 120 displays the message **DO YOU WANT TO CONTINUE? (Y,N)** and then waits for a response to be entered from the keyboard. This response is stored in the string A$. Line 130 compares this string to "Y", and if **A$="Y"** the program branches back to line 20, and the area of another triangle is found. Any other response will terminate the program.

The BASIC listing of this modified program is shown in Figure 7.1, and a sample run is shown in Figure 7.2.

```
]LIST

10   REM    PROGRAM TO FIND THE
15   REM    AREA OF A TRIANGLE
20   PRINT "ENTER THE THREE SIDES
     OF A TRIANGLE"
30   INPUT A,B,C
40   IF A > B THEN L = A: GOTO 60
50 L = B
60   IF C > L THEN L = C
70 S = (A + B + C) / 2
80   IF L > S THEN  PRINT "NO TRIA
     NGLE POSSIBLE": GOTO 20
90 AREA = (S * (S - A) * (S - B) *
     (S - C)) ^ 0.5
100  PRINT "THE AREA OF THE TRIAN
     GLE IS ";AREA
110  PRINT
120  INPUT "DO YOU WANT TO CONTIN
     UE? (Y,N)";A$
130  IF A$ = "Y" THEN 20
140  END
```

FIGURE 7.1 BASIC listing of modified triangle program.

FIGURE 7.2 Sample run of program shown in Fig. 7.1.

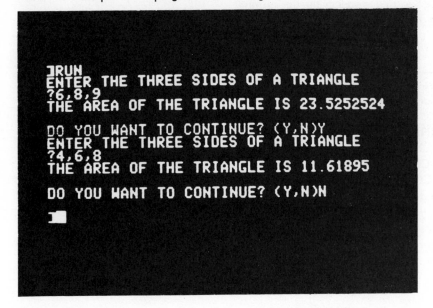

Remember that if the response to an INPUT statement is expected to be a non-numeric value, then a string variable must be used in the INPUT statement. If the INPUT statement contains a numerical variable, and the user types in a letter or other non-numeric value, the Apple II will respond with the message **?REDO FROM START**. It will then wait for a numerical value to be entered. An INPUT statement containing a string variable will accept any input but will treat it as a string. Thus, in line 130 in Figure 7.1 the variable A$ must be compared to the *string* "Y".

The program shown in Figure 7.1 uses an INPUT statement in line 120 to ask the user if he or she wants to continue the program. The user must press Y or N followed by RETURN to answer. The GET statement can be used to eliminate the need to press RETURN.

Substitute the following two statements for line 120 in Figure 7.1:

120 PRINT "DO YOU WANT TO CONTINUE (Y,N)?";
125 GET A$

Note that after the message in line 120 is printed on the screen, the program will wait in line 125 for a key to be pressed. As soon as any key is pressed, the program will go on to line 130. If the key pressed is a "Y", the program will branch back to line 20. Otherwise the program will end.

Type in this program and run it. Note that pressing any key other than "Y" in line 125 will stop the program. Also note that the key pressed is not displayed on the screen. If you want to display the key pressed on the screen, add the statement **127 PRINT A$.**

RANDOM STRIPE PATTERNS

In this section we will write a program that will draw a random horizontal stripe pattern. The pattern will contain 40 horizontal lines each 40 spaces long. In other words the picture will take up the entire 40 × 40 screen area in the low-resolution graphics mode. Each horizontal line plotted will have a 50/50 chance of being one of two possible colors, which can be specified by the user.

A pseudocode description and a structured flowchart for this program are shown in Figure 7.3. After entering the low-resolution graphics mode, specify two color numbers, C1 and C2, in an INPUT statement. The variable Y is used to specify the line number (0–39) at which a particular horizontal line is drawn.

FIGURE 7.3   (a) Pseudocode of program to draw random stripes.

```
loop: enter low resolution graphics
      input 2 colors C1, C2
      Y=0
      loop: R=RND(1)
            if R<0.5
            then COLOR=C1
            else COLOR=C2
            Draw horizontal line at Y
            Y=Y+1
      repeat while Y<=39
      input another picture?"; A$
      clear screen
repeat while A$ = "Y"
```

Each time through the inner *repeat while* loop a single horizontal line is drawn. The line number Y is increased by one each time through this loop. The color of each line is determined by the value of a random number R. The value of this random number is between 0 and 1. If it is less than 0.5 (which will be a

FIGURE 7.3   (b) Structured flowchart for program to draw random stripes.

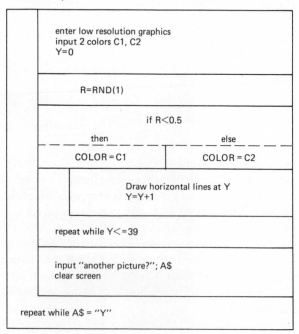

50/50 chance), the color C1 is used for the horizontal line. Otherwise, the color C2 is used. This loop is repeated *while* Y<=39. Therefore, a total of 40 lines (Y=0−39) will be drawn.

After the stripe pattern is plotted, the user is asked if another picture is wanted. If so, the screen is cleared, and the entire program is executed again. Otherwise, the screen is cleared, and the program terminates.

A BASIC listing of this program is shown in Figure 7.4. Compare this listing carefully with the pseudocode and structured flowchart representations of the program shown in Figure 7.3. Note in particular how the *repeat while* and *if . . . then . . . else* constructs are implemented in BASIC. Also note that in line 20 the statement HOME will move the cursor to the upper left-hand corner of the 4-line text area at the bottom of the screen. Line 120 will cause the screen to be cleared of the previous stripe pattern.

You should type in this program and run it. A sample run is shown in Figure 7.5.

```
]LIST
10   REM   RANDOM STRIPES
20   GR : HOME
30   INPUT "ENTER TWO COLORS ";C1,
     C2
40 Y = 0
50 R =   RND (1)
60   IF R < 0.5 THEN   COLOR= C1: GOTO
     80
70   COLOR= C2
80   HLIN 0,39 AT Y
90 Y = Y + 1
100   IF Y < = 39 THEN 50
110   INPUT "ANOTHER PICTURE? (Y O
      R N) ";A$
120   TEXT : HOME
130   IF A$ = "Y" THEN 20
140   END
```

FIGURE 7.4 BASIC listing of program to produce a random stripe pattern.

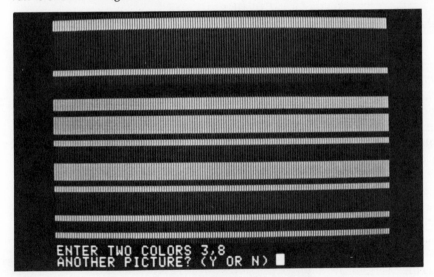

ENTER TWO COLORS 3,8
ANOTHER PICTURE? (Y OR N) ■

FIGURE 7.5 Sample run of program shown in Fig. 7.4.

NESTED LOOPS

The algorithm described in Figure 7.3 really contains two *nested* repeat while loops. The inner loop plots 40 horizontal lines, and the outer loop repeats the entire program if the user types a ''Y''. In this section we will modify this program to plot a random checkerboard pattern rather than a random stripe pattern. This can be done by adding another inner loop that will plot a single spot rather than a horizontal line. Each spot plotted will have a 50/50 chance of being one of two possible colors.

Pseudocode and structured flowchart representa-

tions of this program are shown in Figure 7.6. Compare these algorithms with the corresponding program descriptions given in Figure 7.3 for the random stripe program. Note that for each line plotted on the screen (which occurs within the repeat while Y<=39 loop) there is another nested repeat while X<=39 loop. This inner loop will plot 40 spots (with random color) on each line. Note that the value of X must be initialized to zero at the beginning of this inner loop, (that is, at the beginning of each new line).

63

```
loop: enter low resolution graphics
      input 2 colors C1, C2
      Y=0
      loop: X=0
            loop: R=RND(1)
                  if R<0.5
                  then COLOR=C1
                  else COLOR=C2
                  PLOT X,Y
                  X=X+1
            repeat while X<=39
            Y=Y+1
      repeat while Y<=39
      input "another picture?";A$
      clear screen
repeat while A$="Y"
```

FIGURE 7.6 (a) Pseudocode for program to plot a random checkerboard pattern.

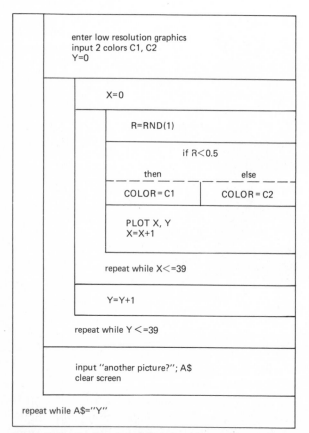

FIGURE 7.6 (b) Structured flowchart for program to plot a random checkerboard pattern.

The BASIC listing of this program is shown in Figure 7.7. Compare this listing carefully with the program description shown in Figure 7.6. Make sure you understand clearly how each of the nested repeat while loops is implemented in BASIC and what its function is in the execution of the program.

Type in this program and run it. A sample run is shown in Figure 7.8.

```
]LIST
10    REM     RANDOM CHECKERBOARD
20    GR : HOME
30    INPUT "ENTER TWO COLORS ";C1,
      C2
40  Y = 0
45  X = 0
50  R =   RND (1)
60    IF R < 0.5 THEN   COLOR= C1: GOTO
      80
70    COLOR= C2
80    PLOT X,Y
85  X = X + 1
90    IF X <  = 39 THEN 50
95  Y = Y + 1
100   IF Y <  = 39 THEN 45
110   INPUT "ANOTHER PICTURE? (Y O
      R N) ";A$
120   TEXT : HOME
130   IF A$ = "Y" THEN 20
140   END
```

FIGURE 7.7 BASIC listing of program to plot random checkerboard pattern.

FIGURE 7.8 Sample run of program shown in Fig. 7.7.

There are really four different elementary loop structures. You can test the logical expression at the beginning of the loop or at the end of the loop. In addition, you can branch out of the loop when the logical expression is either *true* or *false*. We will call the two loops with the test at the end the *repeat while* and the *repeat until* loops. We will call the two loops with the test at the beginning the *do while* and the *do until* loops. In addition to these elementary loops, it is possible to use a more general loop structure in which the test of the logical expression is done in the middle of the loop. Depending upon whether the loop is exited when the logical expression is true or when it is false, we will call these two general loop structures *loop . . . exit if . . . endloop* and *loop . . . continue if . . . endloop*.

All of these loop structures can be implemented in BASIC, although some are easier to implement than others. Most good programmers only use two or three of these loop structures in all of their programs. The choice depends on the programming language being used and to some extent personal preference.

The Repeat While Loop

This is the loop we have been using in all of the programs in this chapter. Its general form is shown in Figure 7.9. In this figure *logical exp.* is any logical expression that is either true or false. This loop is repeated *while* the logical expression is *true*. Figure 7.9 shows what this loop looks like in our train track model of a computer program. Note that the train continues to loop around through the station as long as the logical expression is true.

The Repeat Until Loop

The general form of the *repeat until* loop is shown in Figure 7.10. Note in this case that the loop is *exited* if the logical expression is true. That is, the loop is repeated *until* the logical expression is true. In general you should choose to use either the *repeat while* or the *repeat until* loop in your programs. This will help you avoid logical errors because you will always be thinking either *while* or *until*. Many people prefer the *repeat until,* and some languages implement this loop directly. However, by comparing Figures 7.9 and 7.10, you can see that it is easier to implement a *repeat while* loop in BASIC. The *repeat until* implementation requires an additional GOTO statement. For this reason any time we form a loop with the test at the end of the loop we will make it a *repeat while* loop. After you finish this book you can use whichever loop structure you want.

FIGURE 7.10   The *repeat until* loop: (a) pseudocode, (b) BASIC implementation, (c) structured flowchart, (d) train track equipment.

FIGURE 7.9   The *repeat while* loop: (a) pseudocode, (b) BASIC implementation, (c) structured flowchart, (d) train track equivalent.

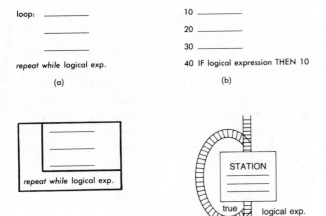

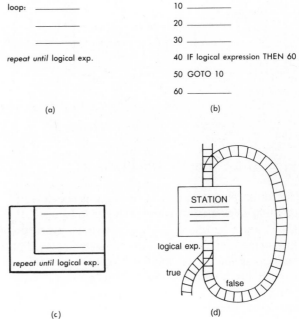

The Do While Loop

The *do while* (sometimes called *while . . . do*) loop is one of those useful programming statements found in newer languages such as PASCAL. Its general form is shown in Figure 7.11. In this loop the test of the logical expression is done at the *beginning*. This means that if the logical expression is initially *false,* the train will *never* go to the station. That is, the statements within the loop will never be executed. Note that the BASIC implementation of the *do while* loop requires *two* GOTO statements, one following the IF . . . THEN statement to skip over the loop statements if the logical expression is false, and one at the end of the loop to branch back to the IF . . . THEN statement.

FIGURE 7.11   The *do while* loop: (a) pseudocode, (b) BASIC implementation, (c) structured flowchart, (d) train track equivalent.

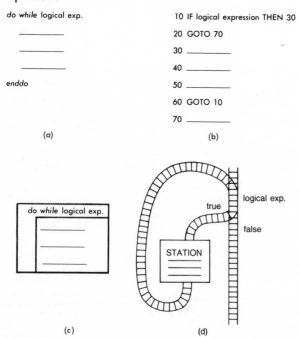

```
do while logical exp.

  _____

  _____

  _____

enddo
```
(a)

```
10 IF logical expression THEN 30
20 GOTO 70
30 _____
40 _____
50 _____
60 GOTO 10
70 _____
```
(b)

(c)   (d)

The Do Until Loop

The fourth elementary loop structure is the *do until* loop whose general structure is shown in Figure 7.12. In this loop the test of the logical expression is also done at the beginning. However, the statements within the loop are only executed if the logical expression is *false,* that is, *until* the logical expression is *true.* Note that if the logical expression is initially *true,* the train will never get to the station, and the statements within the loop will never be executed.

Note also that the BASIC implementation of the *do until* loop requires only one GOTO statement rather than the two needed for the *do while* loop. For this reason we will normally implement the *do until* loop rather than the *do while* loop when we need a test at the beginning of the loop.

People who write structured programs using a "good" structured programming language use the *do while* and the *repeat until* loops. As we have seen, it will save us some code (and therefore some memory) if we use the *do until* and the *repeat while* loops instead. However, any of these loops can be used without much difficulty.

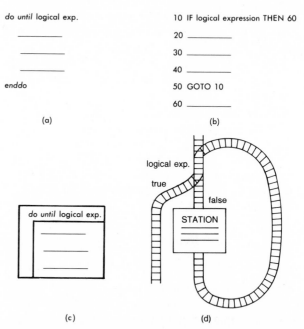

```
do until logical exp.

  _____

  _____

  _____

enddo
```
(a)

```
10 IF logical expression THEN 60
20 _____
30 _____
40 _____
50 GOTO 10
60 _____
```
(b)

(c)   (d)

FIGURE 7.12   The *do until* loop: (a) pseudocode, (b) BASIC implementation, (c) structured flowchart, (d) train track equivalent.

The loop . . . exit if . . . endloop Loop

Occasionally it is convenient to use a more general looping structure. Such a loop is the *loop . . . exit if . . . endloop* construct whose general form is shown in Figure 7.13. This is really a generalized UNTIL loop. That is, if the *exit if* statement is at the top of the loop, it reduces to the *do until* loop. If the *exit if* statement is at the bottom of the loop, it reduces to the *repeat until* loop.

The loop . . . continue if . . . endloop Loop

To complete the discussion of loops, the general form of the *loop . . . continue if . . . endloop* is shown in

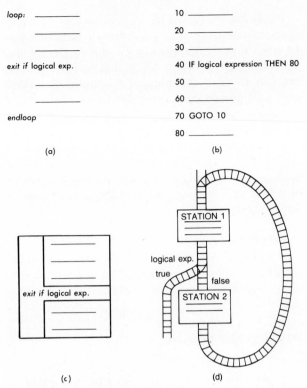

loop: _____

_____

_____

exit if logical exp.

_____

_____

endloop

(a)

10 _____

20 _____

30 _____

40 IF logical expression THEN 80

50 _____

60 _____

70 GOTO 10

80 _____

(b)

exit if logical exp.

(c)

STATION 1

logical exp.

true   false

STATION 2

(d)

FIGURE 7.13   The *loop . . . exit if . . . endloop* loop: (a) pseudocode, (b) BASIC implementation, (c) structured flowchart, (d) train track equivalent.

FIGURE 7.14   The *loop . . . continue if . . . endloop* loop: (a) pseudocode, (b) BASIC implementation.

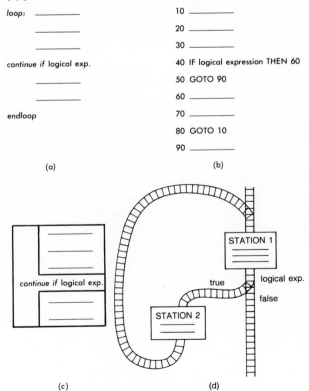

loop: _____

_____

_____

continue if logical exp.

_____

_____

endloop

(a)

10 _____

20 _____

30 _____

40 IF logical expression THEN 60

50 GOTO 90

60 _____

70 _____

80 GOTO 10

90 _____

(b)

continue if logical exp.

(c)

STATION 1

true   logical exp.

false

STATION 2

(d)

Figure 7.14. This is really a generalized WHILE loop. That is, if the *continue if* statement is at the top, it reduces to the *do while* loop. If the *continue if* statement is at the bottom, it reduces to the *repeat while* loop.

Any of the loops described above can be used in your program, but as we have pointed out, the easiest ones to implement in BASIC are the *repeat while,* the *do until,* and the *loop . . . exit if . . . endloop* structures.

EXERCISE 7-1

The dimensions, in feet, of a tract of land are shown in Figure 7.15:

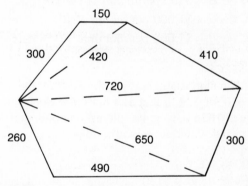

150

300   420   410

720

260   650   300

490

FIGURE 7.15

Modify the program shown in Figure 7.1 to calculate the acreage of this tract of land. The total acreage can be found by computing the area of each of the four triangles, adding these results, and using the fact that 1 acre = 43,560 square feet.

EXERCISE 7-2

Suppose that the tract of land shown in Exercise 7.1 contains a circular pond 200 feet in diameter completely within its boundaries. Write a program that will compute the acreage of the land, excluding the water.

EXERCISE 7-3

The Fibonacci sequence

$$1 \ 1 \ 2 \ 3 \ 5 \ 8 \ 13 \ 21 \ . \ . \ .$$

has the property that each number in the sequence (starting with the third) is the *sum* of the two immediately preceding numbers. Write a program that will display on the screen all numbers in the Fibonacci sequence under 1,000.

EXERCISE 7-4

You decide to deposit an amount of money, D, in a

savings account each month. The account pays P percent interest compounded monthly. Write a program that will input D and P and then determine the number of years (and months) that it will take for you to accumulate a million dollars.

The amount of interest added to the account each month is determined in the following way. If B is the balance in the account at the beginning of the month, then at the end of the month an amount of interest B*MR is added to the account. MR is the monthly interest rate (equal to 0.01*P/12). Thus, the total amount of money in the account at the end of the month will be equal to B+B*MR.

Run the program for the following cases:

a. deposit $500 per month at 8% interest
b. deposit $1,000 per month at 10% interest
c. deposit $1,000 per month at 12% interest

EXERCISE 7-5

Manhattan Island was purchased from the Indians in 1626 for $24. If that $24 had been deposited in a bank in 1626 paying 4% interest compounded annually, what would it be worth today?

EXERCISE 7-6

If you deposit $100 each year in a bank account paying 5% interest compounded annually, how much money will you have after 10 years?

EXERCISE 7-7

Population growth. In 1974 the US. birth rate was 14.9 births per 1,000 population, the death rate was 9.1 deaths per 1,000 population, and the net migration rate was 1.7 per 1,000 population. Assume that these rates will remain constant in the future and that the population of the United States at the beginning of 1976 was 214,398,000. For the purpose of simulating this process on the computer assume that all births, deaths, and migrations take place on the last day of each year. Write and run a program that will determine in which year the population of the U.S. will reach 300,000,000.

EXERCISE 7-8

A rocket is fired vertically into the air with an initial velocity of V feet per second. The height H of the rocket above the ground at any time T is given by

$$H = -16.2\,T^2 + VT$$

Write a program that will

a. input a value of V
b. print the letters T and H for a table heading
c. compute H for values of T starting at 0 and increasing by 1 second until the rocket hits the ground
d. print the values of T and H in the form of a table.

Run the program using a value of V = 200 feet per second.

8

DISPLAYING THE FLAG:
LEARNING ABOUT FOR . . . NEXT

In Chapter 7 you learned how to use the IF . . . THEN statement to form various looping structures in BASIC. There is another looping structure available in BASIC that is called a FOR . . . NEXT loop. This loop uses the BASIC statements FOR and NEXT and is particularly useful when you know the number of times you want to go through a loop.

In this chapter you will learn

1. how to form a FOR . . . NEXT loop
2. to draw dashed lines using the FOR . . . NEXT loop
3. to use nested FOR . . . NEXT loops
4. to display the American flag on the Apple II screen.

THE FOR . . . NEXT LOOP

The general form of a FOR . . . NEXT loop is shown in Figure 8.1. When statement 10 is executed, the value of I is equated to M1 and statements 20, 30, and 40 are executed. If M3>0, when statement 50 is executed the value of I is incremented by M3, and if I is less than or equal to M2, statements 20, 30, and 40 are executed again. This process continues until I becomes greater than M2, at which point the program branches to line 60. Every time around the loop, I is incremented by M3. In line 10 the phrase STEP M3 is optional. If omitted, an increment of one is assumed.

FIGURE 8.1   General form of the FOR . . . NEXT loop.

```
10 FOR I = M1 TO M2 STEP M3
20 _____
30 _____
40 _____
50 NEXTI
60 _____
```

If M3<0, then when statement 50 is executed the value of I is decremented by M3, and statements 20, 30, and 40 continue to be executed until I becomes less than M2.

The pseudocode and structured flowchart equivalents of the FOR . . . NEXT loop are shown in Figure 8.2. When writing pseudocode programs or drawing structured flowcharts you can use the representations of the FOR . . . NEXT loop shown in Figure 8.3.

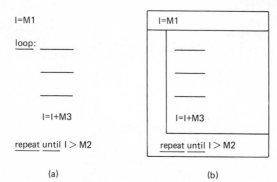

(a)   (b)

FIGURE 8.2   (a) Pseudocode and (b) structured flowchart equivalent of the FOR . . . NEXT loop.

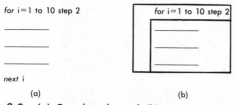

(a)   (b)

FIGURE 8.3   (a) Pseudocode and (b) structured flowchart representation of the FOR . . . NEXT loop.

Immediate Mode Execution of the FOR . . . NEXT Loop

You can execute the FOR . . . NEXT loop in the immediate mode. To see how this loop works, try typing in the following examples in the immediate mode:

```
FOR I=1 TO 10:? I;:NEXTI
FOR I=1 TO 10 STEP 2: ?I;: NEXTI
FOR J=1 TO 10: ? "0";: NEXTJ
FOR J=1 TO 10: ?"- ";: NEXT
```

These examples are shown in Figure 8.4.

Note from the last example that the index variable I on NEXTI is optional,* and NEXTI can be written simply as NEXT. We will normally use only NEXT except in nested FOR . . . NEXT loops where it is helpful to know which next goes with which loop.

Drawing Dashed Lines

The last example shown in Figure 8.4 illustrates how a dashed line can be drawn in the *text* mode. Both vertical and horizontal dashed lines can easily be drawn in the low-resolution graphics mode.

Enter the low-resolution graphics mode by typing **GR: COLOR = 15**. Now type **FOR X = 2 TO 30 STEP 2: PLOT X,5: NEXT**. This will plot the horizontal dashed line shown in Figure 8.5. This single FOR . . . NEXT loop is equivalent to the 15 statements **PLOT 2,5: PLOT 4,5: PLOT 6,5: PLOT 8,5 . . . PLOT 28,5: PLOT 30,5**.

---

*It is not optional in INTEGER BASIC.

FIGURE 8.4   Examples of using the FOR . . . NEXT loop in the immediate mode.

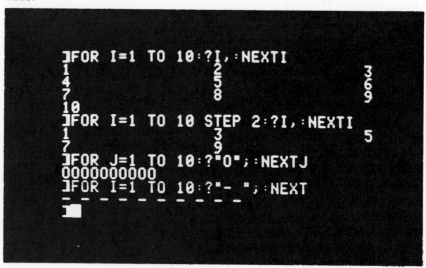

The vertical line shown in Figure 8.5 can be plotted by typing **FOR Y = 10 TO 30 STEP 3: PLOT 25, Y: NEXT.** Note that 7 spots are plotted in this vertical line corresponding to Y values of 10, 13, 16, 19, 22, 25, and 28. Another step of 3 would produce a value of Y equal to 31 which is greater than 30. Therefore, the FOR . . . NEXT loop is exited.

Drawing Areas

The program shown in Figure 8.6a will plot the area shown in Figure 8.6b. This area is plotted by drawing 21 rows (0–20) of horizontal lines, each 18 units long.

Type in this program and run it. Modify the program so that it will draw a square area 15 units on a side with the upper left hand corner of the square at the coordinates X = 10, Y = 10.

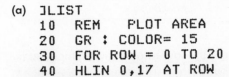

```
(a)  ]LIST
     10   REM    PLOT AREA
     20   GR : COLOR= 15
     30   FOR ROW = 0 TO 20
     40   HLIN 0,17 AT ROW
(b)  50   NEXT ROW
```

FIGURE 8.6   Program shown in (a) will plot area shown in (b).

FIGURE 8.5   Plotting dashed lines using the FOR . . . NEXT loop.

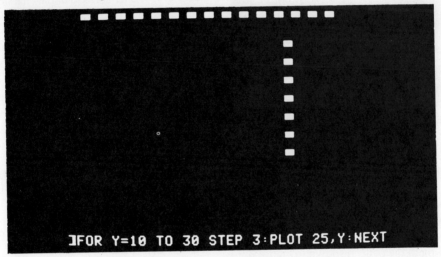

NESTED FOR . . . NEXT LOOPS

FOR . . . NEXT loops may be *nested*. This means that we can put one FOR . . . NEXT loop *completely* within another one. When this is done, the inner FOR . . . NEXT loop is executed completely during *each* pass through the outer loop. This makes it easy to perform fairly complex operations.

Plotting an Array of Points

In Figure 8.5 you saw that in the low-resolution graphics mode the FOR . . . NEXT loop **FOR X = 2 TO 30 STEP 2 : PLOT X,5 : NEXT** will plot 15 spots in a horizontal row with a blank space between adjacent spots. If you change the statement **PLOT X,5** to **PLOT X,Y** and let **Y** change in an outer FOR . . . NEXT loop, you can produce several rows of these dashed lines. The program shown in Figure 8.7 will do this.

FIGURE 8.7   Program to plot an array of points.

```
]LIST
10   REM    ARRAY OF POINTS
20   GR : COLOR= 15
30   FOR Y = 2 TO 30 STEP 2
40   FOR X = 2 TO 30 STEP 2
50   PLOT X,Y
60   NEXT X: NEXT Y
```

71

Line 20 enters the low-resolution graphics mode and sets the color to white. The inner FOR . . . NEXT loop starting at line 40 produces one row of 15 spots at line number Y. The outer FOR . . . NEXT loop starting at line 30 plots 15 rows of these dashed lines as Y varies from 2 to 30 in steps of 2.

Type in this program and run it. You should obtain the array of spots shown in Figure 8.8. Modify this program by changing the number of rows, the number of points plotted in each row, and the spacing between the spots.

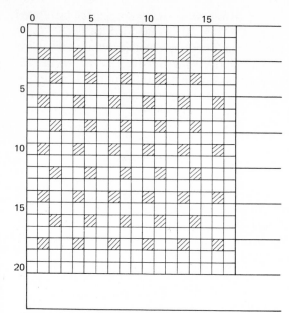

FIGURE 8.9   Pattern used to display the star field in the flag.

FIGURE 8.8   Array of points plotted using the program in Fig. 8.7.

You should be convinced that these two sets of statements will, in fact, produce the pattern shown in Figure 8.9.

A program that will plot this star field is shown in Figure 8.10a. The result of running this program is shown in Figure 8.10b.

Plotting the Star Field

When we display the flag later in this chapter, we will need to plot the star field. We will do this by plotting an array of low-resolution graphic spots. These will be arranged according to the pattern shown in Figure 8.9. Note that in this pattern all of the spots are not positioned exactly as they should be, but it is the best we can do using the low-resolution graphics mode.

If you look carefully at this pattern, you will see that it consists of two rectangular arrays of points; one is 5 × 6 and the other is 4 × 5. These two rectangular arrays will be plotted separately.

The first can be plotted using the following statements:

```
230 FOR Y = 2 TO 18 STEP 4
240 FOR X = 1 TO 16 STEP 3
250 PLOT X, Y : NEXTX : NEXTY
```

The second array can be plotted using the following statements:

```
260 FOR Y = 4 TO 16 STEP 4
270 FOR X = 2 TO 14 STEP 3
280 PLOT X, Y:NEXTX : NEXTY
```

FIGURE 8.10   (a) BASIC program to display star field (b) star field displayed by executing program in (a).

(a)

```
]LIST
215    REM    PLOT STAR FIELD
217    GR :C2 = 15
220    COLOR= C2: REM    WHITE STARS

230    FOR Y = 2 TO 18 STEP 4
240    FOR X = 1 TO 16 STEP 3
250    PLOT X,Y: NEXT X: NEXT Y
260    FOR Y = 4 TO 16 STEP 4
270    FOR X = 2 TO 14 STEP 3
280    PLOT X,Y: NEXT X: NEXT Y
290    END
```

(b)

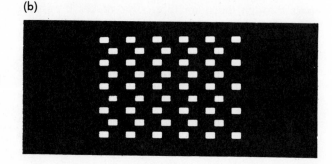

The one further thing we need to learn in order to display our flag is how to make stripes. In this section we will write a general program that can display any size striped pattern made from any two colors. The program will ask the user to enter the following values from the keyboard:

1. the number of stripes, N, to be plotted

2. the width of each stripe, W

3. the length of each stripe, L

4. the two colors, C1 and C2, from which the stripes will be formed.

Given these variables, Figure 8.11 shows an algorithm that will display N stripes, each of width W and length L, starting with the C1 color.

In this algorithm the inner NL *for . . . next* loop will plot one stripe consisting of W rows of lines, each with a length of L. The color of the first stripe will be C1. After the NL *for . . . next* loop is completed, the contents of C is changed to the other color number, using

the *if . . . then . . . else* statement. The outer NS *for . . . next* loop will continue to plot stripes until N stripes have been plotted.

A listing of the BASIC program corresponding to this algorithm is shown in Figure 8.12. You should type in this program and run it. A sample run of this program is shown in Figure 8.13. You should try making different kinds of stripes using this program. Another sample run of this program is shown in Figure 8.14. We will use the values shown in this example to help display our flag.

FIGURE 8.11   Algorithm for displaying N stripes, each of width W and length L, starting with the color C1

```
clear screen
C = C1
ROW = 0
for NS = 1 to N
    COLOR = C
    for NL = 1 to W
        HLIN 0,L−1 at ROW
        ROW = ROW + 1
    next NL
    if C = C1
    then C = C2
    else C = C1
next NS
```

FIGURE 8.12   BASIC listing of program to make stripes.

```
]LIST
10   REM    PROGRAM TO MAKE STRIPES

15   HOME
20   INPUT "ENTER NUMBER OF STRIPE
     S ";N
30   INPUT "ENTER WIDTH OF EACH ST
     RIPE ";W
40   INPUT "ENTER LENGTH OF EACH S
     TRIPE ";L
50   INPUT "ENTER TWO COLORS (1-15
     ) ";C1,C2
60   GR :C = C1:ROW = 0
70   FOR NS = 1 TO N
75   COLOR= C
80   FOR NL = 1 TO W
90   HLIN 0,L − 1 AT ROW
100  ROW = ROW + 1
110   NEXT NL
120   IF C = C1 THEN C = C2: GOTO
      140
130  C = C1
140   NEXT NS
```

FIGURE 8.13   Sample run of program shown in Fig. 8.12.

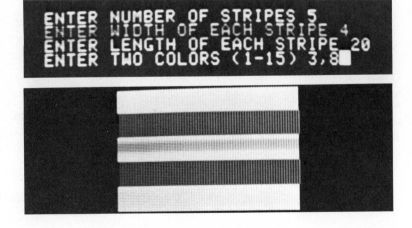

FIGURE 8.14   A second run of program shown in Fig. 8.12.

DISPLAYING THE FLAG

The American flag has 13 stripes. If we use 3 low-resolution lines for each stripe, we will require 39 lines. Since there are 40 rows in low-resolution graphics, this will work out fine. The star field shown in Figure 8.9 is 21 rows high, which corresponds to the top 7 stripes of the flag. This is the correct size of the star field.

The BASIC program shown in Figure 8.15 will display the 13 stripes of the flag. Lines 50–150 are the algorithm shown in Figure 8.11 with N=13, W=3,

and L=39. This will produce the same 13 stripes shown in Figure 8.14b.

We now need to add the blue field to Figure 8.14b. This will be done by plotting a 21 × 18 blue area in the upper left-hand corner of the screen. The following algorithm will do this:

> set color to blue
> *for* ROW=0 to 20
>   HLIN 0,17 at ROW
> *next* ROW

This algorithm is accomplished by adding lines 170–210 to our program, as shown in Figure 8.16. The result of executing this new program is shown in Figure 8.17.

We now need to add the star field. This is done by adding lines 215–290 as shown in Figure 8.18 (see Figure 8.10a). The resulting flag is shown in Figure 8.19.

FIGURE 8.15   Program to display the 13 stripes of the flag.
```
]LIST-150
10   REM     PROGRAM TO DISPLAY FLAG

20 C1 = 1: REM    RED
30 C2 = 15: REM    WHITE
40 C3 = 6: REM    BLUE
50   GR :C = C1:ROW = 0
70   FOR NS = 1 TO 13: REM   RED &
     WHITE STRIPES
80   COLOR= C
90   FOR NL = 1 TO 3
100  HLIN 0,39 AT ROW
110 ROW = ROW + 1
120  NEXT NL
130  IF C = C1 THEN C = C2: GOTO
     150
140 C = C1
150  NEXT NS
```

FIGURE 8.16   Subroutine to add the blue field to the flag.
```
]LIST170-210
170   REM     PLOT BLUE FIELD
180   COLOR= C3
190   FOR ROW = 0 TO 20
200   HLIN 0,17 AT ROW
210   NEXT ROW
```

74

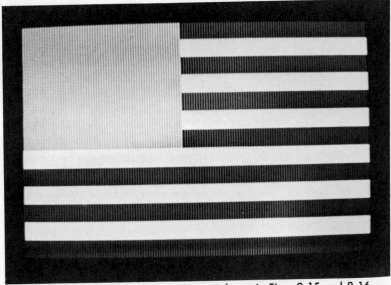

FIGURE 8.17   Result of executing program shown in Figs. 8.15 and 8.16.

FIGURE 8.18   Program to add the star field to the flag.

```
]LIST215-
215   REM    PLOT STAR FIELD
220   COLOR= C2: REM    WHITE STARS
230   FOR Y = 2 TO 18 STEP 4
240   FOR X = 1 TO 16 STEP 3
250   PLOT X,Y: NEXT X: NEXT Y
260   FOR Y = 4 TO 16 STEP 4
270   FOR X = 2 TO 14 STEP 3
280   PLOT X,Y: NEXT X: NEXT Y
290   END
```

EXERCISE 8-1

Use FOR . . . NEXT loops to implement the random checkerboard algorithm given in Figure 7.6. Run the program and compare your result with Figure 7.8.

EXERCISE 8-2

Write a program that will compute and print the cubes of the odd integers between 1 and 20.

EXERCISE 8-3

There are certain three digit numbers, here called "magic" numbers, which have the property that the sum of the cubes of their digits equals the number itself.

Write a program that will print the value of all such magic numbers in a column in which each line is of the form A MAGIC NUMBER IS _____.

Use three nested FOR . . . NEXT loops with index variables I, J, and K. The values of I, J, and K are taken as the digits of a number between 100 and 999. The number N is computed as N = 100*I + 10*J + K. N

FIGURE 8.19   Flag produced by program shown in Figs. 8.15, 8.16, and 8.18.

can then be compared to the sum of the cube of its digits to see if it is magic.

EXERCISE 8-4

Write a program that will draw a large red-and-blue checkerboard (8 × 8) suitable for playing a game of checkers on the screen.

EXERCISE 8-5

Use a FOR . . . NEXT loop to implement the random stripe algorithm given in Figure 7.3. Run the program and compare your result with Figure 7.5.

EXERCISE 8-6

Write a program that will plot a large, 3 × 3 red-and-blue checkerboard for playing tic-tac-toe. Each square of the checkerboard should contain 12 × 12 low-resolution plotting spots. Plot a yellow X on square I,J if you input I,J,X. Plot a green O on square I,J if you input I,J,O. For example, if you input 1,2,X, a large yellow X should be plotted in the second square of the first row. If you input 2,2,0, a large green circle should be plotted in the center square. Make the large circle occupy 8 × 8 squares. Make the large X occupy 7 × 7 squares.

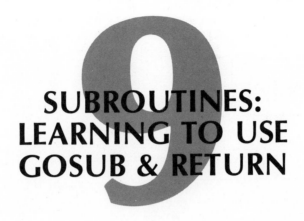

SUBROUTINES: LEARNING TO USE GOSUB & RETURN

Often you will have a sequence of BASIC statements that you would like to execute at several different locations within a program. Instead of having to repeat this same sequence of statements every time you want to use it, you can write the statements only once as a subroutine and then *call* the subroutine each time you want to execute these statements.

Subroutines are also useful as a means of writing programs in a modular fashion. This becomes more and more important as the size of a program grows. Program segments that perform particular functions can be written as subroutines and then called when that function needs to be performed. Inasmuch as the Apple II screen can display a maximum of 22 program lines (leaving two lines at the bottom for the cursor), you should try to keep your main program and all

subroutines less than 22 screen lines long. This will allow you to read and study a complete program segment without having to scroll the screen. This technique of modularizing your program will greatly simplify the process of debugging and modifying your program. It is the secret that allows you to write long programs with almost the same ease that you write short programs.

In this chapter you will learn

1. to use the GOSUB and RETURN statements

2. to plot the same figure at different locations on the screen

3. to plot figures of varying sizes

4. to display your name anywhere on the screen.

THE GOSUB & RETURN STATEMENTS

The general form of the GOSUB statement is **GOSUB line number.** When this statement is executed, the program branches to the statement at line **line number.** For example, the statement **GOSUB 500** will cause the program to branch to line 500. It looks as if **GOSUB 500** behaves the same was as **GOTO 500.** However, there is an important difference. The Apple II *remembers* where the statement **GOSUB 500** is located in the

program. Line number 500 is the first line of a *subroutine* that is just a collection of BASIC statements that perform a particular task. At the end of this subroutine you must include the statement **RETURN.** When the **RETURN** statement is executed, the program will branch back to the next statement following **GOSUB 500.** This process is shown in Figure 9.1.

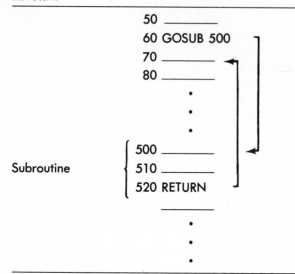

FIGURE 9.1   Forming a subroutine using GOSUB and RETURN.

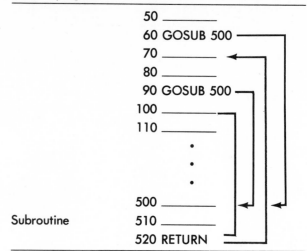

FIGURE 9.2   Calling a subroutine from two different locations within a program.

Now it looks as if you would accomplish the same result in Figure 9.1 by using the two statements **60 GOTO 500** and **520 GOTO 70**. Although this would be true in Figure 9.1, it would not work if you wanted to call the same subroutine from two *different* locations in the program, as shown in Figure 9.2. In this case the statement **60 GOSUB 500** will branch to the subroutine at line 500 then RETURN to line 70. However, the statement **90 GOSUB 500** will also branch to the subroutine at line 500 but will then RETURN to line 100. Recall that the Apple II always remembers the point from which it branched to a subroutine, and it will always return to that point.

You can even call a subroutine from within another subroutine. The Apple II will always find its way back by retracing its steps as shown in Figure 9.3. Line 60 branches to the subroutine at line 500. Line 510, which is within this subroutine, branches to a second subroutine at line 600. The RETURN statement on line 620 will branch back to line 520, the statement following the GOSUB 600 statement. This happens to be the RETURN statement of the subroutine that begins at line 500. It will then branch back to line 70, the statement following the GOSUB 500 statement.

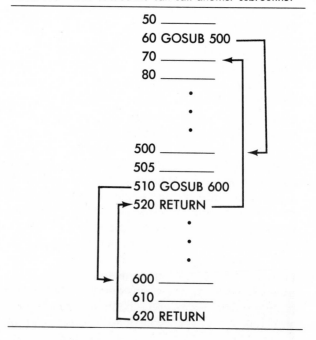

FIGURE 9.3   One subroutine can call another subroutine.

PLOTTING MULTIPLE FIGURES

The graphic figure shown in Figure 9.4a can be plotted using the subroutine given in Figure 9.4b. All points in this figure are defined relative to the X, Y coordinate of the upper left-hand corner of the figure. Lines 100–130 in Figure 9.4b draw the box in a clockwise fashion starting at the position X,Y. Line 140 plots the two eyes.

Line 150 plots the nose, and the mouth is drawn in lines 160–180. Note that line 190 is the RETURN statement. Study the subroutine in Figure 9.4b carefully and make sure you understand how it draws the face in Figure 9.4a.

(a)

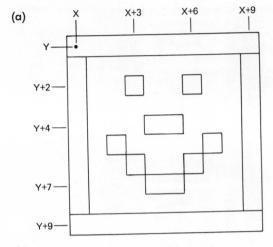

(b)

```
]LIST100-
100   HLIN X,X + 9 AT Y
110   VLIN Y + 1,Y + 8 AT X + 9
120   HLIN X + 9,X AT Y + 9
130   VLIN Y + 8,Y + 1 AT X
140   PLOT X + 3,Y + 2: PLOT X + 6
      ,Y + 2
150   HLIN X + 4,X + 5 AT Y + 4
160   PLOT X + 2,Y + 5: PLOT X + 3
      ,Y + 6
170   HLIN X + 4,X + 5 AT Y + 7
180   PLOT X + 6,Y + 6: PLOT X + 7
      ,Y + 5
190   RETURN
```

FIGURE 9.4 (a) Definition of graphic figure and (b) subroutine to plot the figure in (a).

This subroutine must have values for X and Y before it is called. To test this subroutine, type it in as shown in Figure 9.4b. Then in the immediate mode, type **GR: COLOR = 15**. This will put you into the low-resolution graphics mode. Now type **X=10: Y=10: GOSUB 100**. This should display the figure shown in Figure 9.5.

FIGURE 9.5 Test of subroutine given in Fig. 9.4(b).

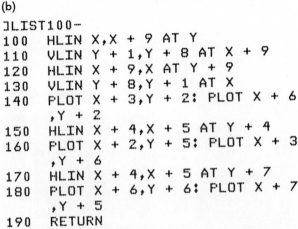

Note that you can execute the statement GOSUB 100 in the immediate mode. This is very useful for testing subroutines.

Now that you know that the subroutine works, you can plot multiple faces by simply calling this subroutine several times with different values for X and Y. The program shown in Figure 9.6 calls the statement GOSUB 100 nine times using a nested FOR . . . NEXT loop. This loop will produce the following nine pairs of values for X and Y:

X	Y
0	0
15	0
30	0
0	15
15	15
30	15
0	30
15	30
30	30

```
]LIST
10    REM    MULTIPLE FIGURES
20    GR : COLOR= 15
30    FOR Y = 0 TO 30 STEP 15
40    FOR X = 0 TO 30 STEP 15
50    GOSUB 100: NEXT X: NEXT Y
60    END
100   HLIN X,X + 9 AT Y
110   VLIN Y + 1,Y + 8 AT X + 9
120   HLIN X + 9,X AT Y + 9
130   VLIN Y + 8,Y + 1 AT X
140   PLOT X + 3,Y + 2: PLOT X + 6
      ,Y + 2
150   HLIN X + 4,X + 5 AT Y + 4
160   PLOT X + 2,Y + 5: PLOT X + 3
      ,Y + 6
170   HLIN X + 4,X + 5 AT Y + 7
180   PLOT X + 6,Y + 6: PLOT X + 7
      ,Y + 5
190   RETURN
```

FIGURE 9.6 Program to plot nine faces on the screen.

These nine pairs of values will correspond to the coordinates of the upper left-hand corner of the nine faces.

You should type in and run the program shown in Figure 9.6. (If you already have the subroutine typed in you only need to add lines 10–60). The result of executing this program is shown in Figure 9.7. Modify this program so as to plot only four faces.

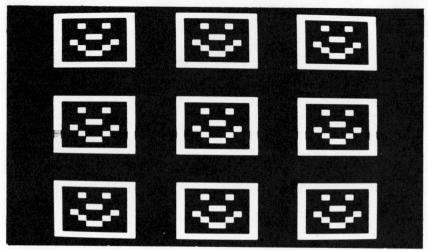

FIGURE 9.7   Result of executing the program given in Fig. 9.6.

Plotting Figures of Different Sizes

In addition to making the location of a figure variable, you can also change the size of a figure. For example, Figure 9.8a shows a square centered at X,Y whose width is 2*H+1. The subroutine shown in Figure 9.8b will plot this square. Note in this subroutine that the four corners of the square each get plotted twice (once with an HLIN and once with a VLIN), but this simplifies the programming.

Type in this subroutine and then test it by typing **GR: COLOR = 15** to enter the low resolution graphics

FIGURE 9.8   (a) Definition of square of width 2*H+1 and (b) subroutine to plot the square in (a).

(a)

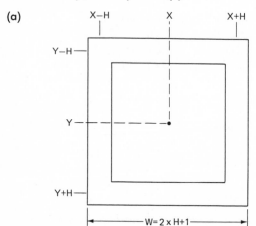

(b)
```
]LIST200
200   REM    SQUARE OF WIDTH 2*H+1
210   HLIN X - H,X + H AT Y - H
220   VLIN Y - H,Y + H AT X + H
230   HLIN X + H,X - H AT Y + H
240   VLIN Y + H,Y - H AT X - H
250   RETURN
```

mode, followed by **X=20: Y=20: H=10: GOSUB 200**. This should display the figure in Figure 9.9.

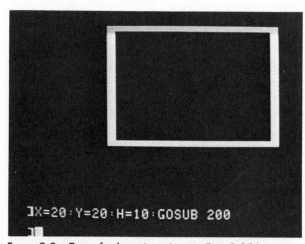

FIGURE 9.9   Test of subroutine given in Fig. 9.8(b).

You can now plot multiple squares of different sizes by calling the subroutine in Figure 9.8b with different values of H. For example, the program shown in Figure 9.10 will plot seven concentric squares, all centered at X=20, Y=20.

FIGURE 9.10   Program to plot concentric squares.
```
]LIST
10    REM     CONCENTRIC SQUARES
20    GR : COLOR= 15
30    X = 20:Y = 20
40    FOR H = 1 TO 19 STEP 3
50    GOSUB 200: NEXT
60    END
200   REM     SQUARE OF WIDTH 2*H+1
210   HLIN X - H,X + H AT Y - H
220   VLIN Y - H,Y + H AT X + H
230   HLIN X + H,X - H AT Y + H
240   VLIN Y + H,Y - H AT X - H
250   RETURN
```

You should type in this program by adding lines 10–60 to the "square" subroutine in Figure 9.8b. If you run the program, you should obtain the figure shown in Figure 9.11. Note that because of the nature of the TV screen, the "squares" do not appear perfectly square. Try running this program after changing the step size in line 40 to 2,4,6, and 1.

FIGURE 9.11   Result of running the program shown in Fig. 9.10.

PLOTTING YOUR NAME

You can use the ideas described in the previous sections of this chapter to plot your name anywhere on the screen in letters of varying sizes. The trick is to define each letter in terms of the X,Y coordinate of its upper left-hand corner and the width, W, and height, H, of the letter. Then you can plot each letter wherever you want by using subroutines.

As an example, Figure 9.12 shows a subroutine that will plot the letter J. In this figure W is the width of the letter and H is the height of the letter. The upper

left-hand corner of the H × W rectangle containing the letter defines the position X,Y of the letter. Study the subroutine shown in Figure 9.12 and make sure you understand how lines 210–230 plot each part of the J.

In a similar way Figure 9.13 shows a subroutine that will plot the letter F. Note that the short horizontal bar in the F is located at row number $Y+(H-1)/2$. If H is an odd number, this will place the horizontal bar at the middle of the F. Also note that the length of this bar is $(W-1)/2$.

FIGURE 9.12   (a) Definition of the letter J and (b) subroutine to plot the letter J shown in (a).

(a)

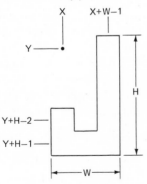

FIGURE 9.13   (a) Definition of the letter F and (b) subroutine to plot the letter F shown in (a).

(a)

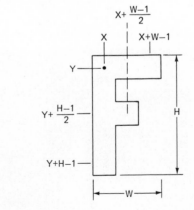

(b)
```
]LIST200-240
200   REM    PLOT A J  (H X W)
210   VLIN Y,Y + H - 1 AT X + W -
      1
220   HLIN X,X + W - 2 AT Y + H -
      1
230   PLOT X,Y + H - 2
240   RETURN
```

(b)
```
]LIST300-340
300   REM    PLOT AN F  (H X W)
310   VLIN Y,Y + H - 1 AT X
320   HLIN X + 1,X + W - 1 AT Y
330   HLIN X + 1,X + (W - 1) / 2 AT
      Y + (H - 1) / 2
340   RETURN
```

Figure 9.14a defines the letter E. The subroutine in Figure 9.14b begins by plotting an F in line 410. Line 420 then adds the bottom horizontal bar to produce an E.

(a)

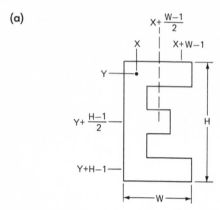

(b)
```
]LIST400-430
400   REM    PLOT AN E  (H X W)
410   GOSUB 300: REM    PLOT F
420   HLIN X + 1,X + W - 1 AT Y +
      H - 1
430   RETURN
```

FIGURE 9.14   (a) Definition of the letter E and (b) subroutine to plot the letter E shown in (a).

To test these subroutines, type in the lines shown in Figures 9.12b, 9.13b, and 9.14b. Then enter the low-resolution graphics mode by typing **GR: COLOR = 15.** You can then plot a J by typing **X=10: Y=10: W=3: H=5: GOSUB 200** as shown in Figure 9.15. To test the

FIGURE 9.15   Testing the subroutine shown in Fig. 9.12.

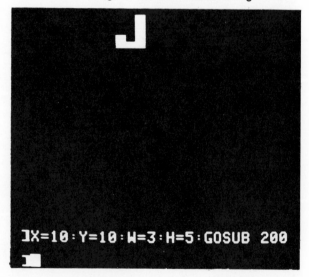

subroutines for plotting the F and the E, type **X=20: GOSUB 300** and **X=30: GOSUB 400** as shown in Figure 9.16.

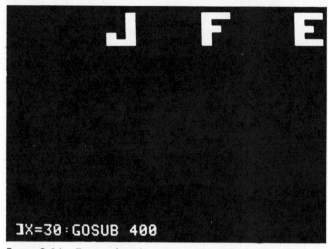

FIGURE 9.16   Testing the subroutine to plot individual letters.

Figure 9.17 shows a subroutine that will combine the letters J, E, and F to plot the name JEFF.

```
]LIST500-
500   REM    PLOT JEFF (H X W)
510   GOSUB 200: REM    J
520 X = X + W + 2: GOSUB 400: REM
      E
530 X = X + W + 2: GOSUB 300: REM
      F
540 X = X + W + 2: GOSUB 300: REM
      F
550   RETURN
```

FIGURE 9.17   Subroutine to plot the name JEFF.

Before calling this subroutine, X,Y,W, and H must have been assigned values. Line 510 plots a J at location X,Y. Line 520 plots an E where the X location has been increased by W+2. This will leave a blank column between the J and the E. Similarly, lines 520–540 plot the two Fs.

A main program that plots three JEFFs of different sizes is shown in Figure 9.18. Lines 20–30 will plot the

FIGURE 9.18   Main program that plots the name JEFF three times.
```
]LIST-80
10   REM    PLOT 3 JEFFS
15   GR : COLOR= 15
20 X = 2:Y = 2:W = 3:H = 5
30   GOSUB 500
40 X = 5:Y = 10:W = 5:H = 7
50   GOSUB 500
60 X = 1:Y = 20:W = 7:H = 11
70   GOSUB 500
80   END
```

name with 5 × 3 sized letters. Lines 40–50 will plot the name at a different location using 7 × 5 sized letters. Finally, the name with 11 × 7 sized letters is plotted in lines 60–70. The result of running this program is shown in Figure 9.19.

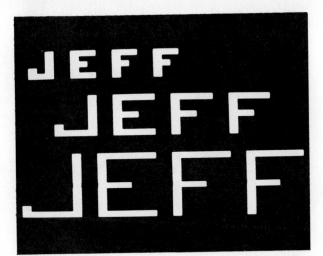

FIGURE 9.19   Result of running the program shown in Fig. 9.18.

EXERCISE 9-1

Write a program that will plot your name at two different locations on the screen. The size of the two names should be different.

EXERCISE 9-2

A baseball player hits a ball with an initial velocity V (in feet per second) at an angle of A (degrees) to the gound as shown in Figure 9.20. The height H (in feet) of the ball above the ground is given in terms of the distance X (in feet) from home plate by the equation

$$H = \frac{-16.1X^2}{V^2\cos^2 A} + X\tan A$$

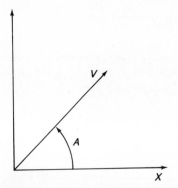

FIGURE 9.20   Diagram for Exercise 9-2.

Write a program that will (1) input the values of V and A, (2) compute H for 1-foot increments in X until the ball hits the ground, and (3) plot the trajectory of the ball on the screen.

Run the program for values of V = 40 feet per second and A = 45°.

CAUTION: The functions COS(A) and TAN(A) must have A expressed in radians. Remember that 180° = π radians.

EXERCISE 9-3

Write a program that will plot a 3 × 3 cross in the center of the screen (see Figure 9.21), and then have

FIGURE 9.21   Diagram for Exercise 9-3.

the cross move around the screen in response to rotating the game paddles.

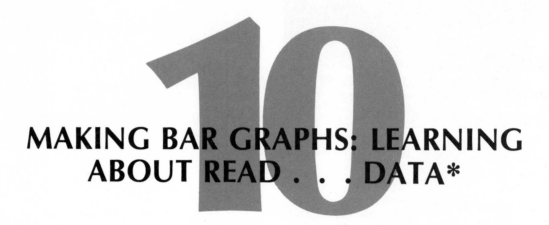

MAKING BAR GRAPHS: LEARNING ABOUT READ . . . DATA*

You know three ways to assign a value to a memory cell name. One is to use an assignment statement such as A=3. The second is to use an INPUT statement such as INPUT A. The third is to use the GET statement. In the last two cases the value is entered through the keyboard.

In this chapter you will learn another method of assigning values to memory cell names. The values to be assigned are stored *in the program* in DATA statements. They are assigned to memory cell names by using a READ statement.

In this chapter you will learn

1. to use the READ, DATA, and RESTORE statements

2. to make horizontal bar graphs

3. to make vertical bar graphs containing multiple bars

4. to scale and label bar graphs.

THE READ, DATA, AND RESTORE STATEMENTS

The READ and DATA statements must be used in the *deferred mode*. Type in the following statements:

```
10 DATA 5,10
20 READ A: PRINT A
30 READ A: PRINT A
40 READ A: PRINT A
```

*Not available in INTEGER BASIC.

Now run the program as shown in Figure 10.1. The first time the statement **READ A** was executed in line 20, the first data value in the DATA statement (5) was stored in A. The second time that **READ A** was executed in line 30, the second data value in the DATA statement (10) was stored in A. The third time **READ A** was executed in line 40 an error message, **?OUT OF DATA**, was displayed. This is because there were no more data values in the DATA statement to use.

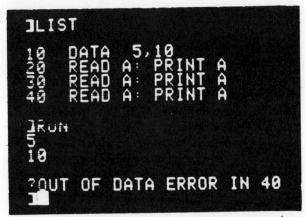

FIGURE 10.1 The READ statement reads successive values from a DATA statement.

When a program is executed, a *pointer* points to the first data value in the DATA statement. (Two or more DATA statements in a program are treated as a single long DATA statement.) As data values are "used up" by being read in READ statements, the pointer keeps moving along to the next unused data value. If the pointer gets to the end of the data values in the DATA statement and another READ statement is executed, then the ?OUT OF DATA error message will be displayed.

The pointer can be reset at any time to the first data value in the DATA statement using the statement **RESTORE**. Also, more than one value can be read with a single READ statement. In order to see this, type in and run the following program as shown in Figure 10.2.

```
10 DATA 5,10,15,20
20 READ A,B,C
30 PRINT A,B,C
40 RESTORE
50 READ B,C
60 PRINT A,B,C
```

Note in this case that the first READ statement stores the values 5, 10, and 15 in A, B, and C respectively. The RESTORE statement then moves the pointer back to the first data value (5). Therefore, the next READ statement will store the values 5 and 10 in B and C respectively. Note that the value of A remains unchanged and is still equal to 5.

Now type in and run the following program as shown in Figure 10.3.

```
10 DATA 5,10,15,20
20 DATA 25,30,35
30 READ A,B,C
40 PRINT A,B,C
50 READ A,B,C
60 PRINT A,B,C
70 READ A,B
```

FIGURE 10.3 There must be data values for *all* variable names in a READ statement.

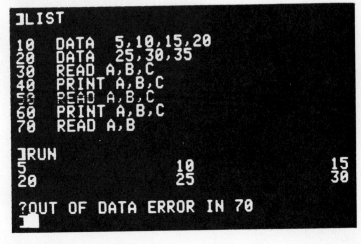

FIGURE 10.2 The RESTORE statement moves the pointer to the first data value in the DATA statement.

30 READ A,B,C,D,A$,B$
40 PRINT A,B,C,D,A$,B$

Note that the two DATA statements are treated as one long DATA statement. DATA statements may occur anywhere in a program. They are effectively combined into one long DATA statement in the order in which they occur in the program. In the last READ statement in Figure 10.3, although there is a value for A (35), there is no value for B and therefore the **?OUT OF DATA** error message is displayed.

Strings can be included in a DATA statement. In this case the corresponding variable name in the READ statement must be a string variable. For example, type in and run the following program as shown in Figure 10.4.

10 DATA 5,10,15,20
20 DATA ACE, "*"

Note that the string ACE in the DATA statement does not have to be enclosed between quotation marks. However, strings containing blanks, commas, and colons must be enclosed between quotation marks. Note also that the numerical variables A and B are completely different memory cells from the string variables A$ and B$. The Apple II will not get these mixed up.

The READ and DATA statements are particularly useful when you have a list of data whose values do not change in the program and which are read by the same READ statement. Examples of using the READ and DATA statements will be given in the following sections.

FIGURE 10.4   String variables can be used in a READ statement to read strings in a DATA statement.

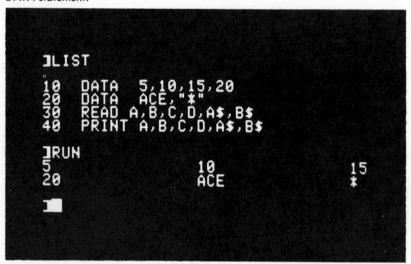

HORIZONTAL BAR GRAPHS

Bar graphs are very useful for providing a quick visual picture of the relative sizes of various quantities. The simplest kind of bar graph that you can draw on the Apple II is to plot a horizontal line whose length is proportional to the quantity of interest.

As an example, suppose you want to compare graphically the four values 12, 25, 5, and 17. You can plot four lines with lengths 12, 25, 5, and 17 using the program shown in Figure 10.5.

In this program line 20 is a DATA statement that contains the lengths of the four bars to be plotted. Line

30 defines the character (the symbol # in this case) that will be used to draw the lines and stores this character in the string variable G$. Other characters such as hyphens or asterisks could also be used. Lines 50–70 form a FOR . . . NEXT loop that is executed once for each bar to be plotted (4 in this case).

Within this loop line 60 reads the next length from the values given in the DATA statement and stores this length in the memory cell L. A bar of length L is then plotted using the subroutine in line 400. This subroutine prints L copies of the symbol (#) stored in G$

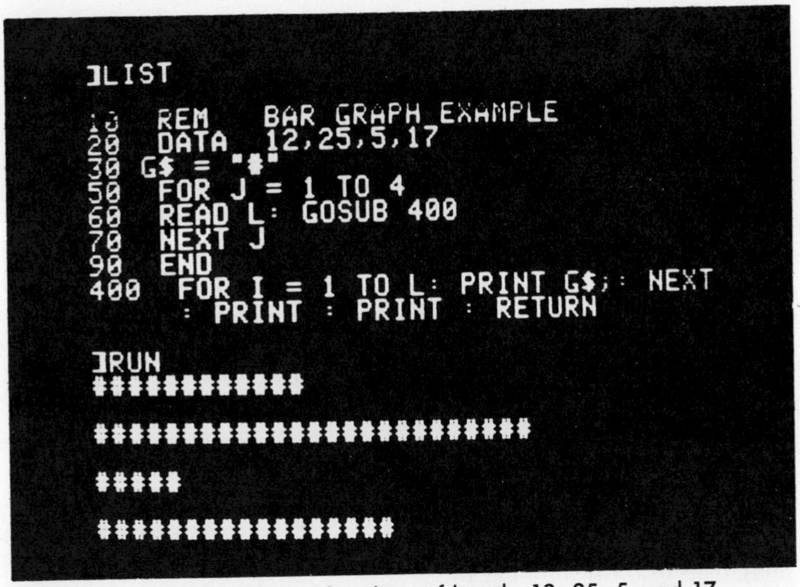

FIGURE 10.5 Program to plot four lines of lengths 12, 25, 5, and 17.

right next to each other to form the bar. The first PRINT statement at the end of the line 400 causes the cursor to be moved to the beginning of the next line. The second PRINT statement causes a line to be skipped.

Note that the END statement in line 90 is necessary to prevent the program from executing line 400 again. (This would produce the error message **?RETURN WITHOUT GOSUB ERROR IN 400**).

The basic ideas shown in Figure 10.5 can be used to produce useful bar graphs of real data as illustrated in the following section.

FIGURE 10.6 Program to produce a bar graph of the data in Table 10.1.

```
]LIST
10   REM     POPULATION BAR GRAPH
20   N = 6
30   G$ = "#"
40   HOME : PRINT " POPULATION OF
     NEW ENGLAND STATES": PRINT :
     PRINT
50   FOR J = 1 TO N
60   READ S$,P
70   L = P / 200000 + .5: GOSUB 400

80   NEXT J
90   END
100   DATA  ME,993663
110   DATA  NH,737681
120   DATA  VT,444732
130   DATA  MA,5689170
140   DATA  CT,3032217
150   DATA  RI,949723
400   PRINT S$;" ";: FOR I = 1 TO
      L: PRINT G$;: NEXT : PRINT :
      PRINT : RETURN
```

Population of the New England States

The populations (1970 census) of the six New England states are shown in Table 10.1. The program given in Figure 10.5 has been modified as shown in Figure 10.6 to plot six bar graphs of the data in Table 10.1.

TABLE 10.1 Population of the New England States

State	Population
ME	993,663
NH	737,681
VT	444,732
MA	5,689,170
CT	3,032,217
RI	949,723

Lines 100–150 are six DATA statements containing the information in Table 10.1. Note that each DATA statement contains a string (the name of the state) and a numerical value (the state's population). For each pass through the FOR . . . NEXT loop (lines 50–80), line 60 stores the next state name in S$ and its population in P.

Each symbol # defined in line 30 will represent a certain number of people. In order to determine how many people this should be, you must choose a value that will insure that the longest bar will fit on the screen. The state name plus a space will use 3 columns of a screen line. Therefore, the longest bar possible is 37 spaces. The maximum population is that of Massachusetts, 5,689,170. Therefore, each symbol # must represent more than 5689170/37=153761 persons. We will therefore choose each symbol to represent a population of 200,000.

Given a population P, line 70 calculates the number of symbols to be plotted, that is, the length of the bar, L. In the equation

$$L = P/200000 + .5$$

the .5 will round to the nearest 200,000 persons, inasmuch as the above equation is equivalent to the equation

$$L = \frac{P+100000}{200000}$$

Note that the number of symbols plotted in the subroutine in line 400 will be equal to the integer part of L.

The subroutine in line 400 has been modified to print the state name, stored in S$, to the left of each bar. Line 40 clears the screen, prints the title to the graph, and then skips two lines. The result of running this program is shown in Figure 10.7.

Adding a Scale

Although the bar graph shown in Figure 10.7 illustrates the relative size of the six state populations, it does not provide any information on the actual values of these populations. We can correct this by adding a scale to the bottom of the graph.

Since each symbol # represents a population of 200,000, five symbols will represent one million people. A subroutine that prints such a scale is shown in Figure 10.8. The subroutine is called in line 85 of the revised main program shown in Figure 10.9. The result of executing this new program is shown in Figure 10.10.

FIGURE 10.8 Subroutine to display scale.

```
]LIST600-
600    REM    ADD SCALE
610    PRINT "   +";: FOR I = 1 TO 6
       : PRINT "----+";: NEXT : PRINT

620    PRINT "   ";: FOR I = 0 TO 6:
        PRINT I;"    ";: NEXT : PRINT
       : PRINT
630    PRINT  TAB( 8);"MILLIONS OF
       PEOPLE"
640    RETURN
```

FIGURE 10.9 Revised main program that calls subroutine to add a scale.

```
]LIST-400
10    REM    POPULATION BAR GRAPH
20    N = 6
30    G$ = "#"
40    HOME : PRINT " POPULATION OF
       NEW ENGLAND STATES": PRINT :
       PRINT
50    FOR J = 1 TO N
60    READ S$,P
70    L = P / 200000 + .5: GOSUB  400

80    NEXT J
85    GOSUB 600: REM    ADD SCALE
90    END
100    DATA  ME,993663
110    DATA  NH,737681
120    DATA  VT,444732
130    DATA  MA,5689170
140    DATA  CT,3032217
150    DATA  RI,949723
400    PRINT S$;" ";: FOR I = 1 TO
       L: PRINT G$;: NEXT : PRINT :
       PRINT : RETURN
```

FIGURE 10.7 Result of running the program shown in Fig. 10.6.

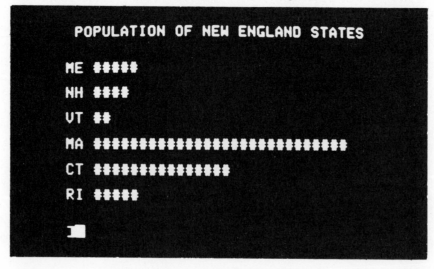

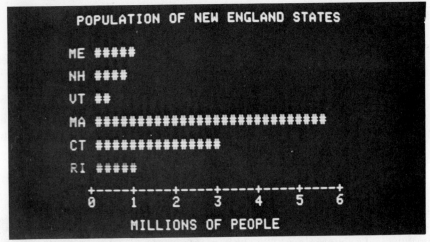

VERTICAL BAR GRAPHS

In addition to the horizontal bar graphs described above, you can draw vertical bars by using low-resolution graphics. As you already know, the statement **VLIN Y1, Y2 AT X** will plot a vertical bar from Y1 to Y2 at the horizontal location X. If Y2 is less than Y1, the bar will be plotted from bottom to top.

Suppose you want to plot a vertical bar with a length proportional to the value V. The value of V can be either positive or negative. For a negative value of V, the bar should be plotted in the negative direction. Figure 10.11 shows the ranges of values for which various numbers of squares will be plotted. The bottom of row 37 on the screen will define the "zero" value of V. From Figure 10.11 you see that a value of V between

0.5 and 1.5 will result in one square being plotted in row Y=37. Similarly, a value of V between −0.5 and −1.5 will result in one square being plotted in row Y=38.

A positive bar of length L can be plotted using the statement **VLIN Y1, Y1 − L + 1 at X**. Note that if L=1, then a single square will be plotted. The case of L=0 must be tested for separately in order to plot no square at all.

A negative bar of length L (absolute value) can be plotted using the statement **VLIN Y1, Y1 + L − 1 AT X**.

In Figure 10.11 note that Y1=37 for a positive bar and Y1=38 for a negative bar. Also note that the number of squares to be plotted, (that is, the length of the bar) is given by **L = INT(ABS(V) + 0.5)**.

These ideas are summarized in the algorithm shown in Figure 10.12, which will plot a vertical bar at position X with a length proportional to V.

FIGURE 10.11   Screen layout for plotting vertical bar with length proportional to the value V.

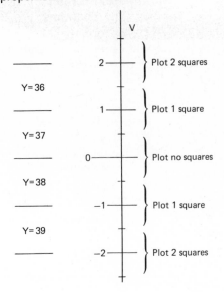

FIGURE 10.12   Algorithm to plot a bar of length proportional to the value V.

L = INT(ABS(V) + 0.5)
if L=0
then return
else if V < 0
    then Y1=38
           VLIN Y1, Y1 + L − 1 AT X
    else Y1=37
           VLIN Y1, Y1 − L + 1 AT X

A BASIC subroutine that implements this algorithm is shown in Figure 10.13. Lines 540–550 plot the bar for positive values of V, and lines 570–580 plot the bar for negative values of V.

89

```
]LIST500-
500   REM    PLOT BAR OF LENGTH V
510   L =  INT ( ABS (V) + 0.5)
520   IF L = 0 THEN  RETURN
530   IF V < 0 THEN 570
540   Y1 = 37
550   VLIN Y1,Y1 - L + 1 AT X
560   GOTO 590
570   Y1 = 38
580   VLIN Y1,Y1 + L - 1 AT X
590   RETURN
```

FIGURE 10.13   Subroutine to plot a bar of length V.

To test this subroutine, type it in as shown in Figure 10.13. Then enter the low-resolution graphics mode by typing **GR : COLOR = 15**. Then type **V = 20 : X = 15 : GOSUB 500**. You should obtain the result shown in Figure 10.14.

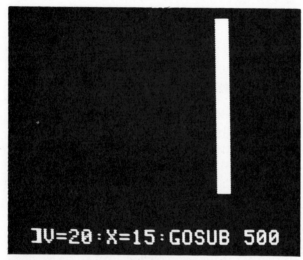

FIGURE 10.14   Testing subroutines given in Fig. 10.13.

As another example, type

GR: COLOR = 15
V = +3.0 : X = 10 : GOSUB 500

The line beginning with V = +3.0 is "live" on the screen. This means that if you edit this line (using ESC I and the retype key) by changing the values of V and X, the new statement will be executed when you press RETURN, and a new bar will be plotted. Edit this line to plot the following bars:

V = +0.6 : X = 11 : GOSUB 500
V = −0.6 : X = 12 : GOSUB 500
V = +1.3 : X = 13 : GOSUB 500
V = −1.3 : X = 14 : GOSUB 500

You should obtain the bars shown in Figure 10.15. Try some other values.

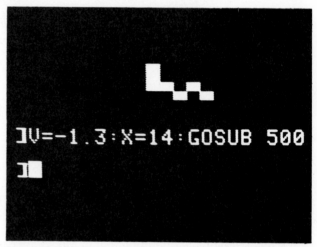

FIGURE 10.15   Further tests of subroutine given in Fig. 10.13.

This technique of using the immediate mode of execution to test subroutines is a good method because you can make many tests without disturbing the program that you have stored in the computer.

We will now use this subroutine to plot a "multiple" bar graph that will display 5-year economic data.

Multiple Bar Graph for the "The Economy"

In this section we will develop a program to plot a "multiple" bar graph of the economic data given in Table 10.2.

TABLE 10.2   Economic Data

	1976	1977	1978	1979	1980	
Inflation % change in C.P.I.	4.7	6.8	9.0	13.3	18.2	Jan. change at compound annual rate
Unemployment % of civilian labor force	7.8	7.0	6.0	5.8	6.2	Jan.
Growth % change in real G.N.P.	4.8	5.8	4.9	0.8	1.7	Projected 1st Q.
Personal Income % change per capita	2.8	4.5	3.4	−0.8	−0.5	Projected 1st Q.

Adapted from data on p. 67 of the March 10, 1980 issue of *Time* Magazine.

For each year we will plot four bars, one for each economic factor. Each of them will be plotted in a different color. Colors used are given in Table 10.3.

TABLE 10.3 Colors used in economy bar graph

		Number	Color
Inflation	C1:	9	Orange
Unemployment	C2:	6	Blue
Growth	C3:	12	Green
Personal Income	C4:	11	Pink

The main program for plotting this bar graph is shown in Figure 10.16.

```
]LIST-150
5   REM    THE ECONOMY
10  GR
15  C1 = 9: REM    ORANGE
16  C2 = 6: REM    BLUE
17  C3 = 12: REM    GREEN
18  C4 = 11: REM    PINK
20    DATA  4.8,7.8,4.8,2.8
30    DATA  6.8,7.0,5.8,4.5
40    DATA  9.0,6.0,4.9,3.4
50    DATA  13.3,5.8,0.8,-0.6
60    DATA  18.2,6.2,1.7,-0.4
65  X = 2
70    FOR J = 1 TO 5
80    GOSUB 200: REM    PLOT 4 BARS
90    NEXT J
100   GOSUB 400: REM    PRINT HEADIN
      G
150   GOTO 150
```

FIGURE 10.16 Main program for plotting economy bar graph.

Line 10 enters the low-resolution graphics mode. Lines 15–18 define the four colors C1–C4 given in Table 10.3. Lines 20–60 are DATA statements containing the data given in Table 10.2. Note that each DATA statement contains the data for one year, starting with 1976. The value of X is initialized to two in line 65. This is the column number in which the first bar will be plotted. The FOR . . . NEXT loop in lines 70–90 is executed five times (once for each year). Each time through this loop, four bars are plotted, corresponding to the data for that year. This is done in a subroutine starting at line 200. Line 100 calls a subroutine at line 400 that prints the heading and scale for the graph. Line 150 branches on itself to prevent the cursor from being displayed.

The subroutine to plot the next four bars of the graph is shown in Figure 10.17. The READ statement in line 210 reads the next four values of inflation, unemployment, growth, and income and stores these values in the memory cells I,U,G, and M. The orange inflation bar is plotted in lines 230–240 using the subroutine at line 500 shown in Figure 10.13. Note that the value of

```
]LIST200-350
200   REM    PLOT NEXT 4 BARS
210   READ I,U,G,M
230   V = 2 * I: COLOR= C1
240   GOSUB 500: REM    PLOT BAR
250   X = X + 1
260   V = 2 * U: COLOR= C2
270   GOSUB 500
280   X = X + 1
290   V = 2 * G: COLOR= C3
300   GOSUB 500
310   X = X + 1
320   V = 2 * M: COLOR= C4
330   GOSUB 500
340   X = X + 5
350   RETURN
```

FIGURE 10.17 Subroutine to plot the next four bars of the graph.

V has been equated to twice the inflation value I. This is done because the maximum data value in Table 10.2 is 18.2. Twice this value is 36.4, which will fit on the screen if we plot 36 squares. Line 250 increments the column number by one so that the next bar will be plotted in the next adjacent column. Lines 260–270 plot the blue unemployment bar. Line 280 moves to the next column, and lines 290–300 plot the green growth bar. Lines 310–330 plot the pink income bar in the next column. Line 340 increases the column number X by 5. This will leave a four-column space between each group of four bars.

The subroutine to display the years and heading at the bottom of the graph is shown in Figure 10.18. Line 420 prints the five years under the appropriate bar graphs. Line 430 prints the title of the graph and a statement indicating the scale of the graph. Lines 440–450 print a legend to explain the four colors. Note that all text in the low-resolution graphics mode must be confined to the bottom four lines on the screen.

FIGURE 10.18 Subroutine to display heading and scale.

```
]LIST400-460
400   REM    DISPLAY YEARS AND TITL
      E
410   HOME
420   PRINT "  1976    1977    197
      8    1979    1980"
430   PRINT "      THE ECONOMY"; SPC(
      9);"1 SQUARE=0.5%"
440   PRINT "INFLATION-ORANGE    GR
      OWTH-GREEN"
450   PRINT "UNEMPLOYMENT-BLUE    PE
      RSONAL INCOME-PINK";
460   RETURN
```

The entire program to plot the economy bar graph is given by the statements in Figures 10.16, 10.17, 10.13, and 10.18. The result of running this program is shown in Figure 10.19.

Although this entire program is relatively long, you can see that by breaking it up into functional modules, you can more easily keep track of what is going on. This will also make it easier for you to modify this program to suit your own needs.

EXERCISE 10-1

The following table shows the amount of gasoline required to fill the gas tank of a certain station wagon:

Speedometer Reading	Gallons to Fill Tank
93769.3	15.5
94034.6	15.2
94249.1	14.8
94376.6	9.0
94558.0	10.5
94778.2	12.8
95037.0	14.9
95258.0	14.7
95499.3	15.3
95732.7	20.3
95941.2	15.0

Write and run a program that will

a. store the above data in DATA statements

b. compute the gas mileage in miles/gallon for each fill-up, and plot the results as a bar graph

c. compute and print out the average miles/gallon for all fill-ups shown in the table.

EXERCISE 10-2

Each entry in the following table gives a nation, its population, and its area (in square miles):

Nation	Population	Area
Australia	13,467,500	2,967,909
Bangladesh	69,087,000	55,126
Britain	56,235,500	94,500
Canada	22,648,200	3,851,809
China	830,453,000	3,691,502
India	587,503,700	1,178,995
Japan	108,152,900	143,689
Soviet Union	253,268,300	8,649,489
United States	212,031,000	3,615,122

a. store the above data in DATA statements

b. compute the population density for each nation in persons per square mile

c. plot the results as a bar graph.

FIGURE 10.19   Bar graph of economic data given in Table 10.2.

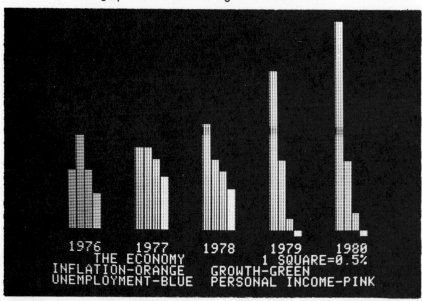

LEARNING TO USE ARRAYS

You have learned that numerical values are stored in memory cells with names like A and B3. Similarly, strings are stored in memory cells with names like A$ and B3$. Sometimes it is desirable to identify a collection of memory cells by the same name. Such a collection of memory cells is called an *array,* and the individual memory cells within the array are identified by means of a *subscript.*

In this chapter you will learn

1. to represent arrays in BASIC
2. the difference between one-dimensional and multidimensional arrays
3. to use the DIM statement
4. to use arrays when plotting bar graphs
5. to sort data stored in a one-dimensional array

ARRAYS

You will often encounter data that are related in some way. For example, Table 10.1 lists the six New England states and their populations. In the program in Figure 10.6 we read each state into the memory cell S$ and each population into the memory cell P. This means that at any one time only one state name and one population were in named memory cells. We printed the state name and plotted a bar with a length proportional to the population. Then we read another state name and population which replaced the previous ones in S$ and P.

Some programs, however, require that all of the state names and populations be stored in different memory cells at the same time. We would therefore need twelve different memory cells—six for the state names and six for the populations. This will require twelve different memory cell names. It is convenient to store all the state names in an *array* called S$ and all the populations in an *array* called P. The individual memory cells within the array are distinguished by a *subscript* I. An individual element within the array is sometimes called a *subscripted variable* P(I) or S$(I).* The arrays S$ and P are shown in Figure 11.1.

---

*String arrays are not available in INTEGER BASIC.

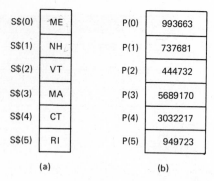

FIGURE 11.1 (a) The six subscripted variables S$(I), I=0,5 contain the state names, and (b) the six subscripted variables P(I), I=0,5 contains the state populations.

Note in Figure 11.1 that subscripts are enclosed in parentheses in BASIC. The variable name P(2), for example, is just the name of a memory cell that contains the value 444732. You can use these subscripted variables any place that you would use a simple variable name. For example, type

S$(2)="VT"
? S$(2)
P(2)=444732
?P(2)

as shown in Figure 11.2. The names S$(2) and P(2) are just the names of two memory cells. They happen to be elements of an array, but individually they can be treated like any other memory cell name.

FIGURE 11.2 Subscripted variables can be used just like simple variables.

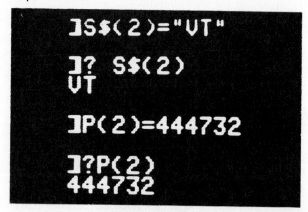

Having a memory cell name contain a subscript, however, can be very useful. For example, type the following two statements as shown in Figure 11.3.

FOR I=0 TO 10: A(I)=2*I: NEXT
FOR I=0 TO 10: ?A(I),: NEXT

The first statement fills each of the 11 memory cells A(I), I=0, 10 with the value 2*I. The second statement prints these 11 values.

Try changing the first statement to FOR I=0 TO 11: A(I)=2*I: NEXT. You will obtain the error message ?BAD SUBSCRIPT ERROR. The reason for this error will be explained in the following section.

The DIM Statement

Whenever an APPLESOFT* program first encounters a subscripted variable, such as A(3), it automatically assigns 11 memory locations to the array. These memory locations are assigned the names A(0)–A(10). Thus, if you try to use the name A(11) there is no such memory cell name reserved in the computer, and you therefore get the error message ?BAD SUBSCRIPT ERROR.

If you want to use an array with more than 11 memory cells, you must explicitly define the array with a DIM (for DIMension) statement. For example, to assign 16 memory cells to the array B you would type DIM B(15). You could then use the 16 memory cells B(0)–B(15). The constant 15 in the above DIM statement (which could also be a variable or an expression) represents the upper subscript limit of the array. The lower subscript limit is always assumed to be zero.

You can define more than one array with a single DIM statement. For example, you can write DIM B(15), A(3), C(24), which defines three arrays containing 16, 4, and 25 memory cells respectively.

Although it is not necessary to use a DIM statement when the array contains 11 or fewer memory cells, it is always a good idea to use the DIM statement to define arrays. For one thing it gives you a convenient place to define what the array means (by following the DIM statement with a REM statement). Also, if you only need five memory cells in an array, using the statement

---

*INTEGER BASIC requires all arrays to be DIMensioned.

FIGURE 11.3 Filling the array A(I) with the value 2*I.

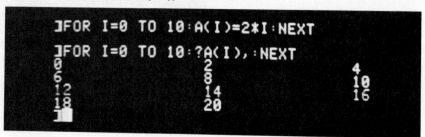

DIM A(4) will save memory, because the computer would automatically reserve 11 memory cells rather than 5 otherwise. This saving is bigger than it may appear because the Apple II uses five bytes of memory for *each* numerical memory cell such as B(3).

There is another way to save considerable memory when using a large array containing only *integers* (whole numbers). If you add a percent sign, %, to an array name, the Apple II will consider all array elements to be integers and will use only *two* bytes of memory (rather than five) to store each integer element. For example, **DIM C%(99)** would define an integer array containing 100 elements and would save 300 bytes of memory when executing the program. You would, of course, use the subscripted variable C%(I) in the program.

Other than using up memory, it does not hurt to reserve more memory locations (by using the DIM statement) than you use in the program. For example, you will reserve 100 memory cells (each containing two bytes of memory) with the statement **DIM C%(99)**. In your program you may only refer to the first 20 of these memory cells. This is O.K. However, if you try to refer to C%(100), you will obtain the error message **?BAD SUBSCRIPT ERROR**.

The DIM statement may occur anywhere in the program, but it must occur *before* you refer to the corresponding subscripted variable. An array can only be dimensioned once in a program. If you try to dimension it more than once, you will obtain the error message **?REDIM'D ARRAY ERROR**. Remember that if a subscripted variable such as A(3) is encountered *before* a DIM statement has been executed, the Apple II will automatically dimension the array equivalent to DIM A(10). If it then encounters a DIM statement, the above error message will be displayed.

For example, try typing the following: **FOR I=0 TO 11: A(I)=2*I:NEXT**. (You may have already done this above.) If you haven't DIMensioned the array A, you will obtain the error message **?BAD SUBSCRIPT ERROR** as shown in Figure 11.4. The problem, of course, is that you tried to refer to A(11), and the Apple II has automatically dimensioned the array equivalent to A(10). But if you try to correct this by typing **DIM A(11)**, you will obtain the error message **?REDIM'D ARRAY ERROR** as shown in Figure 11.4. This is because the array is already dimensioned (automatically) to A(10). What can you do? Type **CLEAR** as shown in Figure 11.4. This *clears,* or reinitializes, the Apple II's system pointers, which has the effect of wiping out any DIMensioning information. You can then type

       DIM A(11)
       FOR I=0 TO 11: A(I)=2*I: NEXT
       FOR I=0 TO 11: ?A(I); SPC(3);: NEXT

without errors as shown in Figure 11.4.

```
]FOR I=0 TO 11:A(I)=2*I:NEXT

?BAD SUBSCRIPT ERROR
]DIM A(11)

?REDIM'D ARRAY ERROR
]CLEAR

]DIM A(11)

]FOR I=0 TO 11:A(I)=2*I:NEXT

]FOR I=0 TO 11:?A(I);SPC(3);:NEXT
0    2    4    6    8   10   12   14    16
18   20   22
]
```

FIGURE 11.4 Examples of using the DIM and CLEAR statements.

The maximum number of elements in an array will be limited by the amount of memory in your Apple II. If the total amount of memory used by your program, variables, and arrays exceeds the amount of memory in your Apple II, you will obtain the error message **?OUT OF MEMORY ERROR.**

Any time you want to know how many bytes of free memory you have left, type **?FRE(1).*** For example, Figure 11.5 shows that an array containing 100 elements uses 507 bytes of memory (5 for each of the 100 elements in the array and 7 for an array header). If the number of free bytes of memory is greater than 32,767, the function FRE(1) will return a *negative* number. To find the actual number of free bytes of memory, add the number 65,536 to this negative number. For example, in Figure 11.5,

$$\text{initial \# of bytes} = -29188 + 65536 = 36348$$
$$\text{final \# of bytes} = -29695 + 65536 = \underline{35841}$$
$$\text{difference} = \qquad\qquad \text{(bytes) } 507$$

*Not available in INTEGER BASIC.

FIGURE 11.5 The statement ?FRE(1) will print the number of free bytes of memory left.

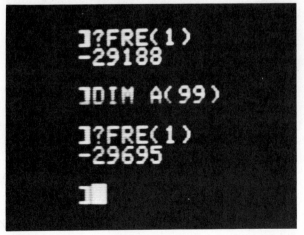

```
]?FRE(1)
-29188

]DIM A(99)

]?FRE(1)
-29695

]
```

95

Multidimensional Arrays*

An array that contains a single subscript is called a one-dimensional array. An array that contains more than one subscript is called a multidimensional array. For example, the DIM statement **DIM A(2,3)** defines a two-dimensional array containing 12 elements. It can be thought of as a two-dimensional *matrix* containing 3 rows and 4 columns, as shown in Figure 11.6. In the array A(I,J) the first subscript, I, is the *row* number in Figure 11.6 and the second subscript, J, is the column number. Thus, for example, in Figure 11.6 the value of A(1,2) is 8 and the value of A(2,1) is 12.

J

	0	1	2	3
0	11	7	0	13
1	3	15	8	4
2	5	12	9	1

I

FIGURE 11.6   The array A(I,J) containing 12 elements.

A three-dimensional array containing a total of 7 × 9 × 3 = 189 elements can be defined by the DIM statement **DIM F(6,8,2)**. We will begin by writing some programs using one-dimensional arrays.

BAR GRAPHS USING ARRAYS

The program shown in Figure 10.5 in the previous chapter plots four bars of lengths 12, 25, 5, and 17. Review that program, and make sure you understand how it works. Line 400 plots a bar of length L using the character stored in G$. In this section we will modify this program to plot the same length bars using a different character for each bar.

The modified program and its execution are shown in Figure 11.7. Line 15 is a new DATA statement that contains the 4 characters that will be used for the 4 bars. Line 25 is the DIM statement **25 DIM G$(4),L(4)**. This statement defines an array G$(I) that will contain the four characters and an array L(I) that will contain the four lengths. Although this DIM statement defines *five* elements for each array, we will use only the elements G$(1)–G$(4) and L(1)–L(4) and just ignore G$(0) and L(0).

Line 30 reads the four characters in the DATA statement on line 15 into the four subscripted variables G$(1)–G$(4). Line 40 reads the four values 12, 25, 5, and 17 from line 20 into the four subscripted variables L(1)–L(4) respectively.

The loop defined by lines 50–70 plots the four bars. Each time through the loop a new length L(J) and a new character G$(J) are assigned to L and G$ to be plotted in line 400. Note how the subscript J gets incremented from 1 to 4 each time through the loop. Also note that the subscripted variable L(J) (and G$(J)) and the simple variable L (and G$) are not confused by the Apple II and are treated as separate memory cells.

The four bars in Figure 11.7 can be plotted adjacent to each other by eliminating one of the PRINT statements in line 400 as shown in Figure 11.8.

FIGURE 11.7   Bar graph example using arrays.

```
]LIST
10   REM    BAR GRAPH EXAMPLE
15   DATA  #,O,*,I
20   DATA  12,25,5,17
25   DIM G$(4),L(4)
30   FOR I = 1 TO 4: READ G$(I): NEXT

40   FOR I = 1 TO 4: READ L(I): NEXT

50   FOR J = 1 TO 4
60   L = L(J):G$ = G$(J): GOSUB 400

70   NEXT J
90   END
400   FOR I = 1 TO L: PRINT G$;: NEXT
      : PRINT : PRINT : RETURN
```

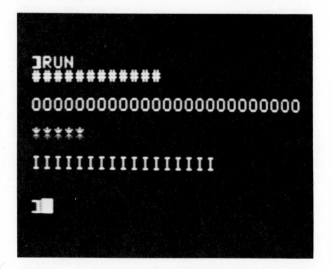

---

*Multidimensional arrays are not available in INTEGER BASIC.

```
]LIST
10    REM    BAR GRAPH EXAMPLE
15    DATA   #,O,*,I
20    DATA   12,25,5,17
25    DIM G$(4),L(4)
30    FOR I = 1 TO 4: READ G$(I): NEXT

40    FOR I = 1 TO 4: READ L(I): NEXT

50    FOR J = 1 TO 4
60    L = L(J):G$ = G$(J): GOSUB 400

70    NEXT J
90    END
400   FOR I = 1 TO L: PRINT G$;: NEXT
      : PRINT : RETURN
]RUN
############
OOOOOOOOOOOOOOOOOOOOOOOOO
*****
IIIIIIIIIIIIIIII
```

FIGURE 11.8   Plotting the bars adjacent to each other.

Suppose you would like to plot the bars shown in Figure 11.8 in *increasing* order of length—that is, the shortest bar first, the next shortest second, etc. You can do this if you rearrange the array L(I) so that the elements are in *increasing*, or ascending, order. One simple method of sorting an array in ascending order will now be described.

Sorting an Array in Ascending Order

There are many algorithms that have been devised for sorting an array of elements in ascending order. Some are more efficient, that is, faster to execute, than others. Some (not necessraily the same ones) are easier to understand than others. The method of sorting the array L illustrated in Figure 11.9 is fairly easy to understand.

FIGURE 11.9   Sorting an array by moving the smallest succeeding value to location I, I=1 TO N−1 (N = number of elements in array).

	I=1	I=2	I=3		Array sorted
L(1)	12	5	5	5	5
L(2)	25	25	12	7	7
L(3)	5	12	25	25	12
L(4)	7	7	7	12	25

The method begins by comparing the first element in the array (I=1) with all succeeding elements. Any time a succeeding element is found that is smaller than the first element, it is interchanged with the first element. Thus, after the first element (whose value may

have changed a few times) is compared with *all* succeeding values, we will have moved the *smallest* value to the first position in the array.

If we repeat this procedure starting with the *second* element (I=2), after comparing the second element with all succeeding elements and interchanging the values if the succeeding element is smaller than the second one, the next-to-smallest value will end up in the second position in the array.

This process continues until we have compared the next-to-last element with the last element in the array. At this point the array is sorted in ascending order as shown in Figure 11.9. The algorithm for this procedure is shown in pseudocode in Figure 11.10. Compare Figures 11.9 and 11.10 and make sure you understand how this sorting algorithm works.

FIGURE 11.10   Pseudocode representation of sorting algorithm shown in Figure 11.9.

```
for I=1 TO N−1
    for J=I+1 TO N
        if L(I)<=L(J)
        then do nothing
        else interchange L(I) and L(J)
    next J
next I
```

The algorithm shown in Figure 11.10 looks as if it will be fairly easy to write in BASIC. The only problem is how to interchange the contents of L(I) and L(J). Note that the two statements

$$L(I) = L(J)$$
$$L(J) = L(I)$$

will not work because the original value in L(I) will be destroyed when the value of L(J) is put in L(I) in the first statement. This means that the second statement will really be assigning the value in L(J) to itself. Thus, L(I) and L(J) will end up with the same value. It requires *three* statements to interchange the values of L(I) and L(J) as shown in Figure 11.11.

FIGURE 11.11   Three statements are required to interchange L(I) and L(J).

L(I) = L(J) L(J) = L(I)	will *not* interchange L(I) and L(J)
T = L(I) L(I) = L(J) L(J) = T	*will* interchange L(I) and L(J)

The value in L(I) must temporarily be stored in another memory cell, T, before the value in L(J) is put in L(I). Then the value in T, which used to be in L(I), can be put in L(J).

The sorting algorithm shown in Figure 11.10 is written as a BASIC subroutine in Figure 11.12. Note that line 2040 interchanges the values in L(I) and L(J). Add this subroutine to the program shown in Figure 11.8. Then add the statement **45 N=4: GOSUB 2000: REM SORT L(I)** to the main program as shown in Figure 11.13. The result of running this program is also shown in Figure 11.13. Line 45 sets the number of elements in the array L to 4 and then sorts this array by calling the subroutine shown in Figure 11.12.

FIGURE 11.12   BASIC subroutine to sort array L(I) containing N elements in ascending order.

```
]LIST2000-
2000   REM    SORT L(I)
2010   FOR I = 1 TO N - 1
2020   FOR J = I + 1 TO N
2030   IF L(I) <  = L(J) THEN 2050

2040   T = L(I):L(I) = L(J):L(J) =
       T
2050   NEXT J: NEXT I
2060   RETURN
```

FIGURE 11.13   Plotting bar graphs in increasing order using the subroutine in Fig. 11.12.

```
]LIST-400
10   REM    BAR GRAPH EXAMPLE
15   DATA  #,O,*,I
20   DATA  12,25,5,17
25   DIM G$(4),L(4)
30   FOR I = 1 TO 4: READ G$(I): NEXT

40   FOR I = 1 TO 4: READ L(I): NEXT

45   N = 4: GOSUB 2000: REM    SORT
50   FOR J = 1 TO 4
60   L = L(J):G$ = G$(J): GOSUB 400

70   NEXT J
90   END
400  FOR I = 1 TO L: PRINT G$;: NEXT
     : PRINT : RETURN
]RUN
#####
OOOOOOOOOOOO
*****************
IIIIIIIIIIIIIIIIIIIIIIIII
```

If you compare Figure 11.13 with Figure 11.8, and you will notice that the four characters are plotted in the same relative order. That is, they did not get sorted as the data did. However, it probably makes more sense to associate a particular character with a particular data value, such as inflation, growth, and so on, so that if the data is rearranged (sorted), the corresponding character will also be rearranged. We can do this by adding the statement **2045 T$=G$(I):G$(I)= G$(J):G$(J) =T$** to the subroutine given in Figure 11.12 as shown in Figure 11.14. This statement will cause G$(I) and G$(J) to be interchanged each time that L(I) and L(J) are interchanged, which will permit a given data value to keep its particular character, as shown in Figure 11.15.

FIGURE 11.14   Sorting subroutine that interchanges G$(I) and G$(J) each time that L(I) and L(J) are interchanged.

```
]LIST2000-
2000   REM    SORT L(I)
2010   FOR I = 1 TO N - 1
2020   FOR J = I + 1 TO N
2030   IF L(I) <  = L(J) THEN 2050

2040   T = L(I):L(I) = L(J):L(J) =
       T
2045   T$ = G$(I):G$(I) = G$(J):G$(
       J) = T$
2050   NEXT J: NEXT I
2060   RETURN
```

FIGURE 11.15   Plotting bar graphs using the subroutine in Fig. 11.14.

```
]LIST-400
10   REM    BAR GRAPH EXAMPLE
15   DATA  #,O,*,I
20   DATA  12,25,5,17
25   DIM G$(4),L(4)
30   FOR I = 1 TO 4: READ G$(I): NEXT

40   FOR I = 1 TO 4: READ L(I): NEXT

45   N = 4: GOSUB 2000: REM    SORT
50   FOR J = 1 TO 4
60   L = L(J):G$ = G$(J): GOSUB 400

70   NEXT J
90   END
400  FOR I = 1 TO L: PRINT G$;: NEXT
     : PRINT : RETURN
]RUN
*****
#############
IIIIIIIIIIIIIIIII
OOOOOOOOOOOOOOOOOOOOOOOOO
```

Sorting an Array in Descending Order

The subroutine in Figure 11.14 can easily be modified to sort the array L(I) in descending order rather than ascending order by changing line 2030 to **2030 IF L(I)>=L(J) THEN 2050** as shown in Figure 11.16. Running the main program with this subroutine will produce the result shown in Figure 11.17.

```
]LIST2000-
2000   REM    SORT L(I)
2010   FOR I = 1 TO N - 1
2020   FOR J = I + 1 TO N
2030   IF L(I) >  = L(J) THEN 2050

2040   T = L(I):L(I) = L(J):L(J) =
       T
2045   T$ = G$(I):G$(I) = G$(J):G$(
       J) = T$
2050   NEXT J: NEXT I
2060   RETURN
```

FIGURE 11.16 Subroutine to sort array L(I) containing N elements in *descending* order.

```
]LIST-400
10    REM    BAR GRAPH EXAMPLE
15    DATA  #,0,*,I
20    DATA  12,25,5,17
25    DIM G$(4),L(4)
30    FOR I = 1 TO 4: READ G$(I): NEXT

40    FOR I = 1 TO 4: READ L(I): NEXT

45    N = 4: GOSUB 2000: REM    SORT
50    FOR J = 1 TO 4
60    L = L(J):G$ = G$(J): GOSUB 400

70    NEXT J
90    END
400   FOR I = 1 TO L: PRINT G$;: NEXT
      : PRINT : RETURN
]RUN
00000000000000000000000000
IIIIIIIIIIIIIIIII
#############
*****
```

FIGURE 11.17 Plotting bar graphs in descending order using the subroutine in Fig. 11.16.

EXERCISE 11-1

Write a program that:

a. stores the six New England states and their populations in the arrays S$(I) and P(I) as shown in Figure 11.1

b. plots a vertical bar graph of the population using low-resolution graphics

c. sorts the populations in increasing order

d. plots a second bar graph (after key "S" is pressed) with the populations in ascending order.

EXERCISE 11-2

Write a program that:

a. stores N test scores in DATA statements, with the value of N stored as the first entry of the first data statement

b. reads the test scores into an array S(I)

c. computes and prints out the average of the N test scores.

EXERCISE 11-3

If AV is the average of the N test scores stored in the array S(I), then the *standard deviation* is defined as:

$$SD = \sqrt{\frac{1}{N} \sum_{I=1}^{N} (S(I)-AV)^2}$$

where the notation $\sum_{I=1}^{N}$ means the sum from I = 1 to N. Modify the program in Exercise 11-2 to compute and print out the standard deviation of the test scores. Run the program for the following test scores:

Test Scores							
75	36	60	92	80	72	68	48
65	82	88	72	76	85	72	98
48	57	73	66	76	88	73	82
44	90	70	56	81	75	87	90

EXERCISE 11-4

The weights shown below are the weights of a group of males and females. Write a computer program that will compute and print out the means and standard deviations of the two groups of weights. Modify the program so as to compute and print the mean and standard deviation of all weights (both male and female). (See Exercise 11-3.)

Male		Female
200	138	103
185	205	105
185	159	112
125	230	102
140	150	160
195	140	120
190	170	115
155	145	130
185	169	140
140	215	118

EXERCISE 11-5

A person makes the following monthly deposits in a savings account paying 5% interest compounded monthly:

Month:	1	2	3	4	5	6	7	8	9	10	11	12
Deposit: (dollars)	25	20	30	15	25	40	20	30	35	35	35	25

The identical pattern of deposits is repeated for a second and third year. Write a computer program that will compute the amount of money the person has deposited and the total amount in the account at the end of 6, 12, 18, 24, 30, and 36 months. Read in the monthly deposits as an array D(I). (Note: If R is the annual interest rate, and it is compounded monthly, then each month the added interest is equal to R/12 times the amount in the account.)

EXERCISE 11-6

The polynomial

$$P(x) = a_1x^4 + a_2x^3 + a_3x^2 + a_4x + a_5$$

can be written in the following nested form:

$$P(x) = a_5 + x(a_4 + x(a_3 + x(a_2 + x(a_1))))$$

If the coefficients a_i are stored as subscripted variables A(I), then the polynomial P can be evaluated, using the nested form, by the algorithm:

> P = A(1)
> *for* I = 2 *to* 5
>   P = A(I) + X * P
> *next* I

Write a program that will use a similar nesting algorithm to evaluate the polynomial

$$P(x) = 3x^5 + 4x^4 - 2x^3 + 5x - 7$$

for values of x between -2 and $+2$ in steps of 0.2. Print out a table of x and P(x). Make your program general so that the coefficients are stored in DATA statements, and the program can handle a polynomial of any order.

12

$$$ WITH STRINGS ATTACHED: LEARNING ABOUT LEFT$, RIGHT$, AND MID$

You have learned in previous chapters of this book that memory cells with names like A$ and C3$ contain *strings*. The dollar sign, $, is used in BASIC to identify string-related names. APPLESOFT BASIC has a number of special functions which make it easy for you to manipulate strings. Learning how to use these functions will permit you to write many interesting programs. In this chapter you will learn

1. to use the string functions LEFT$, RIGHT$, MID$, and LEN

2. to use the numeric/string functions STR$ and VAL

3. to use the ASCII code functions ASC and CHR$

4. to display dollars and cents on the screen

5. to write a program to shuffle and display a deck of playing cards

6. to write a program to deal a hand of playing cards.

THE STRING FUNCTIONS LEFT$, RIGHT$, MID$, AND LEN*

The string functions LEFT$, RIGHT$, and MID$ are used to extract some portion of a string. The function LEN is used to determine the length of a string.

LEFT$

The function **LEFT$(A$,I)** is a string that contains the left-most I characters of the string A$. For example, if **A$="ABCDE"**, then **LEFT$(A$,2)** will be the string "AB". To verify this, type

```
A$="ABCDE"
? LEFT$(A$,2)
```

as shown in Figure 12.1.

RIGHT$

The function **RIGHT$(A$,I)** is a string that contains the right-most I characters of the string A$. For example, if **A$="ABCDE"**, then **RIGHT$(A$,2)** will be the string "DE". To verify this, type **? RIGHT$(A$,2)** as shown in Figure 12.1.

*Only the function LEN is available in INTEGER BASIC.

101

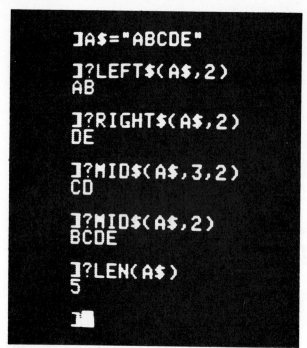

FIGURE 12.1 Examples of using the string functions LEFT$, RIGHT$, MID$, and LEN.

MID$

The function MID$(A$,I,J) is a string that contains the J characters of A$ that start at position I (the first character of A$ is position 1). For example, if A$="ABCDE", then MID$(A$,3,2) will be the string "CD". To verify this, type ?MID$(A$,3,2) as shown in Figure 12.1.

The function MID$ can also be written with only two arguments. In this case MID$(A$,I) is a string that contains the characters of A$ starting at position I and continuing to the end of the string A$. For example, if A$="ABCDE", then MID$(A$,2) will be the string "BCDE". To verify this, type ? MID$(A$,2) as shown in Figure 12.1. Note carefully the difference between MID$(A$,2) and RIGHT$(A$,2). The former is a string containing the right-most characters starting at position 2 of A$, while the latter is a string containing the right-most 2 characters of A$.

LEN

The function LEN(A$) is equal to the length of the string A$. Note that it is a *numerical* value (not a string). For example, if A$="ABCDE" then the value of LEN(A$) is 5. To verify this type ?LEN(A$) as shown in Figure 12.1.

THE NUMERIC/STRING FUNCTIONS VAL AND STR$*

It is important that you understand the difference between the numerical value 456 and the string "456". It is like the difference between BOSTON and "BOSTON". BOSTON is a city in Massachusetts containing buildings, roads, and so on. "BOSTON" is a six-letter word that is the name of a city. Similarly, 456 is a number that you can add to other numbers. "456" is just the three characters 4, 5, and 6 sitting next to each other. Sometimes you will need to convert a string like "456" to its corresponding numerical value 456. The function VAL will do this. You may also need to convert a numerical value like 456 to its corresponding string "456". The function STR$ will do this.

VAL

The function VAL(A$) is equal to the numerical equivalent of the string A$. If A$ does not have a numerical equivalent then VAL(A$) is equal to zero.

As an example of using the VAL function, clear the screen and type

$$A\$="456"$$
$$?\ A\$$$
$$?\ VAL(A\$)$$

as shown in Figure 12.2. It looks as if both PRINT statements print the same value 456. However, in order to see the difference between VAL(A$) and A$, type

$$?VAL(A\$)+10$$
$$?A\$+10$$

as shown in Figure 12.2. Note that the number VAL(A$) can be added to 10, whereas trying to add the string A$ to the number 10 will produce the error message ?TYPE MISMATCH ERROR. Finally, type ?VAL("K") as shown in Figure 12.2. This shows that the value of the function VAL is zero if the string does not have a numerical equivalent.

---

*Not available in INTEGER BASIC.

```
]A$="456"

]?A$
456

]?VAL(A$)
456

]?VAL(A$)+10
466

]?A$+10

?TYPE MISMATCH ERROR
]?VAL("K")
0
```

FIGURE 12.2 Examples of using the numeric/string function VAL.

STR$

The function **STR$(A)** is the string equivalent of the numerical value A. As an example of using the STR$ function, clear the screen and type

A=456

?A

?STR$(A)

as shown in Figure 12.3. Note that both print statements print the number 456. However, STR$(A) is actually a string containing the three characters 4,5 and 6. To verify this, type **?LEN(STR$(A))** as shown in Figure 12.3.

Strings can be added together (concatenated) to form longer strings. For example, type **?"$"+STR$ (A)+".00"** as shown in Figure 12.3. The total string consists of the dollar sign, "$", plus "456," plus ".00" that is "$456.00".

The functions STR$ and VAL are reciprocal functions, as you can verify by typing

?STR$(VAL("246"))

?VAL(STR$(246))

as shown in Figure 12.4.

FIGURE 12.3 Examples of using the numeric/string function STR$.

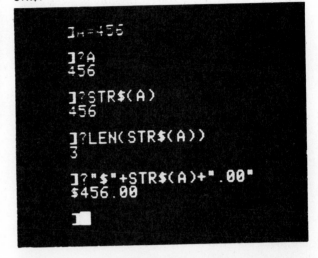

```
]A=456

]?A
456

]?STR$(A)
456

]?LEN(STR$(A))
3

]?"$"+STR$(A)+".00"
$456.00
```

FIGURE 12.4 STR$ and VAL are reciprocal functions.

```
]?STR$(VAL("246"))
246

]?VAL(STR$(246))
246
```

THE ASCII CODE FUNCTIONS ASC AND CHR$*

The name ASCII stands for "American Standard Code for Information Interchange." In this standard code a certain number is associated with each character (let-

---

*CHR$ is not available in INTEGER BASIC. The value of ASC(A$) is normally 128 larger in INTEGER than in Applesoft.

ter, digit, or special character). This code is used extensively throughout the computer industry for sending information from one computer to another or for sending data from a terminal to a computer. The BASIC function ASC can be used to find the ASCII number associated with any character, and the function CHR$

can be used to find the character associated with any ASCII number.

ASC

The function **ASC(A$)** is equal to the ASCII code of the first character in the string A$. To find some ASCII codes, clear the screen and type

?ASC("A")

?ASC("?")

?ASC("ABC")

?ASC("*")

?ASC("7")

as shown in Figure 12.5. Letters, digits, and special character keys all have ASCII numbers. Note that the ASCII number for a digit is different from the digit itself (55 is the ASCII code for 7). Also note that the function ASC("ABC") is the ASCII code of the first character A.

If you want to see what some other ASCII numbers are, try typing the following two-line program:

30 GET A$

40 ?A$; " "; ASC(A$); SPC(2);: GOTO 30

This program will print any character you type, followed by its ASCII code. A sample run is shown in Figure 12.6. The ASCII codes for all of the characters are given in Appendix B.

FIGURE 12.5   Examples of ASCII codes of Apple II characters.

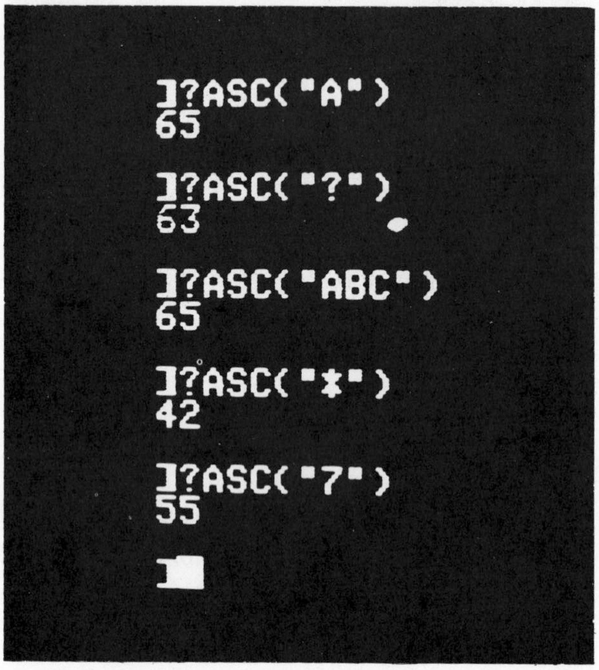

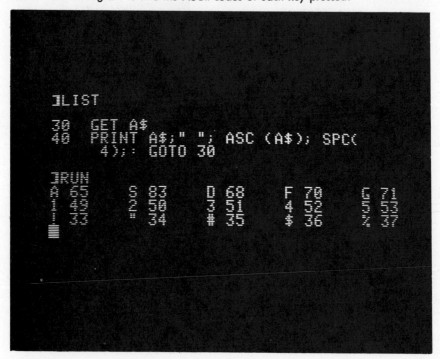

FIGURE 12.6   Program to find the ASCII codes of each key pressed.

CHR$

If you know the ASCII code of a character, you can generate the string of that character using the function **CHR$(A)** where A is the ASCII code of the character.

Using the results in Figure 12.5, try typing the following statements:

```
?CHR$(65)
?CHR$(63)
?CHR$(55)
```

as shown in Figure 12.7.

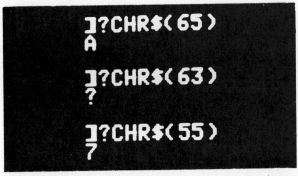

FIGURE 12.7 Examples of printing characters using their ASCII codes.

PRINTING DOLLARS AND CENTS

Lots of practical programs involve money and require you to display dollars and cents on the screen. This is not as easy as it may seem. First of all, if you compute some monetary value, such as interest in a savings account, you will want to round to the nearest cent. You can do this by adding 0.005 to the value and then displaying only two places after the decimal point. In order to try this scheme, type

```
A=208.4978
A1=A+.005
?A1
?INT(A1*100)/100
```

as shown in Figure 12.8. Note that although this method rounded to the nearest cent, the Apple II does not display trailing zeros. Therefore, 50 cents is printed as .5. It would look strange if you printed the amount of a check this way.

FIGURE 12.8 Rounding a monetary value to the nearest cent.

```
]A=208.4978

]A1=A+.005

]?A1
208.5028

]?INT(A1*100)/100
208.5

■
```

One way to print the .5 as .50 is to convert the dollars and cents separately to their string equivalents and then display these strings. To investigate this possibility, type

```
A2=INT(A1)
?A2
A2$=STR$(A2)
?A2$
```

as shown in Figure 12.9. Note that A2 is the dollar value and A2$ is the string representation of this value.

In order to obtain a string representation of the cents value, type

```
A3=A1-A2
?A3
A3$=MID$(STR$(A3),2,2)
?A3$
```

FIGURE 12.9 A2$ is a string representation of the dollar amount.

```
]A2=INT(A1)

]?A2
208

]A2$=STR$(A2)

]?A2$
208

■
```

as shown in Figure 12.10. Note that the cents value A3 is found by subtracting the dollar value from the total rounded amount. A string representing the cents amount consists of the second and third characters in the string STR$(A3) (the first character is a decimal point).

The total dollars and cents can be displayed by typing ?"$";A2$;".";A3$ which will display

$$\underset{\text{A2\$ \quad A3\$}}{\underline{\$208.50}}$$

as shown at the bottom of Figure 12.10.

```
]A3=A1-A2

]?A3
 502799988

]A3$=MID$(STR$(A3),2,2)

]?A3$
50

]?"$";A2$;".";A3$
$208.50
```

FIGURE 12.10   A3$ is a string representation of the cents amount.

The statements shown in Figures 12.8, 12.9, and 12.10 can be combined to form the subroutine shown in Figure 12.11. This subroutine should print the value of A in the form $XX.YY. For the first value of A shown in Figure 12.10 the subroutine works well. However, for a value of A=159.996 the subroutine prints $160..9. The problem can be found by looking at the values of A1 and A3 as shown in Figure 12.11. If the fractional part of A1 (the cents value, A3) is less than 0.001, A3 will be stored in scientific notation. This really creates havoc because now the second and third characters in STR$(A3) are ".9" rather than "00". The subroutine shown in Figure 12.11 can be fixed by adding the statement **925 IF A3<.01 THEN A3$ ="00":GOTO 940** as shown in Figure 12.12. Note that this modified subroutine prints the correct dollars and cents values for all of the examples shown.

```
]LIST

900   REM    PRINT A AS $XX.YY
910   A1 = A + .005:A2 =  INT (A1):
      A3 = A1 - A2
920   A2$ =  STR$ (A2)
930   A3$ =  MID$ ( STR$ (A3),2,2)
940   PRINT "$";A2$;".";A3$;
950   RETURN

]A=208.4978:GOSUB 900
$208.50
]A=159.996:GOSUB 900
$160..9
]?A1
160.001

]?A3
9.99987125E-04
```

FIGURE 12.11   This subroutine for displaying dollars and cents will not work for cents values less than 0.001.

The last example shown in Figure 12.12 rounds 999,999.999 to $1,000,000.00. A check written for this value (or any value over $1,000.00) would look better and easier to read if you included the commas in the dollar amount by the method which follows.

FIGURE 12.12   Modified subroutine that displays correct dollars and cents value.

```
]LIST

900   REM    PRINT A AS $XX.YY
910   A1 = A + .005:A2 =  INT (A1):
      A3 = A1 - A2
920   A2$ =  STR$ (A2)
925   IF A3 < .01 THEN A3$ = "00":
      GOTO 940
930   A3$ =  MID$ ( STR$ (A3),2,2)
940   PRINT "$";A2$;".";A3$;
950   RETURN

]A=208.4978:GOSUB 900
$208.50
]A=159.996:GOSUB 900
$160.00
]A=999999.999:GOSUB 900
$1000000.00
```

Adding Commas to the Dollar Amount

Suppose you want to add commas to the value

$$\underset{\text{A2\$}\qquad\text{A3\$}}{\underline{\$2357829.49}}$$

First of all, the largest dollar value that our subroutine can handle is 999999999 because after this value the Apple II will store A1 and A2 in scientific notation. Actually, because the Apple II does not keep more than nine digits of precision when storing numbers, to get the correct cents you should limit the dollar values to 9,999,999.99. Therefore, at most we need to insert two commas. We will therefore divide the string A2$ into the three sub-strings A4$, A5$, and A6$ as follows:

$$\underset{\text{A6\$}\quad\text{A5\$}\quad\text{A4\$}\quad\text{A3\$}}{\$2, \quad 357, \quad 829. \quad 49}$$

That is, if L=LEN(A2$), then

$$A4\$ = \begin{cases} A2\$ & (L<=3) \\ MID\$(A2\$,L-2,3) & (L>3) \end{cases}$$

$$A5\$ = MID\$(A2\$,L-5,3) \qquad (L>3)$$

and

$$A6\$ = LEFT\$(A2\$,L-6) \qquad (>6)$$

The algorithm for adding the commas will then be

> if L<=3
> then print $A2$.A3$
> else if L<=6
> then print $A5$,A4$.A3$
> else print $A6$,A5$,A4$.A3$

Figure 12.13 shows how this algorithm can be added to the subroutine shown in Figure 12.12. Lines 940–975 implement the algorithm described above. Two examples of using this subroutine are also shown in Figure 12.13.

FIGURE 12.13   Subroutine that includes commas when displaying dollars and cents.

```
]LIST

900   REM    PRINT A AS $XX.YY
910 A1 = A + .005:A2 =   INT (A1):
      A3 = A1 - A2
920 A2$ =  STR$ (A2)
925   IF A3 < .01 THEN A3$ = "00":
      GOTO 940
930 A3$ =  MID$ ( STR$ (A3),2,2)
940 L =  LEN (A2$)
945   PRINT "$";
950   IF L < = 3 THEN A4$ = A2$: GOTO
      975
955   IF L < = 6 THEN A5$ =  LEFT$
      (A2$,L - 3): GOTO 967
960 A6$ =  LEFT$ (A2$,L - 6): PRINT
      A6$;",";
965 A5$ =  MID$ (A2$,L - 5,3)
967   PRINT A5$;",";
970 A4$ =  MID$ (A2$,L - 2,3)
975   PRINT A4$;".";A3$;
980   RETURN
```

```
]A=999999.999:GOSUB 900
$1,000,000.00
]A=2357829.49:GOSUB 900
$2,357,829.49
]
```

As another example of using string functions, we will now develop some subroutines that will be useful in card game programs. The first thing to decide is how to represent a deck of cards within the computer. It is convenient to associate a number between 1 and 52 with each card in the deck. We will use the numbering system shown in Figure 12.14. For example, the seven of hearts is number 33, the jack of diamonds is number 24, and so on.

FIGURE 12.14 Each card in the deck is associated with a number between 1 and 52.

	Club	Diamond	Heart	Spade	Value No. V
A	1	14	27	40	1
2	2	15	28	41	2
3	3	16	29	42	3
4	4	17	30	43	4
5	5	18	31	44	5
6	6	19	32	45	6
7	7	20	33	46	7
8	8	21	34	47	8
9	9	22	35	48	9
T	10	23	36	49	10
J	11	24	37	50	11
Q	12	25	38	51	12
K	13	26	39	52	13
Suit No. S	1	2	3	4	

The value of a card (A–K) has a value number V, and the four suits have a suit number S as defined in Figure 12.14.

It is usually easier to use the card number, C, as much as possible in a program to distinguish cards, and then use C to find the value and suit of the card when needed. Given a card number C, the corresponding suit number S is obtained by

$$S = INT((C-1)/13)+1$$

You should verify this by trying some examples from Figure 12.14. For example, if $C = 26$ (king of diamonds)

$$S = INT(25/13)+1$$
$$= 1+1 = 2$$

Once you know S then the value number V can be determined from the equation

$$V = C-(S-1)*13$$

For example, if $C = 26$, then $S = 2$ and

$$V = 26-(2-1)*13 = 13$$

It is convenient to store all of the card numbers in an array C%(I) (we will use an integer array to save memory). This array can be initialized with the following statements:

DIM C%(52)
FOR I = 1 TO 52: C%(I) = I: NEXT

Thus, for example, C%(47) = 47 and represents the eight of spades.

Suppose you want to display the nineteenth card in the deck. The card number is C%(19) = 19. The suit number is

$$S = INT((C\%(19)-1)/13)+1$$
$$= INT(18/13)+1$$
$$= 2$$

and the value number is

$$V = C\%(19)-(S-1)*13$$
$$= 19-1*13$$
$$= 6$$

Therefore, according to Figure 12.14, the card is the six of diamonds. To display this value, define the two strings V$ and S$ shown in Figure 12.15. Note that the position of each value character in V$ corresponds to the appropriate value number V in Figure 12.14. Therefore, the single value character V1$ corresponding to the value number V is given by V1$ = MID$(V$,V,1). Similarly, the position of each suit character in S$ corresponds to the appropriate suit number S in Figure 12.14. Therefore, the single suit character S1$ corresponding to the suit number S is given by S1$ = MID$(S$,S,1).

FIGURE 12.15 Definition of the value string V$ and the suit string S$.

```
V$ = "A23456789TJQK"
S$ = "CDHS"
```

The above ideas are incorporated in the two subroutines shown in Figure 12.16. The subroutine given by lines 3000–3050 sets up the deck by dimensioning and initializing C%(I) and defining V$ and S$. This subroutine should be called once at the beginning of any program involving playing cards.

The subroutine given by lines 3100–3150 in Figure 12.16 will find the value string V1$ and the suit string S1$ of the card located at position P in the array C%, that is, the card with card number C%(P). Lines 3110–3120 define the suit number S and value number V using the formulas given above. Lines 3130–3140 find the single character strings V1$ and S1$.

FIGURE 12.16   Subroutines to set up deck (line 3000) and pick card at location P (line 3100).

```
]LIST
3000   REM   PLAYING CARD SETUP
3010   DIM C%(52)
3020   FOR I = 1 TO 52:C%(I) = I: NEXT

3030   V$ = "A23456789TJQK"
3040   S$ = "CDHS"
3050   RETURN
3100   REM   PICK CARD AT LOCATION
       P
3110   S =   INT ((C%(P) - 1) / 13) +
       1
3120   V = C%(P) - (S - 1) * 13
3130   V1$ =   MID$ (V$,V,1)
3140   S1$ =   MID$ (S$,S,1)
3150   RETURN
```

To test these subroutines, type

GOSUB 3000
P=33: GOSUB 3100: ?V1$;S1$
P=52: GOSUB 3100: ?V1$;S1$

as shown in Figure 12.17. Note that card number 33 is the seven of hearts and card number 52 is the king of spades according to Figure 12.14.

```
]GOSUB 3000

]P=33:GOSUB 3100:?V1$;S1$
7H

]P=52:GOSUB 3100:?V1$;S1$
KS

■
```

FIGURE 12.17   Testing the subroutines given in Fig. 12.16.

You can display the entire deck by running the program shown in Figure 12.18. Line 20 sets up the deck, and line 25 skips a line. The FOR . . . NEXT loop in lines 30–60 increments P from 1 to 52, finds V1$ and S1$ for the card at position P (line 40), and prints these values and suit characters in line 50. The result of running this program is shown in Figure 12.19. Note that the cards are printed in the order shown in Figure 12.14. To print them in a random order you must first shuffle the deck.

```
]LIST-100
10    REM    DISPLAY DECK
20    GOSUB 3000: REM   SETUP DECK
25    PRINT
30    FOR P = 1 TO 52
40    GOSUB 3100: REM   GET NEXT CAR
      D
50    PRINT V1$;S1$,: REM   DISPLAY
      CARD
60    NEXT P
100   END
```

FIGURE 12.18   Program to display entire deck of cards.

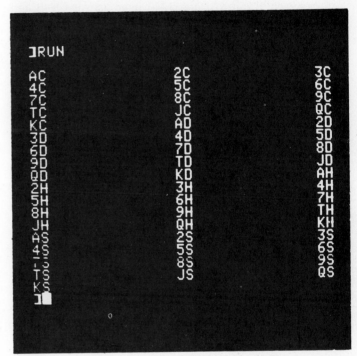

FIGURE 12.19   Result of running program shown in Fig. 12.18.

Shuffling a Deck of Cards

To shuffle a deck of cards, all you have to do is to scramble the order of the card numbers stored in the card array C%(I). The following simple algorithm will do this:

for I=1 TO 52
    find random number J between 1 and 52
    interchange C%(I) and C%(J)
next I

This algorithm interchanges each element in C%(I) in turn with another element selected at random.

RND(1) is a random number with a value greater than 0 and less than 1; therefore J=INT(52* RND(1)+1) will be a random integer between 1 and 52.

A subroutine that will shuffle the deck while displaying a blinking version of the word "SHUFFLING" is shown in Figure 12.20. The FOR . . . NEXT loop in lines 3220–3280 corresponds to the *for . . . next* loop given above. Line 3230 finds a random number J between 1 and 52. Line 3240 interchanges C%(I) and C%(J).

```
]LIST3200-3280
3200   REM    SHUFFLE DECK
3210   FLASH
3215   PRINT "S H U F F L I N G";
3220   FOR I = 1 TO 52
3230   J =   INT (52 *  RND (1) + 1)

3240   T = C%(I):C%(I) = C%(J):C%(J
       ) = T
3250   NEXT I
3260   HTAB 1: NORMAL : INVERSE
3270   PRINT "S H U F F L I N G"
3280   NORMAL : RETURN
```
FIGURE 12.20   Subroutine to shuffle a deck of cards.

Add lines 27 and 28 shown in Figure 12.21 to the main program given in Figure 12.18. This new program will shuffle the deck and then display all of the cards. A sample run is shown in Figure 12.22.

FIGURE 12.21   Main program to display shuffled deck of cards.
```
]LIST-100
10   REM    DISPLAY DECK
20   GOSUB 3000: REM   SETUP DECK
25   PRINT
27   GOSUB 3200: REM   SHUFFLE DECK

28   PRINT : PRINT
30   FOR P = 1 TO 52
40   GOSUB 3100: REM   GET NEXT CAR
     D
50   PRINT V1$;S1$,: REM   DISPLAY
     CARD
60   NEXT P
100   END
```

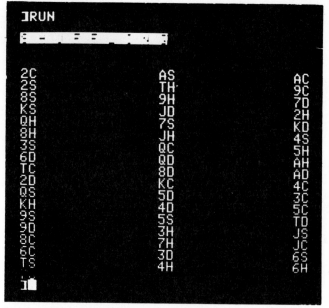

FIGURE 12.22   Sample run of program shown in Fig. 12.21.

Dealing a Hand of Cards

The program shown in Figure 12.21 can easily be modified to deal a hand of cards. All you have to do is divide the cards among a number of players and limit the number of cards dealt to the desired number.

Let NP=number of players and NC=number of cards per hand.

The first card dealt to each player can be displayed on a single line with the statements

```
50 P=1
70 FOR J=1 TO NP
80 GOSUB 3100: REM DEAL NEXT CARD
90 PRINT V1$;S1$;SPC(2);
100 P=P+1
110 NEXT J
```

Note that P points to the next card in the deck, and subroutine 3100 finds the card at C%(P).

To deal NC cards to each player and display them on succeeding lines, add the statements

```
60 FOR I=1 TO NC
120 PRINT
130 NEXTI
```

as shown in Figure 12.23. In this program lines 30–40 allow the user to input the values NP and NC. Line 50 points to the top card of the deck and skips a line. Lines 60–130 are the outer FOR . . . NEXT loop that prints NC rows of cards. Lines 70–110 are the inner FOR . . .

```
JLIST-140
10   REM    DEAL HAND  OF CARDS
20   GOSUB 3000: REM   SETUP DECK
25   PRINT
27   GOSUB 3200: REM    SHUFFLE DECK

28   PRINT : PRINT
30   INPUT "ENTER NUMBER OF PLAYER
     S ";NP
40   INPUT "ENTER NUMBER OF CARDS
     PER HAND ";NC
50 P = 1: PRINT
60   FOR I = 1 TO NC
70   FOR J = 1 TO NP
80   GOSUB 3100: REM   DEAL NEXT CA
     RD
90   PRINT V1$;S1$; SPC( 2);
100 P = P + 1
110  NEXT J
120  PRINT
130  NEXT I
140  END
```

FIGURE 12.23   Program to deal a hand of cards.

NEXT loop that deals NP cards and displays them on one line. Line 100 points to the next card in the deck after each one is dealt. The PRINT statement in line 120 is necessary to move the cursor to the beginning of the next line after each round of cards is dealt.

Two sample runs of this program are shown in Figure 12.24. It would be nice if you could sort each hand by suit. This is easier to do than you may think.

FIGURE 12.24   Sample runs of program shown in Fig. 12.23.

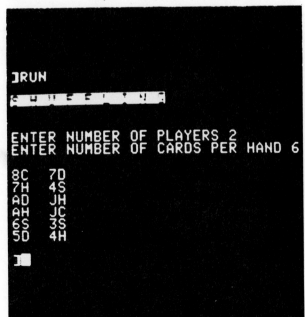

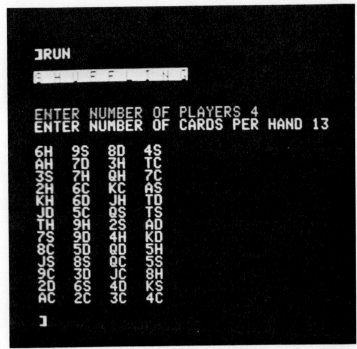

FIGURE 12.24   (cont.)

Sorting a Hand by Suit

Suppose that a hand contains the cards shown in Figure 12.25a, where the number for each card is also given (see Figure 12.14). If the card numbers are sorted in ascending order, then the cards will be sorted in ascending order by suit as shown in Figure 12.25b. This illustrates the advantage of using card numbers to represent playing cards inside the computer.

To sort a hand we will therefore need to store the card numbers for each card in the hand. We can store these in an array. For convenience we will use a *two-dimensional* array, H(I,J), in which each column will contain the card numbers for a different player as shown in Figure 12.26. To sort all hands we will need to sort each column in ascending order.

FIGURE 12.25   A hand of cards can be sorted by suit by sorting the card numbers in ascending order.

Card	Card No.	Card No.	Card
6H	32	2	2C
4D	17	3	3C
8D	21	6	6C
4S	43	17	4D
3C	3	21	8D
JS	50	32	6H
6C	6	35	9H
9H	35	43	4S
2C	2	50	JS
(a)			(b)

111

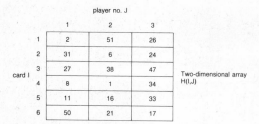

FIGURE 12.26 Each column of the two dimensional array H(I,J) contains the card numbers for one player.

The array H(I,J) must contain NC rows (number of cards per hand) and NP columns (number of players). Since we do not know what these values are until lines 30–40 in Figure 12.23 are executed, we will add the following dimension statement at line 45: **45 DIM H(NC,NP)**. Every time a card is dealt, we need to add the card number to the array H(I,J) by adding the statement **75 H(I,J)=C%(P)** as shown in Figure 12.27.

```
]LIST-140
10   REM    DEAL HAND OF CARDS
20   GOSUB 3000: PRINT
27   GOSUB 3200: PRINT : PRINT
30   INPUT "ENTER NUMBER OF PLAYER
     S ";NP
40   INPUT "ENTER NUMBER OF CARDS
     PER HAND ";NC
45   DIM H(NC,NP)
50   P = 1: PRINT
60   FOR I = 1 TO NC
70   FOR J = 1 TO NP
75   H(I,J) = C%(P)
80   GOSUB 3100: REM   NEXT CARD
90   PRINT V1$;S1$; SPC( 2);
100  P = P + 1
110  NEXT J
120  PRINT
130  NEXT I
135  GOSUB 200: REM   DISPLAY HAND

140  END
```

FIGURE 12.27 Main program to deal a hand of cards and then display the sorted hand.

Note that this statement is inside the two nested FOR . . . NEXT loops and will be filled up one row at a time. In Figure 12.27 we have added the one additional statement **135 GOSUB 200: REM DISPLAY SORTED HAND**, where we will hide everything that we have not yet figured out.

The subroutine at line 200 will have to sort each column in H(I,J) in ascending order and then display the corresponding cards. This subroutine is shown in Figure 12.28. Line 205 prints the word "SORTING" so that if it takes a little time (it will) the user will know what is going on. Line 210 will sort each column in

H(I,J). In the interest of putting off as long as possible what we do not yet know how to do, we will just let the subroutine at line 2000 do this. The nested FOR . . . NEXT loops in lines 220–260 are similar to the ones in lines 60–130 in Figure 12.27 that displayed the original hand. The subroutine at line 3100 will find the card at position P in the array C%, that is, the card with card number C%(P). This was useful in line 80 in Figure 12.27 where we were incrementing P each time through the loop. However, in Figure 12.28 we do not know P, but we *do* know the card number directly—it is just H(I,J). Therefore, we would like to use the subroutine at line 3100 to find the value of the card with card number H(I,J). We must make C%(P) contain the value H(I,J). Inasmuch as the array element C%(0) is not normally used but available, we will use this location to store H(I,J) as shown in line 240 in Figure 12.28. Note that we must set P=0 so that the subroutine at line 3100 shown in Figure 12.16 will use C%(0) which will be equivalent to using H(I,J).

```
]LIST200-260
200   REM   DISPLAY SORTED HAND
205   PRINT : PRINT "SORTING": PRINT

210   GOSUB 2000: REM   SORT COLUMN
      S OF H
220   FOR I = 1 TO NC
230   FOR J = 1 TO NP
240   P = 0:C%(0) = H(I,J)
245   GOSUB 3100: REM   NEXT CARD
250   PRINT V1$;S1$; SPC( 2);
260   NEXT J: PRINT : NEXT I: RETURN
```

FIGURE 12.28 Subroutine to display the sorted hands of cards.

We are finally at the point where we must deal with sorting the columns of H(I,J) in ascending order. If you go back and study the sorting algorithm that we developed in the last chapter (given in Figure 11.10), you will note that all we have to do is apply this same algorithm to each column of H(I,J). The resulting algorithm is given in Figure 12.29. The BASIC implementation of this algorithm is written as a subroutine in Figure 12.30.

FIGURE 12.29 Algorithm for sorting each column of H(I,J) in increasing order.

```
for J=1 TO NP
   for I=1 TO NC−1
      for K=I+1 TO NC
         if H(I,J) <= H(K,J)
         then do nothing
         else interchange H(I,J) and H(K,J)
      nextK
   nextI
nextJ
```

```
]LIST2000-2060
2000   REM  SORT EACH COLUMN OF H(
       NC,NP)
2010   FOR J = 1 TO NP
2020   FOR I = 1 TO NC - 1
2030   FOR K = I + 1 TO NC
2040   IF H(I,J) <  = H(K,J) THEN
       2060
2050   T = H(I,J):H(I,J) = H(K,J):H
       (K,J) = T
2060   NEXT K: NEXT I: NEXT J: RETURN
```

FIGURE 12.30   Subroutine to sort each column of the array H(I,J).

We have now written all of the subroutines needed to run the program shown in Figure 12.27. A sample run is shown in Figure 12.31. Note that each hand is sorted by suit with the suits displayed in order (clubs, diamonds, hearts, and spades).

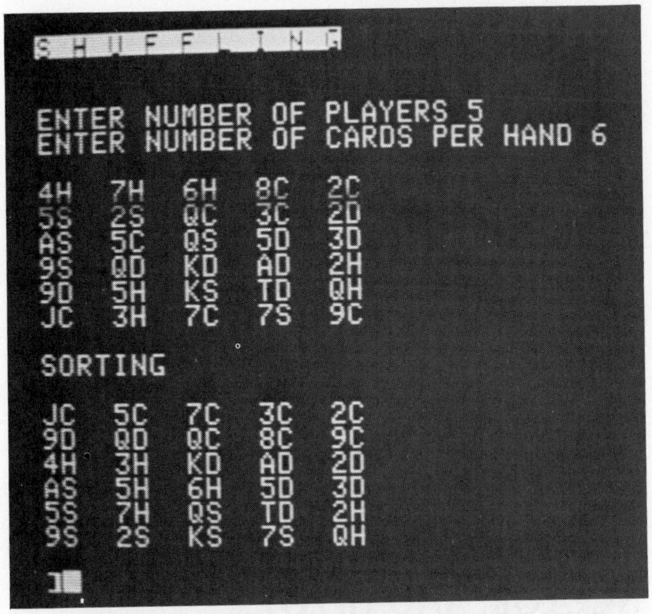

FIGURE 12.31   Sample run of the program shown in Fig. 12.27.

EXERCISE 12-1

Write a program that will input a string A$ and a substring B$, and then search for the first occurrence of the substring B$ in A$. If a match is found, the value of P should be set to the position in A$ of the first character of B$. (P=1 corresponds to the first character in A$.) If no match is found, set P=0.

EXERCISE 12-2

Modify the program in Exercise 12-1 to find all occurrences of B$ in A$. Store the locations of all matches in the array P(I). A value of P(I)=0 will indicate no more matches in the string.

EXERCISE 12-3

Write a program that will replace all occurrences of the substring B$ in A$ with the substring C$. The program should input the string A$ and the two substrings B$ and C$.

EXERCISE 12-4

Write a program that will shuffle a deck of cards and deal a bridge hand. The four hands are to be sorted with the ace as the high card in each suit.

EXERCISE 12-5

Some card games require the players to cut for deal, with either the high card or low card winning the deal. Write a program that will allow NP players to cut for deal and assign the deal to the player cutting the highest card.

EXERCISE 12-6

Write a program that will print a check. The program should input a name, address, date, and the check amount. Print the check in the form

PAY TO THE ORDER OF	DATE	PAY THIS AMOUNT
JOHN DOE	12/13/80	****1,250.41
1234 APPLE DRIVE		
ROCHESTER, MI 48063		

Check to make sure that the amount is in the range 0–9,999,999.00, and print leading asterisks in the amount box on the check.

13
LEARNING TO USE
HIGH-RESOLUTION GRAPHICS

The low-resolution graphics mode was described in Chapter 2, and you have used it in many of your programs in subsequent chapters. The Apple II also has a high-resolution graphics mode that allows you to plot figures on the screen with considerably more detail. In this chapter you will learn

1. to use the high-resolution graphics mode on the Apple II

2. to plot figures in a dot-to-dot fashion by storing the coordinates of the vertices in DATA statements

3. to draw figures of varying size

4. to plot figures at different locations on the screen

5. to plot figures whose coordinates can be calculated

6. to use the statements DRAW, XDRAW, ROT, and SCALE in conjunction with a *shape table*.

THE STATEMENTS HGR, HCOLOR, AND HPLOT

In the high-resolution graphics mode the screen is considered to be divided into a grid with 160 rows and 280 columns, with four lines of text at the bottom as shown in Figure 13.1. The column positions of the grid are numbered 0 through 279 from left to right. The row positions of the grid are numbered 0 through 159 from top to bottom.

To enter the high-resolution graphics mode, type **HOME**, and then type **HGR**. When you do this, the screen will clear, and the cursor will disappear. This is because the cursor is still near the top of the screen. Type **VTAB 21**, and the cursor will show up in the 4-line text area at the bottom of the screen.

Although you can plot 16 different colors in the low-resolution graphics mode, the number of colors that you can plot in the high-resolution graphics mode is much more limited. The color is set in the high-resolution graphics mode by typing **HCOLOR = C** where C is a number from 0 through 7. The colors associated with each number may depend on the type of TV you are using and the setting of the color and tint controls. For some TVs and settings the following colors are associated with each color number:

0. black

1. green (X-odd)

2. violet (X-even)

3. white (X-even violet X-odd green)

4. black

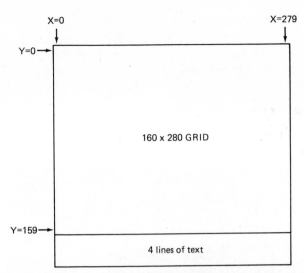

FIGURE 13.1   The high resolution graphics mode divides the screen into a 160 × 280 grid with four lines of text at the bottom.

FIGURE 13.2   Plotting a horizontal line in high resolution graphics.

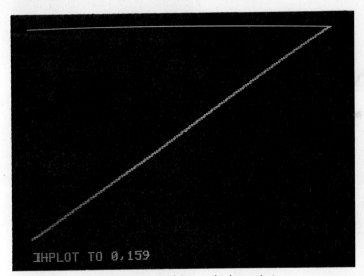

FIGURE 13.3   Plotting a diagonal line in high resolution graphics.

FIGURE 13.4   Plotting a vertical line in high resolution graphics.

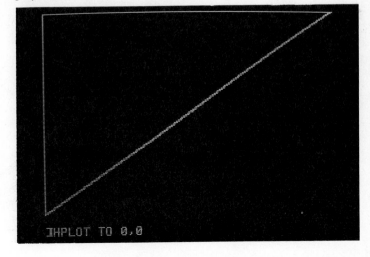

5. red (X-odd)
6. blue (X-even)
7. white (X-even blue
       X-odd red)

Note that there are really only four colors, other than black and white. You will find, however, that each color cannot be plotted at any location on the screen. For example, violet (2) and blue (6) dots can be plotted only in *even* columns on the screen, while green (1) and red (5) dots can be plotted only in *odd* columns on the screen. A white dot will only appear white (on a color TV) if two adjacent dots in a given row are plotted. In addition, it is not always possible to plot different colors very close to each other. Normally, you will not have to worry if the colors of all the lines you plot are not exactly what you thought they were going to be when you wrote the program. It is probably just a function of the TV and the limitation of high-resolution colors in the Apple II.

Set the color to white by typing **HCOLOR = 3**. You can plot a point at any X,Y location (X between 0 and 279 and Y between 0 and 159) by typing **HPLOT X, Y**. For example, if you type **HPLOT 140, 80** you should see a small dot near the center of the screen.

The statement **HPLOT X1, Y1 TO X2, Y2** will plot a line from the location (X1,Y1) to the location (X2,Y2). For example, type **HPLOT 0, 0 TO 279, 0**. This will plot a horizontal line across the top of the screen as shown in Figure 13.2.

The statement **HPLOT TO X, Y** will plot a line from the most recently plotted point to the location (X,Y). For example, typing **HPLOT TO 0, 159** will plot the diagonal line shown in Figure 13.3. This is because the point 279,0 was the last point plotted in Figure 13.2.

If you now type **HPLOT TO 0,0** the vertical line in Figure 13.4 will be plotted.

115

It is possible to plot a sequence of lines in a single statement by using the HPLOT statement in the form **HPLOT X1, Y1 TO X2, Y2 TO X3, Y3.** This statement will plot one line from X1, Y1 to X2, Y2 and then will plot a second line from X2, Y2 to X3, Y3. For example, the statement **HPLOT 0,0 TO 279,0 TO 0,159 TO 0,0 TO 279,159 TO 279,0** will plot the pattern shown in Figure 13.5.

To get out of the high-resolution graphics mode, type **TEXT** as shown in Figure 13.6. Note that the screen does not get filled with "garbage" as it did when leaving the low-resolution graphics mode. Rather, you return to the text mode, and you can see the previous statements that you typed while in the high-resolution graphics mode.

EXERCISE 13-1

Plot a square in high-resolution graphics that is 100 points on a side and has its upper left-hand corner at the coordinates X=90, Y=30.

FIGURE 13.5   Plotting multiple lines in a single HPLOT statement.

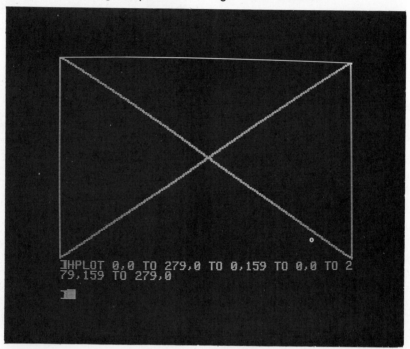

FIGURE 13.6   Typing TEXT returns you to the *text* mode.

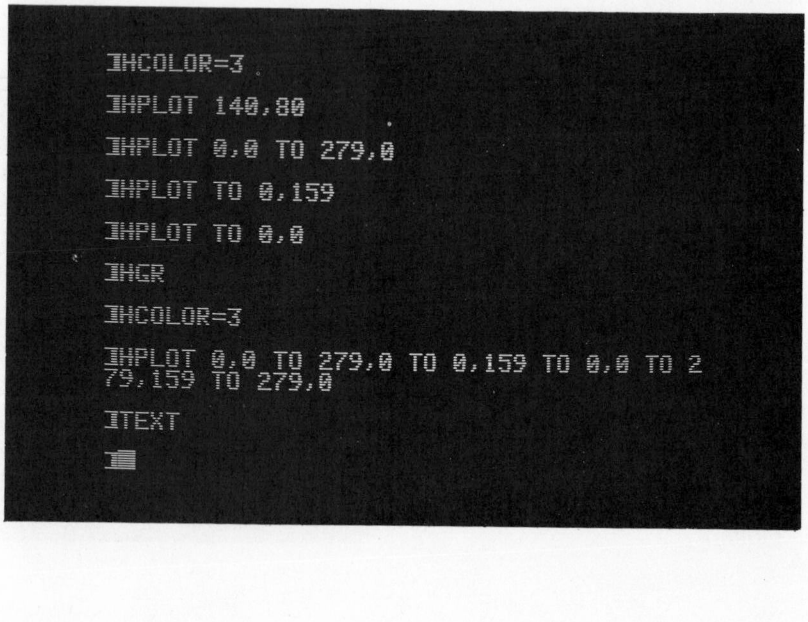

Let us suppose you want to draw some arbitrary figure made up of a sequence of straight line segments. It is convenient to plot the figure on a new X-Y coordinate system that is centered at the screen coordinates XC, YC. For example, in Figure 13.7 a square is shown plotted in such a coordinate system. Note that the Y coordinate is plotted in its "normal" upward direction which is opposite the Y screen coordinate. We will let the computer take care of this difference. Also, note that we have located the origin of our new coordinate system at the center of the square. This means that the coordinates of the vertices of the square may contain negative values as shown in Figure 13.7. Of course, if the square is to fit on the screen, it is necessary for the value of XC (the center of the square) to be in the range 50–229 and the value of YC to be in the range 50–109.

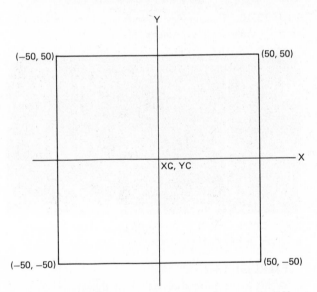

FIGURE 13.7   Defining a square centered on a new X,Y coordinate system.

For any center point XC, YC the square is completely defined by the (X,Y) coordinates of its vertices:

(−50, 50)

(50, 50)

(50, −50)

(−50, −50)

We will store these vertex coordinates in two DATA statements, with all of the X coordinates in the first DATA statement and all of the Y coordinates (in the same order) in the second DATA statement.

The vertex coordinates will be stored in the order you would use to draw the figure in a dot-to-dot fashion. If you return to the starting position, the first (X,Y)

coordinate must also be the last one. Thus, the two DATA statements

250 DATA −50, 50, 50, −50, −50

260 DATA 50, 50, −50, −50, 50

will be used to plot the square shown in Figure 13.7. Statement 250 contains all of the X coordinates, and statement 260 contains the corresponding Y coordinates.

The program shown in Figure 13.8 will plot this square. After entering the high-resolution graphics mode in line 20, the subroutine at line 200 is used to fill the arrays X(I) and Y(I) with the vertex coordinates. These arrays are DIMensioned in line 210, and then the vertex coordinates stored in the DATA statements are read into the arrays X(I) and Y(I) in lines 220 and 230. Note that in line 230 each value stored in Y(I) is changed in sign. This is because the Y coordinate shown in Figure 13.7 (from which the DATA coordinates were determined) is opposite in direction to the Y screen coordinate (see Figure 13.1).

```
]LIST
10   REM    SQUARE
20   HGR : HCOLOR= 3
30   GOSUB 200: REM     FILL ARRAYS
40   XC = 140:YC = 80
50   HPLOT XC + X(0),YC + Y(0)
60   FOR I = 1 TO M
70   HPLOT  TO XC + X(I),YC + Y(I)

80   NEXT I
90   END
200  REM    FILL X,Y ARRAYS
210  M = 4: DIM X(M),Y(M)
220  FOR I = 0 TO M: READ X(I): NEXT

230  FOR I = 0 TO M: READ Y(I):Y(
     I) =  - Y(I): NEXT
240  RETURN
250  DATA  -50,50,50,-50,-50
260  DATA  50,50,-50,-50,50
```

FIGURE 13.8   Program to plot a square.

Line 40 in Figure 13.8 defines the center of the square to be at the screen coordinates (140, 80). Line 50 plots the point located at the upper left-hand corner of the square. Note that the statement HPLOT XC + X(0), YC + Y(0) will actually be equivalent to HPLOT 140−50, 80 + (−50) and will therefore plot the point (−50, 50) shown in Figure 13.7. Remember that all of the signs in Y(I) were inverted in line 230. The statements

> 60 FOR I = 1 TO M
> 70 HPLOT TO XC + X(I), YC + Y(I)
> 80 NEXT I

shown in Figure 13.8 will plot the four sides of the square.

The result of running the program given in Figure 13.8 is shown in Figure 13.9.

FIGURE 13.9   Result of running the program shown in Fig. 13.8.

Note that although we drew a square in Figure 13.7, it did not come out as a square in Figure 13.9. The reason for this is that the distance between adjacent points on a TV is different in the vertical and horizontal direction. You can see from Figure 13.9 that since the same number of points were plotted for both the vertical and horizontal sides of the square, the distance between adjacent vertical points must be larger than the distance between adjacent horizontal points.

There is an easy way to correct for this difference in our program. If we measure the sides of the square on the screen we find that the horizontal length is 2.6 centimeters, and the vertical length is 2.9 centimeters. Therefore, if we reduce the value of all Y coordinates by the factor

$$F = 2.9/2.6 = 1.1$$

then the square should appear *square*. We can do this by adding the statement **215 F = 1.1** and modifying line 230 to read **230 FOR I=0 TO M: READ Y(I): Y(I) = −Y(I)/F: NEXT** as shown in Figure 13.10. The result of running this modified program is shown in Figure 13.11. Note that the square now looks like a square on the screen. You should use this vertical scaling factor (measured for your own screen) in all of your plotting programs to produce properly proportioned figures.

```
]LIST
10   REM    SQUARE
20   HGR : HCOLOR= 3
30   GOSUB 200: REM    FILL ARRAYS
40   XC = 140:YC = 80
50   HPLOT XC + X(0),YC + Y(0)
60   FOR I = 1 TO M
70   HPLOT   TO XC + X(I),YC + Y(I)

80   NEXT I
90   END
200   REM    FILL X,Y ARRAYS
210   M = 4: DIM X(M),Y(M)
215   F = 1.1
220   FOR I = 0 TO M: READ X(I): NEXT

230   FOR I = 0 TO M: READ Y(I):Y(
      I) =  − Y(I) / F: NEXT
240   RETURN
250   DATA  −50,50,50,−50,−50
260   DATA  50,50,−50,−50,50
```

FIGURE 13.10   The changes shown in lines 215 and 230 will properly scale the Y coordinate.

FIGURE 13.11   Result of running the modified "square" program shown in Fig. 13.10.

EXERCISE 13-2

Write a program that will plot the star shown in Figure 13.12 centered at the screen coordinates (140,80).

FIGURE 13.12   Star figure to be plotted in Exercise 13-2.

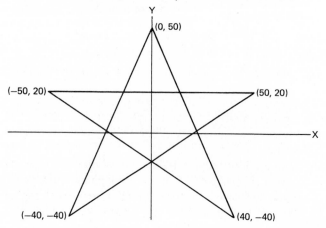

Scaling Figures

If the coordinates of the points in a figure are stored in the arrays X(I) and Y(I) as described above, it is a simple matter to plot the figure a different size. All you have to do is to always use **X(I) * S** and **Y(I) * S** in your plot statements where S is the scale factor. For example, a value of S=2 will cause the figure to be plotted double size, and a value of S=0.5 will cause the figure to be plotted half size.

As an example, the program shown in Figure 13.13 will plot a sequence of concentric squares centered at the screen coordinate (140,80). Note that the *for . . . next* loop

45 FOR S = .2 to 2 STEP .2

—

—

—

85 NEXT S

has been added to the program given in Figure 13.10.

```
]LIST
10   REM    SQUARE
20   HGR : HCOLOR= 3
30   GOSUB 200: REM    FILL ARRAYS
40   XC = 140:YC = 80
45   FOR S = .2 TO 1.8 STEP .2
50   HPLOT XC + X(0) * S,YC + Y(0)
     * S
60   FOR I = 1 TO M
70   HPLOT  TO XC + X(I) * S,YC +
     Y(I) * S
80   NEXT I
85   NEXT S
90   END
200  REM    FILL X,Y ARRAYS
210  M = 4: DIM X(M),Y(M)
215  F = 1.1
220  FOR I = 0 TO M: READ X(I): NEXT

230  FOR I = 0 TO M: READ Y(I):Y(
     I) =  - Y(I) / F: NEXT
240  RETURN
250  DATA  -50,50,50,-50,-50
260  DATA  50,50,-50,-50,50
```

FIGURE 13.13   Program to plot a set of concentric squares.

In addition the HPLOT statements in lines 50 and 70 have been modified to include the scale factor S. The result of running this program is shown in Figure 13.14.

In addition to plotting a figure of different sizes by using the scale factor S, it is a simple matter to plot the figure at different locations on the screen by changing the values of the center coordinates XC and YC.

FIGURE 13.14   Result of running the program shown in Fig. 13.13.

EXERCISE 13-3
Write a program that will plot nine squares in a 3 × 3 arrangement on the screen. The size of each square should be 40 × 40, and the squares should not overlap.

EXERCISE 13-4
Write a program that will plot five stars on the screen at random locations. Take care to insure that no part of any star ever extends beyond the edge of the screen.

EXERCISE 13-5
Modify the program in Exercise 13-4 so that the size of each star, as well as its position, is random.

Plotting Circles

How can you plot a circle in high-resolution graphics? Figure 13.15 shows a circle of radius R with its center

FIGURE 13.15   Relationship between a point (X,Y) on a circle and the radius R and angle A.

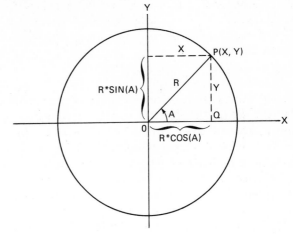

119

at the origin of a local X-Y coordinate system. Recall from trigonometry that for the triangle OPQ the sine of the angle A is defined as

$$SIN(A) = Y/R$$

and the cosine of the angle A is defined as

$$COS(A) = X/R$$

Therefore we see that any point P on the circle has the (X,Y) coordinates

$$X = R*COS(A)$$

$$Y = R*SIN(A)$$

We can therefore plot the circle by letting the angle A increase in steps, calculate new values for X and Y from the equations above, and HPLOT to the new points. If we let A increase from 0 to 360 degrees, we will plot the entire circle. We must remember that when using the built-in functions SIN(A) and COS(A) the angle A must be in *radians*. If AD is the angle in degrees then **AR = AD * PI/180** is the same angle expressed in radians where PI = 3.1415926 (see Figure 4.34).

A program for plotting circles is shown in Figure 13.16. Line 20 clears the screen and moves the cursor

FIGURE 13.16   A program for plotting a circle of radius R using high resolution graphics.

```
LIST
10    REM    PLOTTING CIRCLES
20    HOME : VTAB 21
25    HGR : HCOLOR= 3
30    INPUT "ENTER RADIUS (1-88) ";
      R
35    IF R < 1 OR R > 100 THEN 30
40    INPUT "ENTER ANGLE STEP SIZE
      (DEGREES) ";S
50    PI = 3.1415926:F = 1.1
60    XC = 140:YC = 80
70    HPLOT XC + R,YC
80    FOR AD = 0 TO 360 STEP S
90    AR = AD * PI / 180
100   X = R *  COS (AR)
110   Y = R *  SIN (AR)
120   Y =   - Y / F
130   HPLOT  TO XC + X,YC + Y
140   NEXT AD
150   INVERSE : PRINT "ANOTHER PLO
      T?";: NORMAL : PRINT  SPC( 1
      );
160   GET G$
170   IF G$ = "Y" THEN 20
180   TEXT : HOME : END
```

to row 21. Line 25 enters the high-resolution graphics mode and sets the color to white. The user can specify the radius R and angular step size S in lines 30 and 40. Line 50 defines PI and the vertical scale factor F. The center of the circle will be located at the screen coordinates XC, YC defined in line 60. The first point on the circle located at the screen coordinates XC + R, YC is plotted in line 70. The FOR . . . NEXT loop in lines 80–140 plots the rest of the circle. Notice that the angle AD increases from 0 degrees to 360 degrees in steps of S degrees. Line 90 converts AD to an angle AR in radians. Lines 100–110 calculate the next values of X and Y on the circle. Line 120 inverts and scales the Y values as described above so that the circle will look like a circle. The next segment of the circle is plotted in line 130.

You should type in this program and run it. Some sample runs are shown in Figure 13.17. Note that if the angle step size gets too big, a polygon is plotted rather than a circle. This suggests an easy way to plot some interesting multiple polygon figures. The next section will describe such a program.

FIGURE 13.17   Examples of running the program shown in Fig. 13.16.

(a)

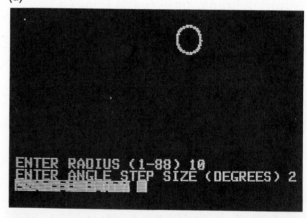

(b)

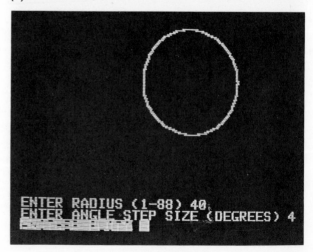

(c)

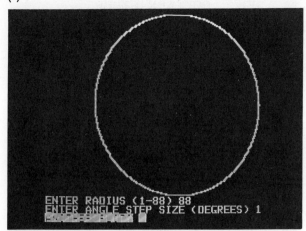

Plotting Polygons

Suppose you would like to plot the picture shown in Figure 13.19. How would you go about it? You could start at the vertex X(1), Y(1) and draw the four lines to X(K), Y(K) (K=2 to 5) as shown in Figure 13.20a. Next you could add the three lines from X(2), Y(2) to X(K), Y(K) (K=3 to 5) as shown in Figure 13.20b. Then you could add the two lines from X(3), Y(3) to X(K), Y(K) (K=4 to 5) as shown in Figure 13.20c. Finally you would add the line from X(4), Y(4) to X(5), Y(5). Note that the four steps shown in Figure 13.20 can be carried out by the algorithm

> *for* J=1 to N−1
> > *for* K = J+1 to N
> > > plot line from X(J), Y(J) to X(K), Y(K)
> > *next* K
> *next* J

EXERCISE 13-6

Write a program to plot the "ball" shown in Figure 13.18a. Think of looking down on the top of the ball and then plotting a series of circles at different angles B as shown in Figure 13.18(b). Both halves of this circle will appear on the screen so you only need to let B increase from 0 to 90 degrees. The X coordinate of each circle will now be **X= R * COS(A) * COS(B)**.

FIGURE 13.18   Plotting a 3-D ball (Exercise 13.6).

(a)

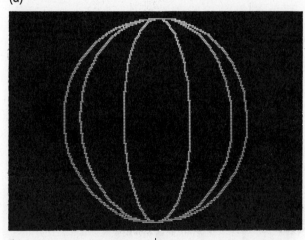

(b)

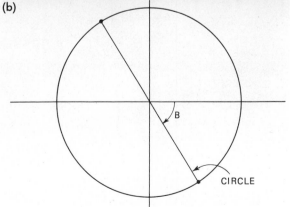

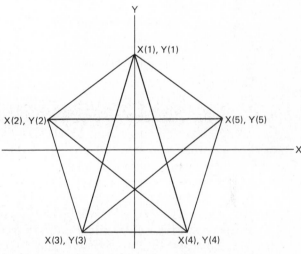

FIGURE 13.19   A polygon with a line down between all vertices.

FIGURE 13.20   Steps in generating the picture shown in Fig. 13.19.

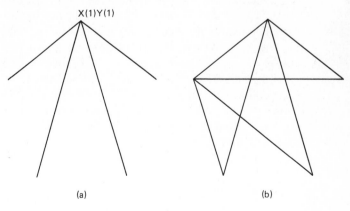

(a)   (b)

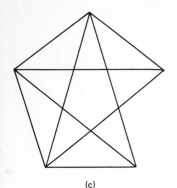
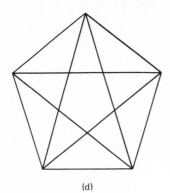

(c)   (d)

FIGURE 13.20   (cont.)

where N is the number of vertices in the polygon (5 in Figure 13.20).

Think of a circle that passes through all of the vertices of the polygon. If R is the radius of this circle, the N coordinate pairs X(I), Y(I) can be calculated from the following algorithm:

$$for\ I = 1\ to\ N$$
$$AD = I * 360/N$$
$$AR = AD * PI/180$$
$$X(I) = R * COS(AR)$$
$$Y(I) = R * SIN(AR)$$
$$next\ I$$

Note that this algorithm divides the circle into N pie-shaped wedges where the angle of each "pie piece" is 360/N degrees. The coordinates X(I), Y(I) are then calculated using the equations of the circle.

A program that will plot this polygon figure for polygons with from 3 to 15 sides is shown in Figure 13.21. The center of the polygon will be at XC, YC which are specified to be 140, 80 in line 50. The radius of the circle that would pass through the polygon vertices is set to 88 in line 50. After inputting the number of sides N in line 60 and checking to make sure that N is between 3 and 15 in line 70, the subroutine at line 200 is called. This subroutine calculates the N coordinates X(I), Y(I) as described above. Note that line 260 inverts and scales the Y coordinates by our usual vertical scale factor F=1.1 (defined in line 40).

Lines 90–120 actually plot the polygon figure using the nested *for . . . next* loops described above. Notice that the HPLOT statement in line 110 will cause the polygon to be centered at XC, YC. After plotting the figure, line 130 will ask the user if another plot is desired. The GET statement in line 140 will wait for a response and then in line 150 will branch back to line 20 if key "Y" is pressed. Any other key will cause line 160 to be executed, which will clear the screen and stop the program.

```
]LIST
10   REM    POLYGON FIGURE
15   DIM X(15),Y(15)
20   HOME : VTAB 22
30   HGR : HCOLOR= 3
40   PI = 3.1415926:F = 1.1
50   XC = 140:YC = 80:R = 88
60   INPUT "ENTER NUMBER OF SIDES
     (3-15) ";N
70   IF N < 3 OR N > 15 THEN 60
80   GOSUB 200: REM    CALCULATE PO
     INTS
90   FOR J = 1 TO N - 1
100  FOR K = J + 1 TO N
110  HPLOT XC + X(J),YC + Y(J) TO
     XC + X(K),YC + Y(K)
120  NEXT K: NEXT J
125  VTAB 24
130  INVERSE : PRINT "ANOTHER PLO
     T?";: NORMAL : PRINT  SPC( 1
     )
140  GET G$
150  IF G$ = "Y" THEN 20
160  TEXT : HOME : END
200  REM    CALCULATE POINTS
210  FOR I = 1 TO N
220  AD = I * 360 / N
230  AR = AD * PI / 180
240  X(I) = R *  COS (AR)
250  Y(I) = R *  SIN (AR)
260  Y(I) =  - Y(I) / F
270  NEXT I: RETURN
```

FIGURE 13.21   Program to plot a polygon figure with from 3 to 15 sides.

Type in this program and run it. Two figures that can be generated by this program are shown in Figure 13.22. Try some different values of N.

FIGURE 13.22   Examples of polygon figures that can be generated by the program shown in Fig. 13.21.

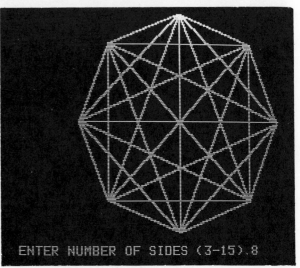

ENTER NUMBER OF SIDES (3-15),8

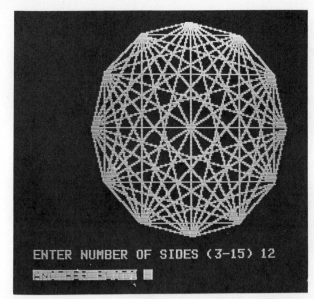

ENTER NUMBER OF SIDES (3-15) 12

FIGURE 13.22 (cont.)

Plotting Functions

The high-resolution graphics capability of the Apple II makes it a useful tool for studying the behavior of mathematical functions. For example, the function

$$y(x) = A \sin(2\pi x/T + \phi)$$

defines a *sine wave* with amplitude A, period T, and phase angle ϕ. You can define this function by using the BASIC statement **DEF FN Y(X) = A * SIN(2*PI*X/T + PH)** where PI = 3.1415926 and PH is the phase angle in radians.

A program that will plot this function is shown in Figure 13.23. The subroutine at line 200 that is called in line 30 will plot the axes shown in Figure 13.24a. Each grid mark on the axes represents an increment of 10 screen units. Lines 50–70 allow the user to enter values for the amplitude A, the period T, and the phase

```
]LIST
10   REM   SINE WAVE
20   HOME : HGR : HCOLOR= 3
25 PI = 3.1415926
30   GOSUB 200: REM   PLOT AXES
35   VTAB 24
40   PRINT "Y=A*SIN(2*PI*X/T+PHASE
     )";
45   VTAB 21: HTAB 1
50   INPUT "ENTER AMPLITUDE A (0-8
     0) ";A
60   INPUT "ENTER PERIOD T ";T
70   INPUT "ENTER PHASE ANGLE ";PH

75 PH = PH * PI / 180
80   DEF  FN Y(X) =  - A *  SIN (2
      * PI * X / T + PH)
90   X =   - 140:Y =  FN Y(X)
95   HPLOT XC + X,YC + Y
100  FOR X =   - 139 TO 139
110 Y =  FN Y(X)
120  HPLOT  TO XC + X,YC + Y
130  NEXT X
140  VTAB 24: HTAB 25: INVERSE
150  PRINT "ANOTHER PLOT?";
160  NORMAL : PRINT " ";: GET A$
170  IF A$ = "Y" THEN 20
180  TEXT : HOME : END
200  REM   PLOT AXES
210 XC = 140:YC = 80
220  HPLOT 0,YC TO 279,YC
230  HPLOT XC,0 TO XC,159
240  FOR X = 0 TO 270 STEP 10
250  HPLOT X,YC TO X,YC - 5
260  NEXT X
270  FOR Y = 0 TO 150 STEP 10
280  HPLOT XC - 5,Y TO XC + 5,Y
290  NEXT Y
300  RETURN
```

FIGURE 13.23   Program to plot a sine wave.

FIGURE 13.24   (a) Axes plotted by the subroutine at line 200 in Fig. 13.23.

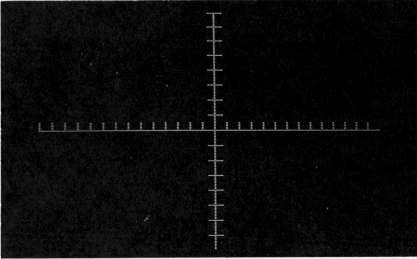

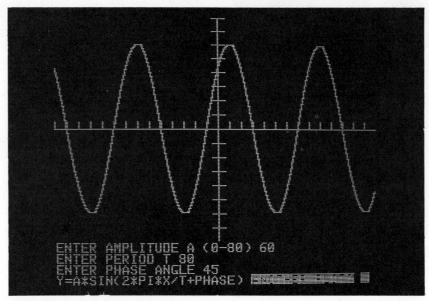

ENTER AMPLITUDE A (0-80) 60
ENTER PERIOD T 80
ENTER PHASE ANGLE 45
Y=A*SIN(2*PI*X/T+PHASE)

FIGURE 13.24   (b) Example of sine wave that is plotted by the program shown in Fig. 13.23.

angle PH (in degrees). Line 75 converts the phase angle from degrees to radians. Line 80 defines the sine wave as a function Y(X).

The origin of the coordinate system plotted in the subroutine at line 200 is located at the screen coordinates XC, YC (defined to be 140, 80 in line 210). The first point of the function that is plotted (in line 95) will be the left-most value of X (−140). This value is assigned in line 90 together with the corresponding value of Y = FN Y(X). The negative sign in the definition of Y(X) in line 80 is our usual inversion because the positive Y screen coordinate points downward.

The FOR . . . NEXT loop in lines 100–130 plots the rest of the curve. Notice that the value of X is increased from −139 to +139 and for each value of X the value of the function Y(X) is calculated in line 110.

Type in this program and run it. A sample run is shown in Figure 13.24b. By entering different values of the amplitude A, period T, and phase angle PH you will be able to get a good idea of how this function behaves.

EXERCISE 13-7
Write programs that the user can use to plot the following functions for different values of the parameters A, C, and N.

a. $Y = A * LOG(X/C)$ $X > 0$
b. $Y = A * EXP(-X/C)$
c. $Y = X \wedge N/C$
d. $Y = A*SQR(X/C)$ $X > 0$

USING A SHAPE TABLE

Earlier in this chapter you learned how to store the vertices of a graphic figure in DATA statements and then use the HPLOT statement to draw the figure in a dot-to-dot fashion. The Apple II has another way of drawing graphic figures. It is possible to define a graphic figure in terms of basic "move only" or "plot and move" operations. Each "move" is one screen unit up, down, left, or right. The numbers 0–7 are used to define the eight basic move operations shown in Figure 13.25. A particular graphic figure is defined by simply listing a sequence of numbers (0–7). For example, the cross shown in Figure 13.26 can be drawn by starting at the center of the cross and carrying out the following operations:

2, 2, 2, 7, 4, 4, 7, 7, 4, 4, 5, 5, 4, 4,

5, 5, 6, 6, 5, 5, 6, 6, 7, 7, 6, 6, 7

Once a shape is defined in terms of a sequence of numbers, these numbers must be stored in the computer memory in the form of a *shape table*. In the next section we will show you how to do this using a simple BASIC subroutine. After the shape table is stored in the computer memory, you can draw the shape anywhere on the screen by using the DRAW and XDRAW statements. In addition, the shape can be drawn with different sizes and orientations by using the statements SCALE and PLOT.

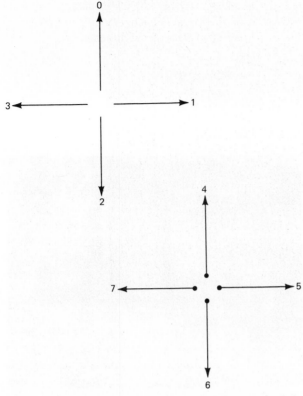

Figure 13.25   Numbers 0-3 define the four "move only" operations and numbers 4-7 define the four "plot and move" operations.

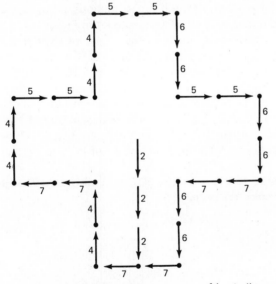

Figure 13.26   Defining a shape in terms of basic "move only" and "plot and move" operations.

A BASIC Subroutine for Storing a Shape Table

As it is described in the APPLESOFT Reference Manual, the process of generating a shape table is a little complicated. It involves figuring out what hexa-decimal numbers need to be stored in a sequence of memory locations. All of this complication can be avoided by using the BASIC subroutine shown in Figure 13.27. Do not be concerned that you don't know how the subroutine works yet. All you need to do is to store your shape definition in a DATA statement at the end of the subroutine. Add the number 8 at the end of the DATA statement to indicate the end of the shape definition. The DATA statement in line 700 in Figure 13.27 stores the shape definition for the cross shown in Figure 13.26.

The subroutine in Figure 13.27 uses the POKE statement (to be described in Chapter 14) to store the shape table in the Apple II memory. Type it in as shown and then type **GOSUB 600**. The shape table for the cross is now stored in the Apple II memory starting at memory location 768.

```
]LIST
600    REM    STORE SHAPE TABLE
610    POKE 768,01: POKE 769,00: POKE
       770,04: POKE 771,00:M = 772
612    POKE 232,00: POKE 233,03
615    READ A
620    IF A = 8 THEN 690
630    READ B
640    IF B = 8 THEN 680
650    X = B * 8 + A
660    POKE M,X:M = M + 1
670    GOTO 615
680    POKE M,A:M = M + 1
690    POKE M,0
695    RETURN
700    DATA   2,2,2,7,4,4,7,7,4,4,5,
       5,4,4,5,5,6,6,5,,5,6,6,7,7,6
       ,6,7,8
```

Figure 13.27   BASIC subroutine that will store a shape table in the Apple II memory.

The Statements SCALE, ROT, DRAW, and XDRAW

After you have stored a shape table (by entering the BASIC subroutine in Figure 13.27 and typing **GOSUB 600**) you can draw the shape by using the statements SCALE, ROT, DRAW, and XDRAW. Enter the high-resolution graphics mode by typing **HGR: HCOLOR=3**. Then, in the immediate mode, type

SCALE = 1

ROT = 0

DRAW 1 AT 140, 80

A small cross should appear near the center of the screen as shown in Figure 13.28.

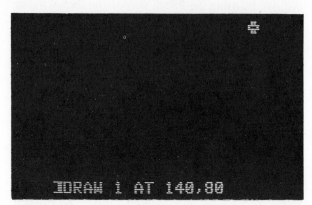

FIGURE 13.28   Using the DRAW statement to plot a shape previously stored in a shape table.

The DRAW statement has the form **DRAW N AT X, Y.** This statement will draw shape number N at location X,Y on the screen. (We can only store one shape using the subroutine in Figure 13.27, and therefore N must be equal to 1). Before the DRAW statement can be used, the scale factor SCALE and the rotation factor ROT must be set. A value of ROT = 0 will cause the shape to be plotted as defined. A value of SCALE = 1 will cause the shape to be plotted at the defined size.

Try changing the scale factor by typing

SCALE = 10

DRAW 1 AT 140, 80

as shown in Figure 13.29. Note that a new cross is plotted that is 10 times as large as the original cross. The value assigned to scale can be from 1 to 255. (A

FIGURE 13.29   The SCALE factor can be used to change the size of the shape plotted.

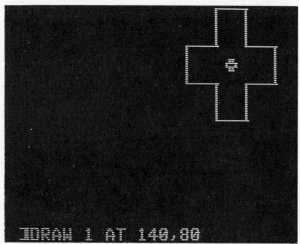

value of SCALE = 0 will produce the *maximum* size.) If the value of SCALE is 5, each "move" or "plot and move" operation is repeated 5 times.

Now type

ROT = 8

DRAW 1 AT 140, 80

as shown in Figure 13.30. Note that the cross is drawn rotated 45 degrees.

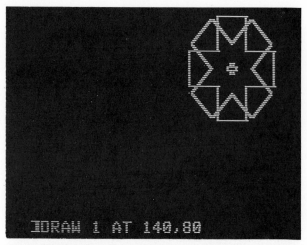

FIGURE 13.30   The statement ROT = 8 will cause the shape to be DRAWN rotated 45 degrees clockwise.

The value of ROT must be between 0 and 255. Values of 16, 32, and 48 will cause rotations of 90, 180, and 270 degrees clockwise as shown in Figure 13.31.

The number of different values of ROT that are recognized depends on the value of SCALE. For a value of SCALE = 1 only the four values (0,16,32,48) shown in Figure 13.31 are recognized. Other values will normally be treated as the next smaller recognized value. For example, values of ROT between 16 and 32 will behave like 16 (90 degree rotation). Larger values of SCALE will cause more values of ROT to be recog-

FIGURE 13.31   Increasing ROT by 16 will cause a 90 degree rotation clockwise.

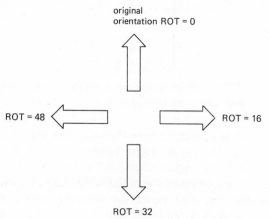

nized. For example, 8 values of ROT are recognized when SCALE is equal to 2.

It is easy to draw multiple plots of the same shape with different locations, sizes, and orientations. For example, Figure 13.32 shows a program that plots 12 crosses. Note that each cross is plotted with a SCALE of 4 and a ROT factor of 0. The effect of changing the value of ROT by 2 for each cross with SCALE = 5 is shown in Figure 13.33.

```
LIST-90
10   REM    TWELVE CROSSES
20   GOSUB 600: REM    STORE SHAPE
       TABLE
25   HOME : VTAB 22
30   HGR : HCOLOR= 3
40   ROT= 0: SCALE= 4
50   FOR Y = 40 TO 120 STEP 40
60   FOR X = 50 TO 200 STEP 50
70   DRAW 1 AT X,Y
80   NEXT X: NEXT Y
90   END
```

FIGURE 13.32   (a) Program to plot 12 crosses.

(b) Result of running the program in (a).

A program that plots six crosses of different sizes is shown in Figure 13.34.

The statement **XDRAW N AT X, Y** behaves much like the DRAW statement. The only difference is that it plots the shape using the *complement* of the color that already exists at that particular location on the screen. If the existing color is white, then XDRAW will plot in black. This makes it easy to erase a figure. For example, if you XDRAW a figure white (HCOLOR = 3) and then XDRAW it again (without changing HCOLOR), it will disappear. Try it by typing (assuming the cross shape table is still stored in memory):

```
]LIST-90
10   REM    TWELVE CROSSES
20   GOSUB 600: REM    STORE SHAPE
       TABLE
25   HOME : VTAB 22
30   HGR : HCOLOR= 3
40   R = 0: SCALE= 5
50   FOR Y = 40 TO 120 STEP 40
60   FOR X = 50 TO 200 STEP 50
62   R = R + 2
65   ROT= R
70   DRAW 1 AT X,Y
80   NEXT X: NEXT Y
90   END
```

FIGURE 13.33   Twelve crosses plotted with different values of ROT.

FIGURE 13.34   (a) Program to plot crosses with different values of SCALE.

```
LIST-90
10   REM    SCALED CROSSES
20   GOSUB 600: REM    STORE SHAPE
       TABLE
25   HOME : VTAB 22
30   HGR : HCOLOR= 3
40   ROT= 0:X = 140:Y = 80
50   FOR S = 1 TO 30 STEP 5
60   SCALE= S
70   DRAW 1 AT X,Y
80   NEXT S
90   END
```

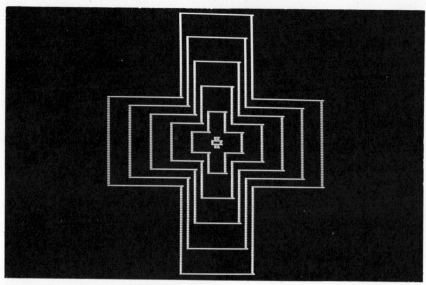

FIGURE 13.34   Result of running the program in (a).

HGR : HCOLOR = 3
SCALE = 5
ROT = 0
XDRAW 1 AT 140, 80
XDRAW 1 AT 140, 80

The program shown in Figure 13.35 will cause the cross to move back and forth across the screen. Type in this program and run it.

FIGURE 13.35   Program that uses XDRAW to move the cross back and forth across the screen.

(a)

```
]LIST-130
10    REM     MOVING CROSS
20    GOSUB 600: REM     STORE SHAPE
      TABLE
25    HOME : VTAB 22
30    HGR : HCOLOR= 3
40    ROT= 0: SCALE= 5:Y = 80
50    FOR X = 50 TO 200 STEP 2
60    XDRAW 1 AT X,Y
70    XDRAW 1 AT X,Y
80    NEXT X
90    FOR X = 200 TO 50 STEP  - 2
100   XDRAW 1 AT X,Y
110   XDRAW 1 AT X,Y
120   NEXT X
130   GOTO 50
```

(b)

EXERCISE 13-8
Write a program that plots a series of crosses, all centered at (140,80) with a value of SCALE = 25, by letting the value of ROT increase from 0 to 16 in steps of 2.

EXERCISE 13-9
Use the game paddles to vary the values of ROT from 0 to 64 (PDL(0)/4) and SCALE from 1 to 52 (PDL(1)/5+1) and then continuously draw crosses of different sizes and orientations by turning the game paddles.

EXERCISE 13-10
Change the shape plotted in Figure 13.33 to an L-shaped figure.

Storing More Than One Shape Table

It is possible for you to store more than one shape table at a time in the Apple II memory. This can be done by using the BASIC subroutine shown in Figure 13.36. To use this subroutine you must include your own DATA statements starting in line 730. The DATA statement in line 730 must contain the number of shape definitions that you want to store. You must then include one DATA statement for each shape definition. Each of these DATA statement shape definitions must end with the number 8.

The DATA statements shown in Figure 13.36 define the shapes for the numbers 1–9 plus 0. If you store N shapes, the shapes are numbered from 1 to N in the order in which you write the DATA statements. For example, line 740 defines the number 1 and is shape number 1; line 755 defines the number 4 and is shape number 4; line 785 defines the number 0 and is shape number 10.

FIGURE 13.36 Subroutine that will store more than one shape table.

```
]LIST
600  REM     STORE SHAPE TABLES
605 S = 768
610 S1 =  INT (S / 256):S2 = S -
     S1 * 256
615  POKE 232,S2: POKE 233,S1
620  READ N:K = N
625  POKE S,N: POKE S + 1,00
630 M = S + 2 * (N + 1):S2 = S +
     2
635 D = M - S
640  IF D > 255 THEN 655
645  POKE S2,D: POKE S2 + 1,0
650  GOTO 665
655 D1 =  INT (D / 256):D2 = D -
     D1 * 256
660  POKE S2,D2: POKE S2 + 1,D1
665 S2 = S2 + 2
668  READ A
670  IF A = 8 THEN 710
675  READ B
680  IF B = 8 THEN 700
685 X = B * 8 + A
690  POKE M,X:M = M + 1
695  GOTO 668
700  POKE M,A:M = M + 1
710  POKE M,0:M = M + 1
715 K = K - 1
720  IF K = 0 THEN  RETURN
725  GOTO 635
730  DATA    10
740  DATA  6,6,6,6,6,6,6,8
745  DATA  2,4,5,5,5,5,6,6,6,7,7,
     7,7,6,6,6,5,5,5,5,5,8
750  DATA    2,4,5,5,5,5,6,6,6,7,
     7,5,5,6,6,6,7,7,7,7,4,4,8
755  DATA  6,6,6,6,6,5,5,5,5,7,2,
     4,4,4,4,4,4,4,8
760  DATA  1,1,1,1,7,7,7,7,6,6,6,
     5,5,5,5,6,6,6,7,7,7,7,8
765  DATA  1,1,1,1,7,7,7,7,6,6,6,
     5,5,5,5,6,6,6,7,7,7,7,4,4,4,
     8
770  DATA  2,4,5,5,5,5,6,6,6,6,6,
     6,6,8
775  DATA  6,6,6,6,6,6,5,5,5,5,4,
     4,4,4,4,4,7,7,7,7,2,2,2,5,5,
     5,5,8
780  DATA  2,2,2,2,2,2,5,5,5,5,4,
     4,4,4,4,4,7,7,7,7,6,6,6,5,5,
     5,5,8
785  DATA    5,5,5,5,6,6,6,6,6,6,7
     ,7,7,7,4,4,4,4,4,4,8
```

Figure 13.37 shows a program that plots these numbers in three different sizes. It should be clear that by using shape tables you can include text in the high-resolution portion of the screen. This can be very useful for labeling graphs for example. You can even rotate the letters 90 degrees to write up the edge of a graph. The shape definitions for the 26 upper case letters and 10 digits are given in Table 13.1. You can, of course, define your own lower case letters or other font types if you wish.

FIGURE 13.37 Using shape tables to plot numbers in high resolution graphics.

(a)

```
]LIST-100
10   REM  PLOT NUMBERS IN
15   REM  HIGH RESOLUTION GRAPHICS
20   GOSUB 600: REM  STORE SHAPE T
     ABLE
30   HGR : HCOLOR= 3
40   ROT= 0: SCALE= 1
50   FOR I = 1 TO 10
55   DRAW I AT 22 * I,40: NEXT
60   SCALE= 2
70   FOR I = 1 TO 10
75   DRAW I AT 22 * I,80: NEXT
80   SCALE= 4
90   FOR I = 1 TO 10
95   DRAW I AT 22 * I,120: NEXT
100  END
```

(b)

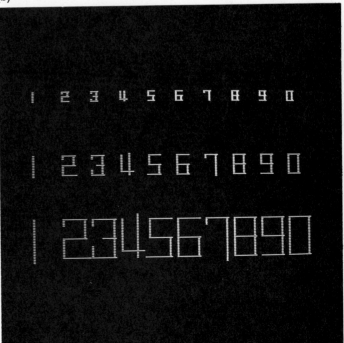

TABLE 13.1   Shape Definitions for Letters and Digits

A: 6,6,6,6,6,6,4,4,4,4,4,4,5,5,5,5,6,6,6,6,6,6,4,4,4,7,7,7,7,8
B: 5,5,5,6,1,6,7,2,7,7,7,5,5,5,6,1,6,7,2,7,7,7,4,4,4,4,4,4,8
C: 5,5,5,5,7,7,7,7,6,6,6,6,6,6,5,5,5,5,8
D: 6,6,6,6,6,6,5,5,5,4,1,4,4,4,4,1,3,7,7,7,8
E: 5,5,5,5,7,7,7,7,6,6,6,5,5,7,7,6,6,6,5,5,5,5,7,8
F: 5,5,5,5,7,7,7,7,6,6,6,5,5,7,7,6,6,6,6,8
G: 5,5,5,5,7,7,7,7,6,6,6,6,6,6,5,5,5,5,4,4,4,7,7,8
H: 6,6,6,6,6,6,4,4,4,5,5,5,5,6,6,6,4,4,4,4,4,4,6,8
I: 6,6,6,6,6,6,4,8
J: 1,1,1,1,6,6,6,6,6,6,7,7,7,7,4,6,8
K: 6,6,6,6,6,6,4,4,4,5,4,1,4,1,4,1,6,2,2,2,2,2,4,3,4,3,4,8
L: 6,6,6,6,6,6,5,5,5,5,7,8
M: 6,6,6,6,6,6,4,4,4,4,4,4,5,2,5,2,4,1,4,1,6,6,6,6,6,6,4,8
N: 6,6,6,6,6,6,4,4,4,4,4,4,5,2,6,5,2,5,2,6,5,6,4,4,4,4,4,6,8
O: 6,6,6,6,6,6,5,5,5,5,4,4,4,4,4,7,7,7,7,8
P: 6,6,6,6,6,6,4,4,4,5,5,5,5,4,4,4,7,7,7,7,8
Q: 2,6,6,6,6,6,1,5,5,5,4,7,5,4,4,4,4,4,3,7,7,7,8
R: 6,6,6,6,6,6,4,4,4,5,5,5,5,4,4,4,7,7,7,7,6,6,6,5,6,1,6,1,6,1,7,8
S: 5,5,5,5,7,7,7,7,6,6,6,5,5,5,5,6,6,6,7,7,7,7,5,8
T: 5,5,5,5,7,7,6,6,6,6,6,6,4,8
U: 6,6,6,6,6,6,5,5,5,5,4,4,4,4,4,6,8
V: 6,6,5,2,6,5,2,6,4,4,1,4,4,1,4,4,6,8
W: 6,6,6,6,6,6,1,4,1,4,4,6,6,6,1,4,1,4,4,4,4,4,6,8
X: 6,6,1,6,1,6,1,6,1,6,7,3,3,3,4,4,1,4,1,4,1,4,1,4,6,8
Y: 6,1,6,1,6,6,6,6,4,4,4,4,4,1,4,1,6,8
Z: 5,5,5,6,6,6,3,6,3,6,3,6,3,6,5,5,5,5,7,8
0: 5,5,5,6,6,6,6,6,6,6,7,7,7,7,4,4,4,4,4,4,8
1: 2,2,6,6,6,6,6,6,4,8
2: 2,4,5,5,5,5,6,6,6,6,7,7,7,7,6,6,6,6,5,5,5,5,7,8
3: 2,4,5,5,5,5,6,6,6,6,7,7,5,5,6,6,6,6,7,7,7,7,4,4,8
4: 6,6,6,6,6,5,5,5,5,7,2,4,4,4,4,4,4,6,8
5: 5,5,5,5,7,7,7,7,6,6,6,6,5,5,5,5,6,6,6,6,7,7,7,7,5,8
6: 5,5,5,5,7,7,7,7,6,6,6,6,5,5,5,5,6,6,6,6,7,7,7,7,4,4,4,8
7: 2,4,5,5,5,5,6,6,6,6,6,6,4,8
8: 6,6,6,6,6,6,5,5,5,5,4,4,4,4,4,7,7,7,7,2,2,2,5,5,5,5,8
9: 2,2,2,2,2,2,5,5,5,5,4,4,4,4,4,7,7,7,7,6,6,6,5,5,5,5,8

EXERCISE 13-11

Modify the program shown in Figure 13.23 so as to label the axes and print SINE WAVE above the graph.

14
LEARNING TO PEEK AND POKE

As you have learned, the Apple II contains a large number of memory locations that are used to store the programs and data. Some of this memory is read/write memory (RAM), some is read only memory (ROM), and some is special input/output memory that allows communication to the outside world. Examples of communication with the outside world include game paddles and getting data from the keyboard, and writing and reading data to and from a diskette.

When writing a program in BASIC, you refer to a memory cell by its name, such as A$, or C3. You do not know exactly which memory location within the Apple II contains the data in C3. The Apple II's BASIC interpreter automatically takes care of assigning these locations. However, in order to use the full power of the Apple II, you must sometimes read and write data to *specific* memory locations within it. To do this with maximum flexibility and speed, you must write the program in assembly language, which will be covered

more fully in a second book entitled *Understanding 6502 Microprocessors Using an Apple II*.

You can, however, read and write data to specific memory locations even in BASIC. You do this by using the PEEK and POKE statements. In this chapter you will learn

1. how data is stored in memory locations in the Apple II

2. how to use the PEEK and POKE statements

3. how to use the pushbuttons on the game paddles

4. how to tell if a key on the keyboard has been pressed

5. how to generate a random seed for the random number generator

6. how to use the Apple II's alternate text and graphics pages

7. how to use the CALL statement

8. how to make sounds on the Apple II's speaker.

THE STATEMENTS PEEK AND POKE

The 6502 microprocessor (see Figure 3.1) that is the "brain" of the Apple II can address a total of 65,536 memory locations (with addresses between 0-65,535). The reason for this is that the 6502 has 16 address lines,

and each line can be either high or low (1 or 0). Thus a typical address might be represented by the 16 bits **0011010111000001**. This *binary* number is equivalent to the *decimal* number 13,761. Thus, this memory

131

location would have an address of 13761. Since each of the 16 bits in the address can be either a 1 or a 0, the total number of addresses possible is

$$2^{16} = 65536$$

Your Apple II will actually contain less than this maximum amount of memory.

When working with binary numbers like the address given above, it is convenient to represent these binary numbers as *hexadecimal* numbers. This is not necessary with BASIC because the PEEK and POKE statements use only *decimal* numbers. However, if you want to program in assembly language, the use of hexadecimal numbers is essential. A brief discussion of hexadecimal numbers is given in Appendix D if you are curious, but you do not need to know anything about them for the purposes of this book.

In addition to the 16 address lines, the 6502 microprocessor has 8 data lines. These lines connect the microprocessor to all of the memory chips in the Apple II. Thus, data is moved between memory locations in groups of 8 bits called *bytes*. The total number of different values that a data byte can have is

$$2^8 = 256$$

Thus, data in a memory location in the Apple II can have a value between 0–255. This relationship between addresses and data is shown in Figure 14.1.

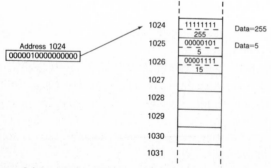

FIGURE 14.1   Each address in the range 0-65535 points to a memory location containing data in the range 0-255.

In this figure, memory location 1024 contains a data value of 255 (8 ones), and memory location 1025 contains a data value of 5.

Although memory addresses must be in the range 0–65535, the Apple II will recognize an equivalent *negative* address found by subtracting 65536 from the actual address. Thus, for example, the address 49249 is equivalent to the negative address

$$49249 - 65536 = -16287$$

Similarly, the negative address −16286 is equivalent to the actual address

$$65536 - 16286 = 49250$$

You can find the data value stored in a particular memory location by using the PEEK statement. You can store a particular data value in a given memory location by using the POKE statement.

PEEK

The function **PEEK(Addr)** returns the data value stored in the memory location with an address **Addr**. The value of **Addr** must be in the range −65535 through 65535. Try printing some value of PEEK to see what you get. For example, try

?PEEK(2048)

?PEEK(2105)

as shown in Figure 14.2. Your Apple II will probably contain different data values in these locations than those shown in Figure 14.2.

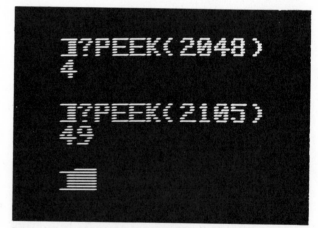

FIGURE 14.2   Memory location 2038 contains the value 4, and memory location 2105 contains the value 49.

Certain memory locations have particular meanings to the Apple II. For example, memory location −16287 (or 49249) will contain a value greater than 127 if the pushbutton on game paddle #0 is being pressed. Similarly, memory location −16286 (or 49250) will contain a value greater than 127 if the pushbutton on game paddle #1 is being pressed.

To see how this works, type and run the following one-line program. **10 ?PEEK(−16287), PEEK(−16286): GOTO 10.** The data values in locations −16287 and −16286 will keep being displayed and scroll off the screen. Press the pushbuttons on game paddles #0 and #1, and watch what happens. Note that as long as the pushbutton is being pressed, the value displayed is greater than 127.

This fact can be used in programs if you want to know if a pushbutton is being pressed. For example, the program shown in Figure 14.3 will cause a ball to bounce back and forth across the screen as long as pushbutton #1 is pressed. When you release the pushbutton the ball will stop. The FOR . . . NEXT loop in lines 30–60 causes the ball to move from left to right across the screen if pushbutton #0 is pressed. The subroutine in lines 200–220 tests whether the pushbutton is being pressed. If it is *not,* line 210 just loops on itself. This means that the last spot plotted in line 35 will remain stationary on the screen. If the pushbutton *is* being pressed, the subroutine will exit at line 220, and line 50 will then erase the most recently plotted spot. A new spot will then be plotted in line 35 just to the right of the previously plotted (and erased) spot as the FOR . . . NEXT loop increments the value of X by 1.

```
]LIST
10    REM     BOUNCING BALL
20    GR
30    FOR X = 0 TO 39
35    COLOR= 15: PLOT X,20
40    GOSUB 200: REM     TEST PUSHBUT
         TON
50    COLOR= 0: PLOT X,20
60    NEXT X
70    FOR X = 38 TO 1 STEP  - 1
80    COLOR= 15: PLOT X,20
90    GOSUB 200: REM     TEST PUSHBUT
         TON
100   COLOR= 0: PLOT X,20
110   NEXT X
120   GOTO 30
200   REM     TEST PUSHBUTTON
210   IF  PEEK ( - 16287) <  = 127
         THEN 210
220   RETURN
```

Figure 14.3   The ball will move back and forth across the screen as long as pushbutton #0 is pressed.

After a spot has been plotted and erased at the right-most position on the screen (X=39) the FOR . . . NEXT loop is exited, and another FOR . . . NEXT loop in lines 70–110 is executed. This loop moves the spot in a similar manner from right to left. When this loop is exited after the spot has been plotted and erased in position X=1, line 120 branches back to line 30 so that the entire process will be repeated as long as the pushbutton is being pressed. Note that since the pushbutton testing subroutine is always called (in lines 40 and 90) after a spot has been plotted and before it has been erased, when you release the pushbutton a single spot will always remain on the screen. Type in this program and run it.

POKE

Whereas PEEK allows you to read the data value in a particular memory location the statement **POKE Adrr, Data** allows you to store the value **Data** in the memory location **Addr.** For example, type

POKE 768, 75
?PEEK(768)

as shown in Figure 14.4. Note that **PEEK(768)** verifies that you actually stored the value 75 in memory location 768.

The 1024 memory locations 1024–2047 are special locations called the TV RAM. Of these 1024 memory locations, 960 contain the special codes corresponding to the 960 characters (24 × 40) that are currently being displayed on the TV screen. (Blanks are characters with their own special code.)

Memory location 1024 corresponds to the upper left-hand corner of the screen, and the memory addresses increase along each row. However, the addresses do not increase in order from row to row. If you POKE a value to one of these addresses, the character corresponding to this value will appear on the screen. For example, clear the screen, move the cursor down two lines (using ESC M) and type **POKE 1024, 193.** Note that the letter A appears at the upper left-hand corner of the screen. This is because 193 is the special code for an A, and you POKEd it into location 1024 which is the first location in the TV RAM.

Figure 14.4   POKE 768, 75 stores the value 75 in memory location 768.

READING THE KEYBOARD

The two memory locations 49152 (or −16384) and 49168 (−16368) are special locations that are used by the Apple II keyboard. As long as no key is pressed, the value stored in memory location −16384 will be *less than* 127. Thus you can see if any key has been pressed by checking memory location −16384 in statements such as

$$\text{if PEEK}(-16384) > 127$$
then key has been pressed

or

$$\text{if PEEK}(-16384) < 128$$
then key has *not* been pressed

If a key has been pressed, the value stored in memory location −16384 will be equal to the ASCII code for that key. This value will, of course, be greater than 127 (otherwise, a key would not have been pressed). But if this is the case, how can you tell when you press a second key? You must somehow reset the value in location −16384 to some value less than 128 so that it can become greater than 127 when you press a second key. You accomplish this reset function by referring to memory location −16368. It doesn't matter how you refer to it—you can either PEEK(−16368) in a statement such as **X = PEEK(−16368)**, or you can POKE any value into −16368 using, for example, the statement **POKE −16368, 0**. Simply referring to location −16368 will cause the value in location −16384 to become less than 128.

In order to verify the above statements, type in and run the following program:

```
100 REM READ ASCII CODES FROM KEYBOARD
110 HOME
120 IF PEEK(−16384) < 128 THEN 120
130 A = PEEK(−16384)
140 PRINT A; SPC(2); CHR$(A),
150 POKE −16368, 0
160 GOTO 120
```

Line 120 will loop on itself until a key is pressed. Line 130 will then read the ASCII value of the key that was pressed. This value, A, and the corresponding character CHR$(A) are printed in line 140. Line 150 will reset the value in location −16384 to some value less than 128. (The new value will be the present value minus 128.) Line 160 branches back to line 120 which waits for another key to be pressed. Examples of running this program are shown in Figure 14.5.

```
JLIST
100    REM    READ ASCII CODES FROM
       KEYBOARD
110    HOME
120    IF  PEEK ( − 16384) < 128 THEN
       120
130 A = PEEK ( − 16384)
140    PRINT A; SPC( 2); CHR$ (A),
150    POKE  − 16368,0
160    GOTO 120
```

FIGURE 14.5   ASCII values read from location −16384 after pressing a key.

FIGURE 14.5   (cont.)

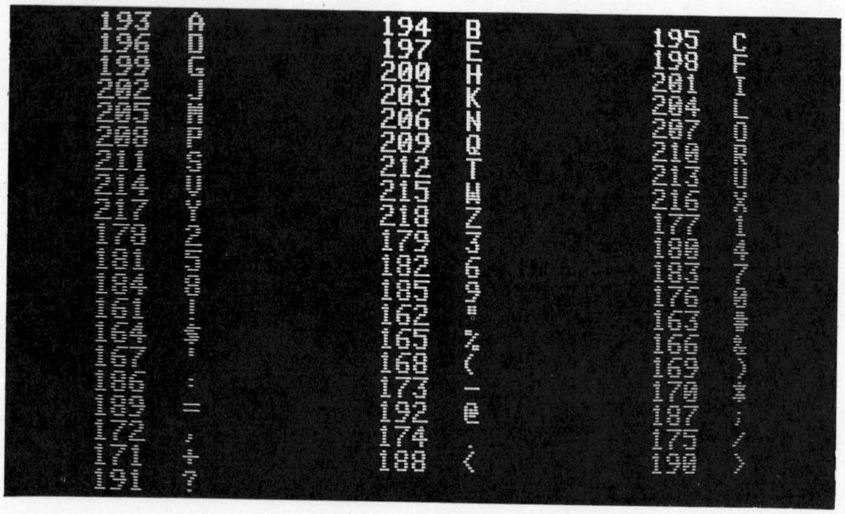

If you renumber line 150 to line 125, you will find that all of the ASCII numbers have been reduced by 128. This is because the value in location −16384 is reset (reduced in value by 128) before the value of A is read in line 130. Note, however, that the correct key value is still printed on the screen. That is, CHR$(A) = CHR$(A − 128) for values of A between 161 and 223.

PEEKing the special keyboard memory location −16384 is useful when you want to take a quick look to see if a key has been pressed, and if not, then go on to do something else. For example, suppose you want to start and stop the bouncing ball in Figure 14.3 by pressing any key on the keyboard. The GET statement is no help here because the program will stop and wait at the GET statement until you press a key. Instead you can modify the subroutine at line 200 in Figure 14.3 to read

> 200 REM CHECK FOR KEY PRESSED
> 210 IF PEEK(−16384) <128 THEN RETURN
> 220 POKE −16368, 0
> 230 IF PEEK (−16384) < 128 THEN 230
> 240 POKE −16368, 0
> 250 RETURN

The resulting program is shown in Figure 14.6. Note that after each new ball is plotted (and before it is erased), the subroutine at line 200 is called. Line 210 checks to see if any key has been pressed. If not, the

FIGURE 14.6 Any key can be used to start and stop the bouncing ball.

```
LIST
10   REM     BOUNCING BALL
20   GR
30   FOR X = 0 TO 39
35   COLOR= 15: PLOT X,20
40   GOSUB 200: REM     TEST PUSHBUT
     TON
50   COLOR= 0: PLOT X,20
60   NEXT X
70   FOR X = 38 TO 1 STEP  - 1
80   COLOR= 15: PLOT X,20
90   GOSUB 200: REM     TEST PUSHBUT
     TON
100  COLOR= 0: PLOT X,20
110  NEXT X
120  GOTO 30
200  REM   CHECK FOR KEY PRESSED
210  IF  PEEK ( - 16384) < 128 THEN
     RETURN
220  POKE  - 16368,0
230  IF  PEEK ( - 16384) < 128 THEN
     230
240  POKE  - 16368,0
250  RETURN
```

subroutine is exited. If a key has been pressed, line 220 will "clear the keyboard strobe", that is, subtract 128 from the value in location −16384. Line 230 will then loop on itself until a key is pressed. During this time the ball will remain stationary on the screen. When a second key has been pressed (any key), line 240 will clear the keyboard strobe before returning to the main program.

Type in this program and run it. Note that you can start and stop the bouncing ball by pressing any key. Also note that it does not matter how long you hold a key down. The Apple II only detects key pressings. It does not detect when you release the key.

Generating a Random Seed

The Apple II has a built-in program that it executes whenever it is waiting for the user to press a key. This program keeps looking at memory location −16384 until the value in that location becomes greater than 127, indicating that a key has been pressed. While it is waiting for a key to be pressed, the program also continually adds 1 to memory location 78. When the value in this location reaches 255, adding 1 causes the value to be reset to 0. When this occurs, a 1 is added to the value in memory location 79. The value in location 78 will cycle through 255 different values over one hundred times per second. This means that at any instant in time the value in location 78 (and 79) will be quite unpredictable. You can see this by running the one line program **10 PRINT PEEK(78)** over and over again.

Recall from Chapter 4 that a different seed can be generated for the random function RND by executing the statement **20 X = RND(−N)** for different values of N (see Figures 4.32 and 4.33). You can generate a pseudo-random seed by using the value of PEEK(78) for N. Thus, the statement **20 X = RND(−PEEK(78))** can be used at the beginning of a program in which you want the random sequence generated by RND(1) to be different every time the program is run. To be even more sure of a different random sequence each time, you can use the values in both memory locations 78 and 79 by writing

> 10 N = PEEK(78) + 256 * PEEK(79)
> 20 X = RND(−N)

The value of N will be some (unpredictable) value between 0 and 65535.

The 6502 microprocessor used in the Apple II computer can address a maximum of 64K (65,536) bytes of memory. This memory space is divided among read-write memory (RAM), I/O or Input/Output memory, and read only memory (ROM). Figure 14.7 shows how this memory is allocated for an Apple II Plus computer with 48K bytes of RAM. Notice from the left-hand and right-hand sides of the figure that locations 0–49151 are the 48K bytes of RAM, locations 49152–53247 are 4K bytes associated with Input/Output, and locations 53248–65535 are 12K bytes of ROM.

As described earlier in this chapter, memory locations 1024–2047 are used to store the ASCII codes that are being displayed on the TV screen. These same memory locations are used to store the color codes used to plot various colored spots in the low-resolution graphics mode. These memory locations (1024–2047) are referred to as Page 1 (or the primary page) of text and low-resolution graphics.

It turns out that there is a Page 2 (or secondary page) of text and low-resolution graphics at memory locations 2048–3071. This secondary page is difficult to use from BASIC because your BASIC programs are normally stored in memory starting at location 2048 (see Figure 14.7).

When you used high-resolution graphics in Chapter

FIGURE 14.7 Memory map of an Apple II Plus with 48K bytes of RAM.

			Memory Location
48K bytes RAM	Systems programs, stack, and keyboard buffer		0
			767
	Available for user to store shape tables or short machines language programs		768
			1007
	Holds special monitor addresses		1008
			1023
	Page 1 - Text & Lo-res Graphics (1,024 bytes)		1024
			2047
	BASIC programs start here	Page 2 - Text & Lo-res Graphics (1,024 bytes)	2048
			3071
			3072
			8191
	Page 1 - Hi-res Graphics (8,192 bytes)		8192
			16383
	Page 2 - Hi-res Graphics (8,192 bytes)		16384
			24575
			24576
			38399
		Used by Disk Operating System (10,752 bytes)	38400
			49151
4K bytes I/O	Input/Output - Keyboard, speaker, game paddles, I/o slots (4,096 bytes)		49152
			53247
12K bytes	System ROM (12,288 bytes) (monitor & Applesoft interpreter)		53248
			65535

13, the information being displayed on the screen was stored in memory at locations 8192–16383. This is called Page 1 (or the primary page) of high-resolution graphics. There is also a Page 2 (or secondary page) of high-resolution graphics (assuming you have enough RAM) at memory locations 16384–24575.

You can switch between these various pages by using the "soft switches" shown in Figure 14.8. There are four switches (shown on the left side of the figure), and the position of each switch is associated with a particular memory address. Note that the addresses of these soft switches are in the I/O area of memory. Figure 14.8 gives the negative equivalent of the positive address. To turn a switch to a particular position, you simply have to refer to the address in a POKE statement of the form **POKE addr, 0.**

There are ten different modes that you can enable by setting the four soft switches. These ten modes are illustrated by the tree graph shown in Figure 14.8. The top of the tree is switch 1 (addresses –16303 and –16304) which selects either *text* or *graphics*. Row 2 of the tree uses switch 2 (address –16300 and –16299) to select either Page 1 or Page 2. Row 3 of the tree uses switch 3 (addresses –16301 and –16302) to select between mixed text and graphics (that is, four lines of text at the bottom of the screen) and all graphics. The bottom row of the tree uses switch 4 (addresses –16298 and –16297) to select between low-resolution graphics and high-resolution graphics.

When setting the soft switches in Figure 14.8, it is a good idea to start at the bottom of the tree and set the text-graphics switch last. This will prevent you from seeing intermediate modes when switching from text to graphics.

The statement TEXT in BASIC is equivalent to setting the switches

$$\text{POKE } -16300,0 \qquad \text{(Page 1)}$$
$$\text{POKE } -16303,0 \qquad \text{(text)}$$

The statement GR is equivalent to setting the switches

$$\text{POKE } -16298,0 \qquad \text{(Lo-Res)}$$
$$\text{POKE } -16301,0 \qquad \text{(Text \& graphics)}$$
$$\text{POKE } -16300,0 \qquad \text{(Page 1)}$$
$$\text{POKE } -16304,0 \qquad \text{(Graphics)}$$

and then clearing the screen. The statement HGR is equivalent to setting the switches

$$\text{POKE } -16297,0 \qquad \text{(Hi-Res)}$$
$$\text{POKE } -16301,0 \qquad \text{(Text \& graphics)}$$
$$\text{POKE } -16300,0 \qquad \text{(Page 1)}$$
$$\text{POKE } -16304,0 \qquad \text{(Graphics)}$$

and then clearing the screen.

FIGURE 14.8   Soft switches used to select text and graphics pages.

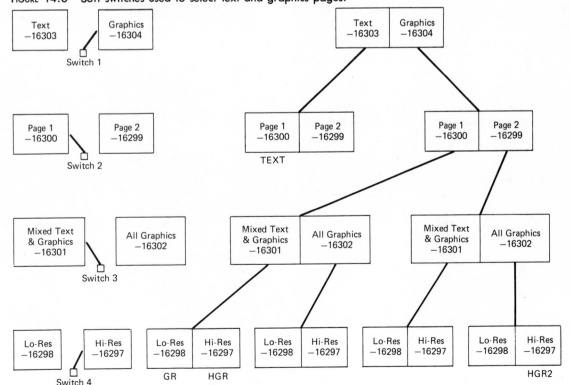

There is also a BASIC statement HGR2 which enters Page 2 of high-resolution graphics with no text at the bottom of the screen. It is equivalent to setting the switches

POKE −16297,0	(Hi-Res)
POKE −16302,0	(All graphics)
POKE −16299,0	(Page 2)
POKE −16304,0	(Graphics)

and then clearing the screen.

You can use these soft switches at any time in a program to change the display mode on the screen. For example, switching between Page 1 and Page 2 of high-resolution graphics allows you to produce animation on your Apple II.

Animated Graphics

If you have one high-resolution graphics figure stored on Page 1 and a second figure stored on Page 2, you can create the appearance of motion by switching quickly between these two pages. If, in addition, you can change the figure on Page 1 while Page 2 is being displayed (and vice versa), you then create a complete animated scene.

In order to cause the statement HPLOT to plot on Page 1 while Page 2 is being displayed on the screen, you must store the value 32 in location 230 using the statement **POKE 230,32 (Draws to Page 1)**. Similarly, HPLOT will plot on Page 2 while Page 1 is being displayed if you store the value 64 in location 230 using the statement **POKE 230,64 (Draws to Page 2)**.

As an example of animated graphics we will write a program that will simulate the motion of a compound pendulum. This is like a stick that is pivoted at one end. The fixed point of the pendulum will be at XC,YC and the other end will move in a circular arc as shown in Figure 14.9.

FIGURE 14.9   Describing the motion of a pendulum of length R.

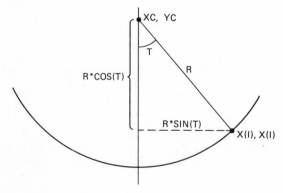

To speed up the program during the animation, we will pre-store all of the coordinate pairs along the circular arc in the arrays X(I) and Y(I). Then while one page is being displayed, the previous line on the other page can be erased and a new line plotted. You can then switch and display the other page.

The subroutine shown in Figure 14.10 will store the points along the circular arc in the arrays X(I) and Y(I). The angle T is varied from +45° to −45° in steps of −2°. The total number of points calculated is N (equal to 45).

```
]LIST500−
500   REM   FILL ARRAY
510   REM   CIRCULAR ARC
515   XC = 140:YC = 10:R = 120
520   D = 2:I = 1:PI = 3.1415926
530   FOR T = 45 TO  − 45 STEP  −
      D
540   T1 = T * PI / 180
550   X(I) = XC + R *   SIN (T1)
560   Y(I) = YC + R *   COS (T1)
570   I = I + 1
580   NEXT T
590   N = I − 1
595   RETURN
```

FIGURE 14.10   Subroutine to store points along a circular arc in the arrays X(I) and Y(I).

The main program to produce the animated pendulum is shown in Figure 14.11. Line 50 clears the Page 1 high-resolution graphics memory and sets the screen to full graphics. Line 60 does the same for Page 2.

Lines 70–140 cause the pendulum to move through a complete arc from right to left on the screen. Lines 80–90 erase the previous pendulum and plot the new one on Page 1. During this time the graphic on Page 2 is being displayed. Line 100 then switches to Page 1 to display this new pendulum. While Page 1 is being displayed, lines 110–120 erase the previous pendulum and plot a new one on Page 2. Line 130 then switches to display Page 2.

After the left-most pendulum has been displayed (on Page 2), line 150 displays Page 1 which starts the pendulum's motion from left to right. Lines 160–250 cause the pendulum to move through a complete arc from left to right. Line 260 branches back to line 70 which repeats the motion endlessly.

Note that every other point along the arc (I and I+2) are used to plot lines on Page 1, and the other points (I+1 and I+3) are used to plot lines on Page 2. In order to avoid leaving an unerased pendulum at the ends of the swing, it is necessary to plot an even number of lines. Try changing the value of D in line 520 to 1 and see what happens.

```
JLIST-260
10   REM   ANIMATED GRAPHICS
20   DIM X(100),Y(100)
35   HOME : PRINT "CALCULATING POI
     NTS"
40   GOSUB 500: REM   FILL ARRAYS
50   HGR : POKE  - 16302,0
60   HGR2
70   FOR I = 1 TO N - 3 STEP 2
80   POKE 230,32: REM   DRAW ON PG
     1
85   HCOLOR= 0: HPLOT XC,YC TO X(I
     ),Y(I)
87   HCOLOR= 3
90   HPLOT XC,YC TO X(I + 2),Y(I +
     2)
100  POKE  - 16300,0: REM  DISPLA
     Y ON PG 1
110  POKE 230,64: REM   DRAW ON P
     G 2
115  HCOLOR= 0: HPLOT XC,YC TO X(
     I + 1),Y(I + 1)
117  HCOLOR= 3
120  HPLOT XC,YC TO X(I + 3),Y(I +
     3)
130  POKE  - 16299,0: REM  DISPLA
     Y PG 2
140  NEXT I
150  POKE  - 16300,0: REM  DISPLA
     Y PG 1
160  FOR I = N - 3 TO 2 STEP  - 2

170  POKE 230,64: REM   DRAW ON PG
     2
180  HCOLOR= 0: HPLOT XC,YC TO X(
     I + 3),Y(I + 3)
190  HCOLOR= 3: HPLOT XC,YC TO X(
     I + 1),Y(I + 1)
200  POKE  - 16299,0: REM    DISPL
     AY PG 2
210  POKE 230,32: REM   DRAW ON PG
     1
220  HCOLOR= 0: HPLOT XC,YC TO X(
     I + 2),Y(I + 2)
230  HCOLOR= 3: HPLOT XC,YC TO X(
     I),Y(I)
240  POKE  - 16300,0: REM  DISPLA
     Y PG 1
250  NEXT I
260  GOTO 70
```

FIGURE 14.11 Program to produce an animated pendulum.

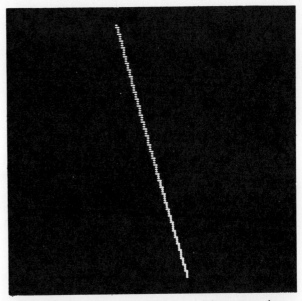

FIGURE 14.12 (a) An instant of time while running the program in Fig. 14.11.

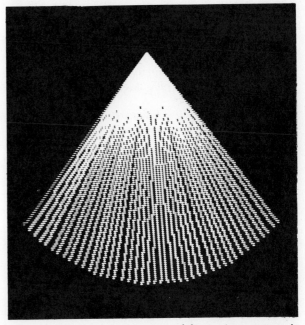

FIGURE 14.12 (b) Time exposure while running program in Fig. 14.11.

What to Do When Your BASIC Programs Get Too Big

At some time you may write very large BASIC programs or programs that use large arrays. When you do, several undesirable things may occur. You may get an **OUT OF MEMORY** message or, if you are using high-resolution graphics, some strange things may appear on the screen. The first thing to do is to make sure that you have the full complement of 48K bytes of RAM as shown in Figure 14.7.

Type in this program and run it. The result of running this program is shown in Figure 14.12.

Assuming that you are using an Apple II Plus with 48K bytes of RAM and a disk drive, the memory between location 2048 and 38399 is available for your BASIC program as shown in Figure 14.13. If you are not using any high-resolution graphics, all of these 36,352 bytes are available for your program. This is a lot of memory, and you should not have any problem unless you have dimensioned very large arrays in your program. You can often reduce drastically the size of arrays that you need by storing data on a diskette instead of in memory. The way to do this will be described in Chapter 15.

Memory problems usually occur when you use high-resolution graphics. As shown in Figure 14.13, your program will run into the high-resolution graphics memory long before you actually run out of memory in the computer. If this happens, you will know it because your high-resolution graphics picture will suddenly go haywire. There are several things you can do to remedy the situation.

When you type in your BASIC program, it will be stored in memory starting at location 2048. When the program is executed, it will use more memory to store simple variables and arrays. It will use memory for this purpose starting at a location called LOMEN. This value is equal to **256*PEEK(106) + PEEK(105)** and is usually right after the end of your BASIC program. As a BASIC program grows, the value of LOMEN is automatically increased. You can see from Figure 14.13 that eventually the numeric and string pointer arrays will run into Page 1 of the high-resolution graphics memory. One way to avoid this is for you to change LOMEN. If you are not using Page 2 of the high-resolution graphics, you could move LOMEN to location 16384 by using the BASIC statement **LOMEN: 16384** at the beginning of your BASIC program. Then simple variables and arrays will be stored after location 16384 in memory. If you are using Page 2 of the high-resolution graphics, you could move LOMEN to location 24576.

There is a total of 6,144 bytes of RAM between location 2048 and the beginning of Page 1 of high-resolution graphics memory. However, there are 13,824 bytes of memory between the top of Hi-Res Page 2 and the last available RAM location at 38399. There are 22,016 bytes of memory between the top of Hi-Res Page 1 and location 38399. If you need more memory for your program (as opposed to just for arrays), you can move your program above the high-resolution graphics memory.

The values stored in locations 103 and 104 define

FIGURE 14.13   Memory locations used by an APPLESOFT BASIC program.

256* PEEK(104 + PEEK(103) →	BASIC Program	2048
256* PEEK(180) + (179) →		
LOMEN = →		
256* PEEK(106) + PEEK(105)	Simple Variables	
256*PEEK(108) + PEEK(107) →	Numeric and string Pointer Arrays	
256* PEEK(110) + PEEK(109) →		
		8191
	Page 1 Hi-Res Graphics	8192
		16383
	Page 2 Hi-Res Graphics	16384
		24575
		24576
256*PEEK(112) + PEEK(111) →	STRINGS	
HIMEN = 256*PEEK(116) + PEEK(115) →		38399

the starting address of your APPLESOFT program. You can see what this address is by typing **? 256*PEEK(104) + PEEK(103)**. This should display 2049. The value stored in location 104 should be 8, and the value stored in location 103 should be 1. If you type **?PEEK(2048)**, you should print 0. This means that your BASIC program starts at location 2049, and location 2048 contains a zero. It is always necessary to have the memory location preceding the start of your program contain a zero.

To move the starting address of your BASIC program to location *addr,* POKE the value

$$INT(Addr/256)$$

in location 104 and the value

$$addr - INT(addr/256)$$

in location 103. For example, to move your program to location 16384, type

POKE 104,64

POKE 103,1

Note that INT(16385/256) = 64. It is also necessary to set the preceding memory location to zero by typing **POKE 16384,0.**

To move the BASIC program above Page 2 of high-resolution graphics, type

POKE 104,96

POKE 103, 1

POKE 24576,0

These statements will not actually move your program. Rather the next time a program is loaded from the disk it will be stored at this new location.

When strings are defined in a program, they are stored in memory starting at the highest available location and moving down in memory. This location is defined by HIMEM and can be found by typing **?256*PEEK(116)+ PEEK(115)**. It is automatically set to the highest available memory location.

If you need some memory to store shape tables or machine language programs, you can move HIMEM down to some other address by including the statement **HIMEM: address** at the beginning of your BASIC program. For example, the statement **HIMEM: 30399** would move HIMEM down to location 30399 in Figure 14.13 and would make 8,000 bytes of memory between 30400 and 38399 available for other uses.

The memory addresses corresponding to the end of program, start of numeric arrays, end of numeric arrays, and end of strings can be determined by printing the various PEEK expressions on the left-hand side of Figure 14.13.

Text Window and Cursor Controls

Memory locations 32–35 control the size of the text window. The normal size is 24 rows of 40 characters. Sometimes you may wish to make a smaller window that will prevent writing outside the window. The top, bottom, left side, and width of the window can be controlled using the POKE statements shown in Figure 14.14.

The statement **POKE 33,20** will set the number of characters that can be written on a line to 20 rather than 40. Do *not* set a value of W equal to zero. This will bomb APPLESOFT.

The statement **POKE 32,6** will set the left margin to 6. This will prevent writing into the first 6 character positions on each line. The width value W is not changed. Therefore, at this point characters can be written in columns 7–26.

The statement **POKE 34,5** sets the top margin to 5. This means that text cannot be written into the first five lines (0–4) of the screen.

FIGURE 14.14   Setting the text window.

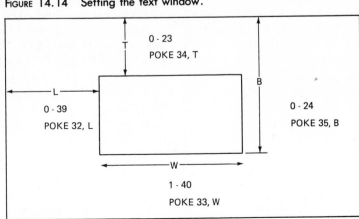

The statement **POKE 35,20** sets the bottom margin to 20. This means that text cannot be written into the last four lines (21–24) of the screen. Do not set the value of B smaller than the value of the top margin T.

Memory locations 36 and 37 contain the horizontal and vertical positions of the cursor.

The statement **CH = PEEK(36)** reads the horizontal cursor position (0–39) relative to the window's left-hand window margin L.

The statement **CV = PEEK(37)** reads the *absolute* vertical cursor position (0–23).

The statement **POKE 36,CH** will move the cursor to the CH+1 position from the left margin of the text window.

The statement **POKE 37, CV** will move the cursor to row CV (0–23) on the screen.

THE CALL STATEMENT

The CALL statement is used to jump to a machine language subroutine. We will have to write a short machine language program in the next section to make sounds on the Apple II's speaker. There are, however, some built-in machine language subroutines that you may find useful.

The general form of the CALL statement is **CALL Addr** where **Addr** is the address of the machine language subroutine. When this statement is executed, the program jumps to the machine language subroutine at location **Addr**. When the subroutine has completed its execution, the program returns to the statement following the CALL statement.

A list of useful built-in machine language subroutines is given in Table 14.1.

TABLE 14.1   Apple II Plus Built-in Machine Language Subroutines

CALL −936	Clears all characters inside text window—same as HOME
CALL −958	Clears all characters inside text window from the current cursor position to the bottom margin—same as ESC F
CALL −868	Clears current line from the cursor to the right margin—same as ESC E
CALL −922	Produces a line feed, that is, moves the cursor down one line
CALL −912	Scrolls all text within the text window up one line
CALL −1994	Clears low-resolution graphics portion of screen when in the mixed text-graphics mode
CALL −1998	Clears entire low-resolution graphics screen when in the full-screen graphics mode
CALL 62450	Clears current high-resolution graphics screen to black
CALL 62454	Changes the background color of the current high-resolution graphics screen to the HCOLOR most recently HPLOTED

MAKING SOUNDS WITH THE APPLE II

The effectiveness of your programs can be greatly enhanced by adding sound effects. The Apple II has a built-in speaker that will allow you to make simple sound effects. Sound is produced by the speaker when a diaphragm made in the form of a paper cone is moved back and forth rapidly. The faster the diaphragm vibrates, the higher the frequency of the resulting sound waves. High notes have higher frequencies than low notes.

The speaker on the Apple II is controlled by memory location −16336. Each time this memory location is referred to, the speaker will toggle. That is, if the diaphragm is out, it will move in; if it is in, it will move out. Thus, if memory location −16336 is referred to over

and over again rapidly, the speaker diaphragm should move in and out rapidly and produce a sound.

To try this, type in the following one-line program and run it: **10 X=PEEK(−16336): GOTO 10**. This program continually PEEKs at location −16336 which will continually toggle the speaker. You should hear a buzzing sound from the speaker. Press CTRL C or RESET to stop the noise.

To produce a higher frequency tone it is necessary to toggle the speaker faster. However, the one-line program given above toggles the speaker about as fast as a BASIC program can. A machine language subroutine must be used to toggle the speaker significantly faster. You can store this machine language subroutine in the Apple II starting at location 770 by executing the BASIC subroutine shown in Figure 14.15. (See Appendix E for a listing of the assembly language program corresponding to this machine language subroutine.)

```
]LIST
9000   REM   STORE SPEAKER ROUTINE
9010   DATA   160,0,174,0,3,173,48,
       192
9012   DATA   136,208,5,206,1,3,240
       ,5
9014   DATA   202,208,245,240,237,9
       6,256
9020   AD = 770
9030   READ X
9040   IF X = 256 THEN  RETURN
9050   POKE AD,X
9060   AD = AD + 1
9070   GOTO 9030
```

FIGURE 14.15 BASIC subroutine that will store a machine language subroutine to produce a tone.

This machine language subroutine will produce a "square wave" tone of duration bL and half-period aP as shown in Figure 14.16. The constant a is 10 microseconds (10^{-5} seconds), and the constant b is 2.569 milliseconds (.002569 seconds). The integers P and L must be values between 1 and 255 and must be POKEd into locations 768 and 769 before the machine language subroutine at location 770 is called.

The BASIC subroutine starting at line 1000 shown in Figure 14.16 will POKE the value P into location 768 and POKE the value L into location 769. It then calls

the machine language subroutine using the statement CALL 770. This will produce a tone of pitch P and duration L.

To try this, type in the subroutine starting at line 9000 shown in Figure 14.15 and also type in the subroutine starting at line 1000 shown in Figure 14.16. Then type **GOSUB 9000**. This will store the machine language subroutine at location 770. Next type **P = 152 : L = 255 : GOSUB 1000**. You should hear a tone that lasts for a little over half a second. To play higher notes, use smaller values of P. Try typing

P = 85 : GOSUB 1000

P = 20 : GOSUB 1000

Try out different values for L and P. If you change the value of L to 5, you should hear a single *click*. We will now write a subroutine to produce multiple clicks.

Producing Multiple Clicks

A single click of pitch P can be produced by letting L=5 in the tone subroutine shown in Figure 14.16. The subroutine shown in Figure 14.17 will produce N clicks with a separation S and pitch P. Lines 1120–1140 loop N times, and a click is produced (using subroutine 1000) each time line 1120 is executed. Line 1130 is a delay proportional to the separation time S.

FIGURE 14.16 The BASIC subroutine at line 1000 will produce a tone of pitch P and duration L.

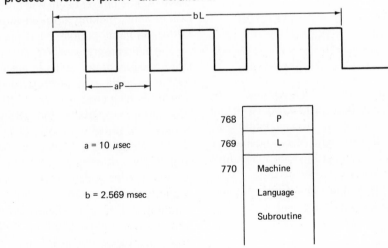

```
]LIST1000-1020
1000   REM   PLAY TONE WITH PITCH P
       AND DURATION L
1010   POKE 768,P: POKE 769,L
1020   CALL 770: RETURN
```

```
]LIST1100-1140
1100   REM      PRODUCE N CLICKS WITH

1105   REM      SPACING S AND PITCH P

1110   L = 5
1120   FOR I1 = 1 TO N: GOSUB 1000

1130   FOR I2 = 1 TO S: NEXT
1140   NEXT I1: RETURN
```

FIGURE 14.17   Subroutine to produce N clicks with separation S and pitch P.

To test this subroutine type **N = 10: S = 300: P = 80: GOSUB 1100.** You should hear 10 clicks. Edit this line by changing the values of N, S, and P to produce different clicking effects.

Producing a Phaser Noise

If you repeatedly call the tone subroutine in Figure 14.16 with different pitch values P, you can produce a variety of effects. For example, the subroutine shown in Figure 14.18 produces a "phaser" noise consisting of NC cycles of a sound in which the pitch varies from P1 to P2 in steps of DP.

```
]LIST1200-1250
1200   REM      PHASER NOISE
1202   REM      NC=# CYCLES
1204   REM      P1=STARTING PITCH
1206   REM      P2=ENDING PITCH
1208   REM      DP=PITCH INCREMENT
1210   L = 5
1220   FOR J = 1 TO NC
1230   FOR P = P1 TO P2 STEP DP
1240   GOSUB 1000: NEXT P
1250   NEXT J: RETURN
```

FIGURE 14.18   Subroutine for making a phaser noise.

To hear what this noise sounds like, type **NC = 6: P1 = 40: P2 = 120: DP = 8: GOSUB 1200.** Note that the sound goes from high to low (corresponding to values of P going from low to high). Also note that L is set to 5 in line 1210 which makes the tone subroutine produce a click sound for a given value of P.

Try a variety of different values for NC, P1, P2, and DP by editing the line shown above.

Producing a Siren Sound

A siren noise can be produced by repeatedly calling the tone subroutine first with increasing values of P and then with decreasing values of P as shown in Figure 14.19. The outer FOR . . . NEXT loop from lines

1310–1360 produces NC complete cycles of the siren sound. The loop in lines 1320–1330 produces the decreasing sound, and the loop in lines 1340–1350 produces the increasing sound. Each of these loops calls the subroutine at line 1000 that produces a tone of pitch P and length L.

To try out this subroutine type it in, and then type **NC = 8: P1 = 70: P2 = 170: DP = 2: L = 10: GOSUB 1300.** Try changing the values of NC, P1, P2, DP, and L to produce different siren sounds.

```
]LIST1300-1360
1300   REM      SIREN NOISE
1302   REM      NC=# CYCLES
1303   REM      P1=STARTING PITCH
1305   REM      P2=ENDING PITCH
1307   REM      DP=PITCH INCREMENT
1308   REM      L=HOLDING TIME
1310   FOR J = 1 TO NC
1320   FOR P = P1 TO P2 STEP DP
1330   GOSUB 1000: NEXT
1340   FOR P = P2 TO P1 STEP  - DP

1350   GOSUB 1000: NEXT
1360   NEXT J: RETURN
```

FIGURE 14.19   Subroutine to produce a siren sound.

Fighter Plane with Phasers

As an example of using sound effects, we will write a program that will move a plane around the screen in response to the game paddles. When the pushbutton on game paddle #0 is pressed, a red phaser beam will fire out of the left wing of the plane making a phaser noise. A blue phaser beam will fire out of the right wing of the plane, making a phaser noise, when the pushbutton on game paddle #1 is pressed.

The main program is shown in Figure 14.20. Line 15 stores the machine language speaker routine. The subroutine to do this was described earlier and is shown at line 9000 in Figure 14.21. Lines 30–50 in Figure 14.20 read the game paddles. Line 40 makes sure that the wing of the plane will not go off the left edge of the screen. The plane is plotted in line 60 using the subroutine shown in Figure 14.22.

Lines 70–90 in Figure 14.20 read the game paddle again. Only if these readings differ from the previous readings will the plane be erased and replotted at the new location in line 110. This will prevent the plane from blinking when it is not being moved. Erasing and replotting the plane is done using the subroutine at line 200 shown in Figure 14.23. Note that after the plane at (X,Y) is erased, the values of X and Y are assigned the new values X1 and Y1. This will be the new location of the plane.

```
]LIST-130
10   REM     PLANE WITH PHASERS
12   HOME
15   GOSUB 9000: REM   STORE SPEAKE
     R ROUTINE
20   GR : COLOR= 15
30   X =  INT ( PDL (0) / 7)
40   IF X < 2 THEN X = 2
50   Y =  INT ( PDL (1) / 7)
60   GOSUB 500: REM   PLOT PLANE
70   X1 =  INT ( PDL (0) / 7)
80   IF X1 < 2 THEN X! = 2
90   Y1 =  INT ( PDL (1) / 7)
100  IF X1 = X AND Y1 = Y THEN 12
     0
110  GOSUB 200: REM   ERASE AND RE
     PLOT PLANE
120  GOSUB 300: REM   CHECK PHASER
     S
130  GOTO 70
```

Figure 14.20 Main program for fighter plane with phasers.

```
]LIST9000-
9000   REM   STORE SPEAKER ROUTINE
9010   DATA   160,0,174,0,3,173,48,
       192
9012   DATA   136,208,5,206,1,3,240
       ,5
9014   DATA   202,208,245,240,237,9
       6,256
9020   AD = 770
9030   READ X
9040   IF X = 256 THEN   RETURN
9050   POKE AD,X
9060   AD = AD + 1
9070   GOTO 9030
```

Figure 14.21 Sound subroutines used to produce a tone.

```
]LIST500-540
500   REM   PLOT PLANE
510   VLIN Y,Y + 3 AT X
520   HLIN X - 2,X + 2 AT Y + 1
530   HLIN X - 1,X + 1 AT Y + 3
540   RETURN
```

Figure 14.22 Subroutine to plot plane.

```
]LIST200-240
200   REM   ERASE AND REPLOT PLANE
210   COLOR= 0: GOSUB 500: REM   ER
      ASE PLANE
220   X = X1:Y = Y1
230   COLOR= 15: GOSUB 500: REM   P
      LOT NEW PLANE
240   RETURN
```

Figure 14.23 Subroutine to erase and replot the plane.

Line 120 in Figure 14.20 checks to see if either phaser should be fired. This is done using the subroutine shown in Figure 14.24. Line 310 in Figure 14.24 checks pushbuttons #0, and line 320 checks pushbutton #1. If pushbutton #0 is pressed, the left phaser is fired using the subroutine at line 350. If pushbutton #1 is pressed, the right phaser is fired using the subroutine at line 400. Each of these subroutines plots a vertical line from the left or right wing tip to the top of the screen. While this phaser line is plotted, a phaser noise is sounded using the subroutine at line 600 shown in Figure 14.25. This is a modified version of the phaser noise subroutine in Figure 14.18 where only two cycles are sounded during each firing.

Figure 14.24 Subroutine to check pushbuttons and fire phasers.

```
]LIST300-440
300   REM   CHECK FOR PHASER FIRING

310   IF  PEEK ( - 16287) > 127 THEN
         GOSUB 350
320   IF  PEEK ( - 16286) > 127 THEN
         GOSUB 400
330   RETURN
350   REM   FIRE LEFT PHASER
360   COLOR= 1
365   VLIN Y,0 AT X - 2
370   GOSUB 600: REM   PHASER SOUND

375   COLOR= 0
380   VLIN Y,0 AT X - 2
390   RETURN
400   REM   FIRE RIGHT PHASER
410   COLOR= 6
415   VLIN Y,0 AT X + 2
420   GOSUB 600: REM   PHASER SOUND

425   COLOR= 0
430   VLIN Y,0 AT X + 2
440   RETURN
```

Figure 14.25 Subroutine to produce phaser noise during phaser firings.

```
]LIST600-1020
600   REM   PHASER SOUND
605 L = 5
610   FOR J = 1 TO 2
620   FOR P = 40 TO 120 STEP 8
630   GOSUB 1000: NEXT P
640   NEXT J: RETURN
1000   REM   PLAY TONE WITH PITCH P
       AND DURATION L
1010   POKE 768,P: POKE 769,L
1020   CALL 770: RETURN
```

The entire program consists of the statements shown in Figures 14.20, 14.23, 14.24, 14.22, 14.25, and 14.21. Type in this program and run it. Figure 14.26 shows the screen during phaser firings from the two wings.

The discussion of the various sound subroutines presented in this chapter should enable you to add interesting sound effects to your programs. Programming your Apple II to actually play music will be described in the next chapter.

EXERCISE 14-1

Write a program that will cause a ball to bounce at a 45° angle off the four sides of the screen. Have the ball stop each time any key is pressed.

EXERCISE 14-2

Write a program that switches between Page 1 and Page 2 of high-resolution graphics to produce an animated graphic of a spoked wheel rotating.

EXERCISE 14-3

Modify the program in Exercise 14-1 to produce a clicking sound each time the ball hits the wall.

EXERCISE 14-4

Write a program that stores a sequence of pitch (P) and length (L) values in a DATA statement and then plays this sequence of tones. The DATA statement (or statements) should be of the form

    20 DATA P1, L1, P2, L2, P3, L3, . . .

where P1 and L1 are the pitch and length of the first tone, P2 and L2 are the pitch and length of the second tone, and so on. To play a complete song, see Exercise 15-5 in Chapter 15.

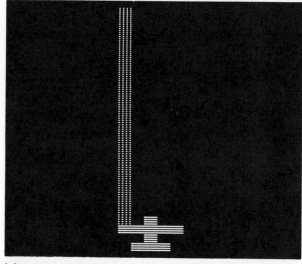
(a)

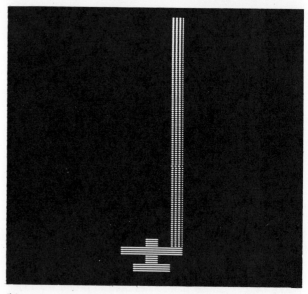
(b)

FIGURE 14.26   Firing phasers during the execution of the program shown in Fig. 14.20.

15

LEARNING TO PUT IT ALL TOGETHER

In the previous 14 chapters you have learned how to use the various features of APPLESOFT BASIC, including its graphic and audio capacities. Now that you know the BASIC language, you will want to write your own programs. How do you go from an idea of something you would like to accomplish to a working BASIC program that does it? That is what this chapter is all about.

To illustrate the various steps involved in developing a program, we will write two complete programs in this chapter. Although both programs are useful and fun to run, it is the process of developing the programs that we are trying to explain.

The first program is a popular word-guessing game called Hangman. The second program converts your Apple II into an electronic organ that plays music.

In this chapter you will learn

1. to define what you want to achieve and give a word-description of the program

2. to define the variables you will need in the program

3. the technique of top-down programming

4. to write a program to play Hangman

5. to store data on a diskette

6. to play music on your Apple II.

HANGMAN

We will now develop a program to play the word-guessing game Hangman. The following six steps will help you develop a program with the minimum amount of difficulty. We will follow these six steps in developing HANGMAN:

STEP 1: Define *what* you want the program to do
STEP 2: Give a word-description of the program

STEP 3: Define program variable names

STEP 4: Write and test the main program and essential subroutines

STEP 5: Write and test the remaining subroutines

STEP 6: Test the entire program and make improvements.

Defining What HANGMAN Will Do

This is the most important step in developing a program, but it is a step that is often omitted or carried out inadequately. There is an almost irresistible temptation to start writing BASIC code immediately, but you *must* resist it at all cost. Do not write any BASIC code until STEP 4.

Poor programming, like poor writing, is usually a sign of confused thinking. If you don't have a clear idea of what you want the program to do, you will have little chance of writing a program to do it. Now you may not know all of the features that your program will eventually have. Indeed, programming is an iterative process in which you will improve a program by rewriting it several times. However, you must understand enough about what you want to get a proper start.

Hangman is a word-guessing game in which the Apple II thinks of a word and displays a blank for each

FIGURE 15.1   Screen layout for Hangman program.

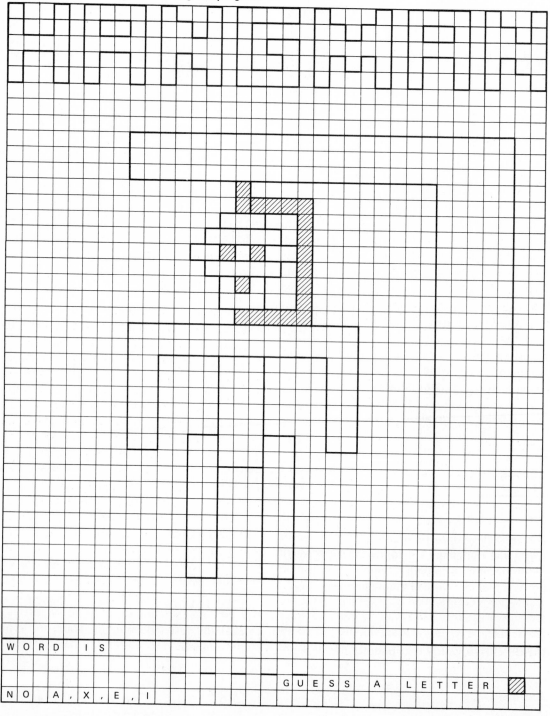

letter in the word. You guess a letter. If the letter occurs in the word, it is inserted at every location it occupies in the word. If the letter does not occur in the word, a part of your body is added to a hanging gallows. You keep guessing letters until you guess the word or until you guess six wrong letters, at which time the body on the gallows is complete, and you are hanged.

The first decisions you must make are what you want the screen to look like and how you want the screen to respond to various inputs and conditions. The best idea is to sketch the screen to scale. Figure 15.1 shows the screen layout for the Hangman game which will use low-resolution graphics to display the gallows.

When the program is first executed, the name **HANGMAN** is written in low-resolution graphics at the top of the screen. The program then displays the gallows in low-resolution graphics, the blanks for the word, and the words **GUESS A LETTER** (in reverse video), followed by a blinking cursor. As each correct letter is guessed, it is filled in at the appropriate blank position(s). When an incorrect letter is guessed, the phrase **NO X** will be printed on the bottom line of the screen, and another part of the body will be added.

If you guess the word correctly, the word will be flashed and the words **YOU ARE SAVED!** will be printed. If you fail to guess the word, the correct word will be displayed above the blanks, and the words **YOU ARE HANGED!** will be printed. The words **PLAY AGAIN?** followed by a blinking cursor will then be displayed at the lower right corner of the screen.

Having laid out what you want the screen to look like and thought about how the game is to be played, you are ready to write a *word-description* of the program.

A Word-Description of HANGMAN

At this point you should write a word-description of the program that will completely describe its logic. Use pseudocode, flowcharts, or whatever you find useful. A word-description for the Hangman program, written in pseudocode is shown in Figure 15.2; study it carefully. Note that it follows closely the screen layout we made in Figure 15.1 and our ideas on how the program should work. Developing the word-description shown in Figure 15.2 is the most creative part of writing the program, and it accounts for most of the hard work involved. This is why it is so important to understand how to write word-descriptions like the one in Figure 15.2. Study it again. Note particularly how the *do until* loop is used to include the entire process of guessing a word. Being able to identify the

FIGURE 15.2 Pseudocode word-description of Hangman program.

```
Loop:  Clear screen
       Display HANGMAN
       Display gallows
       Display the words GUESS A LETTER
       Find a random word
       Display blanks for word
       do until Word is guessed or you are hanged
               Guess a letter
               Search for letter in word
               if letter is in word
               then display letter at proper position
               else display NO "letter"
                    add part to body
       end do
       if word is guessed
       then blink word
            display YOU ARE SAVED!
       else display correct word
            display YOU ARE HANGED!
       Ask to PLAY AGAIN?
repeat while answer is "Y"
```

appropriate looping structure for a particular problem (think *do until*, *repeat while*, or *for . . . next*) is one of the important skills you will need to develop to become a good programmer.

Defining Program Variables

At this stage in the development of the program you should define names for those variables that you know you will need. You will not know all of the variables you will end up using, but do not be concerned about that. Define the important ones that you do know. This will help you to focus in on how you will implement various little algorithms. Be particularly conscious of defining appropriate string variables and arrays.

In the Hangman program we will store the word to be guessed in the string W$. The length of this string (the number of letters in the word) will be L. How can you tell when the word is guessed correctly or when it is time to be hanged? You will need to keep track of the number of blanks that have been correctly filled in. We will call this value NL. You will also need to keep track of the number of incorrect guesses. We will call this value NH. Each letter guessed will be stored in the string G$. You can determine if a guessed letter G$ is in the word W$ by comparing G$ with each letter in W$ and noting where any matches occur. You will also need to know if any match occurred. For this purpose define a flag R and set R to 1 if any match occurs and set

R to 0 if G$ is not in W$. At this point we have therefore defined the variable names given in Figure 15.3. We can now use these variable names to put a little more detail in the pseudocode description of the program given in Figure 15.2. For example, the *do until* loop can be rewritten in the form shown in Figure 15.4. Note that the word is guessed when NL=L, and you are hanged when NH=6. The algorithm to search for a letter in the word is given by the *for . . . next* loop. Note that this algorithm displays each letter that is found in its proper position so that nothing more needs to be done in the *then* part of the following *if . . . then . . . else* statement. Also note that the flag R is used to tell if a letter is in the word.

You have now developed the program to the point where you can begin to write some BASIC code. Since you have already done most of the work, the BASIC code will practically write itself at this point.

FIGURE 15.3 Definition of initial variables to be used in Hangman program.

W$ = word to be guessed
L = length of word to be guessed
G$ = letter guessed
NL = number of correct letter positions guessed
NH = number of incorrect guesses

$$R = \begin{cases} 1 \text{ if G\$ is in W\$} \\ 0 \text{ if G\$ is not in W\$} \end{cases}$$

FIGURE 15.4 More detailed version of *do until* loop used in Hangman program.

```
NL=0
NH=0
do until NL=L or NH=6
    Guess a letter G$
    R=0
    for I=1 to L
        if G$=MID$(W$, I,1)
        then print G$ plus space
            NL=NL+1
            R=1
        else move cursor 2 spaces
    next I
    if R=1
    then do nothing
    else NH=NH+1
        display NO "letter"
        add part to body
enddo
```

Your next step should be to write the main program in BASIC following the pseudocode description given in Figures 15.2 and 15.4. Your goal should be to write this *entire* program so that it fits on a single page and you can read it all at once. To do this, use subroutine calls for anything that takes a lot of coding or for anything you do not know how to do.

The main program for Hangman is shown in Figure 15.5. Line 20 sets the low-resolution graphics mode. Line 30 displays the word HANGMAN and the gallows in subroutine 600. Line 40 finds a random word W$ in subroutine 1000. Line 50 finds the length, L, of the word W$ and moves the cursor to the first "blank" position. Each letter position will be separated by a

FIGURE 15.5 Main program for Hangman.

```
]LIST-210
10   REM    HANGMAN
20   HOME : GR : COLOR= 15
30   GOSUB 600: REM   DISPLAY HANGM
     AN & GALLOWS
40   GOSUB 1000: REM   FIND WORD W$

50 L =   LEN (W$): VTAB 22: HTAB (
     20 - L)
60   FOR I = 1 TO L: PRINT "- ";: NEXT

70   NL = 0:NH = 0:S$ = ""
80   IF NL = L OR NH = 6 THEN 160
90   GOSUB 400: REM    GUESS A LETTE
     R
100  VTAB 22:X = 20 - L: HTAB X:R
     = 0
110  FOR I = 1 TO L
112  X = X + 2
115  IF G$ =  MID$ (W$,I,1) THEN
     PRINT G$;" ";:NL = NL + 1:R
     = 1: GOTO 130
120  HTAB X
130  NEXT I
140  IF R = 1 THEN 80
150 NH = NH + 1: GOSUB 900: GOTO
     80
160  VTAB 23: HTAB 1
170  IF NH = 6 THEN  PRINT "YOU A
     RE HANGED!";: GOSUB 300: GOTO
     190
180  PRINT "YOU ARE SAVED   ";: GOSUB
     700
190  VTAB 24: HTAB 23: INVERSE
195  PRINT "PLAY AGAIN????";: NORMAL
     : PRINT " ";
200  GET G$: IF G$ = "Y" THEN 20
210  TEXT : HOME : END
```

space. Therefore, HTABing to the position 20-L will center each word on the screen. Line 60 prints the L blanks for the word to be guessed.

Lines 70–150 implement the *do until* loop shown in Figure 15.4. (The initialization of S$ to the null string in line 70 was added when the subroutine to guess a letter in line 400 was written.) Line 90 calls subroutine 400 to guess a letter. The words **GUESS A LETTER** that appear on the screen will be written in this subroutine. Line 100 moves the cursor to the first letter position in the word and sets the flag R to 0. Lines 110–130 implement the *for . . . next* loop given in Figure 15.4. Note how the statement HTAB X is used in line 120 to move the cursor 2 spaces in the *else* clause. The value of X is incremented by 2 each time through the *for . . . next* loop (in line 112). The use of the HTAB statement rather than the SPC(2) function is required so that existing letters will not be erased. Lines 140–150 implement the last *if . . . then . . . else* statement in Figure 15.4. Subroutine 900 called in line 150 will display **NO "letter"** and add a part of the body.

Lines 160–180 implement the last *if . . . then . . . else* statement in Figure 15.2. We have actually interchanged the roles of *then* and *else*. That is, line 170 is equivalent to *if* word is *not* guessed. Subroutine 300 called in line 170 will display the correct word. Subroutine 700 called in line 180 will blink the word. Lines 190–195 will ask to **PLAY AGAIN????** in reverse video. Line 200 will then get G$ and cause a new game to be played if the answer to **PLAY AGAIN?** is **"Y"**.

We have therefore written a complete main program that implements the Hangman algorithm given in Figure 15.2. We have also identified all the subroutines that must still be written. These are summarized in Figure 15.6.

FIGURE 15.6   List of subroutines called from main program.

Line No.	Subroutine
600	Initial display (HANGMAN, gallows)
1000	Find a word, W$
400	Guess a Letter, G$
900	Wrong Guess-NO "letter", add to body
300	Print correct word
700	Blink word

The next step is to write the minimum amount of code in each subroutine that will allow you to run and test the main program. This *stub* could be just a RE-TURN statement that does nothing but return to the main program. Once you are certain that the main program is behaving properly, you can then write and test each subroutine separately. They can then be tested, of course, by running the main program which calls the subroutine. This technique of *top-down pro-*

gramming allows you to plan the entire program and begin to test it before you have to get involved in all the details of every subroutine. It also keeps your program well modularized, which will make it much easier for you to debug and modify the program.

In subroutine 600, it will take some thought to figure out how to draw the word HANGMAN and the gallows. Therefore, for now, just type

> **600 REM INITIAL DISPLAY**
> **610 RETURN**

for subroutine 600 and worry about the details later.

To test the main program you should store a known word in W$. Therefore, for subroutine 1000 type

> **1000 REM FIND A WORD**
> **1010 W$= "HANGMAN"**
> **1020 RETURN**

which will assign the word HANGMAN to W$. It is a good idea to pick a test word that contains multiple occurrences of a single letter, to make sure that the main program displays all letters in their proper locations. Later, you can come back and make subroutine 1000 produce random words.

Subroutine 400 will display the words **GUESS A LETTER** and will then have the player guess a letter, G$. At first it looks as if this is just the statement GET G$. However, you do not want to allow letters that have already been guessed. (Otherwise, you could hang yourself by typing the same wrong letter six times.) Therefore, subroutine 400 must keep track of all letters that have been typed and only return new values for G$. We'll figure out how to do this later. For now just type

> **400 REM GUESS A LETTER**
> **410 VTAB 24: HTAB 23: INVERSE**
> **420 PRINT "GUESS A LETTER";: NORMAL: PRINT " ";**
> **430 GET G$**
> **440 RETURN**

For subroutine 900 type

> **900 REM WRONG GUESS**
> **910 VTAB 24: HTAB 1**
> **920 PRINT "NO"; G$**
> **930 RETURN**

You know this will print all wrong guesses at the same location on the screen, but it will help test the main program. You can fix it up later and figure out how to add a new part to the body each time.

Put It All Together   151

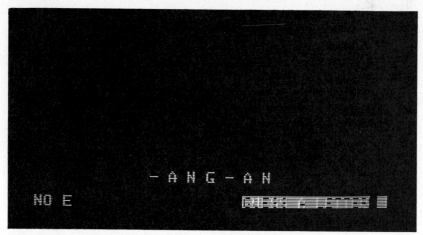

FIGURE 15.7 Testing the main program of Hangman.

For subroutine 300 and 700 just type the stubs

```
300 REM PRINT CORRECT WORD
310 RETURN
```

and

```
700 REM BLINK WORD
710 RETURN
```

and worry about these later.

With this much of the program written you can run the main program and test that it is working properly. Figure 15.7 shows what the screen might look like during such a test.

After you have debugged the main program (it won't work the first time—Figure 15.5 was *not* my first version), you are ready to tackle the remaining subroutines one by one.

Writing the Remaining Subroutines

You can now go through and finish the subroutines listed in Figure 15.6. Figure 15.8 is a listing of subroutine 600. Lines 605–670 plot the word HANG-MAN. Subroutines at lines 510, 540 and 560 are used to plot the letters H, A, and N respectively. Lines 675–685 draw the blue gallows. The result of running the main program after adding the subroutines given in Figure 15.8 is shown in Figure 15.9.

The guess-a-letter subroutine 400 is shown in Figure 15.10, where lines 440–470 have been added to insure that no letter is guessed more than once. Line 470 keeps track of all letters that have been guessed by adding each new letter to the string S$. (This is why we initialized S$ to the null string '''' in line 70 of the main program. Each time that line 430 GETs a new letter G$, it is compared with all previous letters (stored in S$) in the loop in lines 440–460. If a match is found in line 450, the program GETs a new letter in line 430.

FIGURE 15.8 Initial display subroutine that plots the word Hangman and draws the gallows.

```
]LIST500-690
500    REM    LETTERS H,A,N
510    VLIN Y,Y + 4 AT X: REM    H
520    VLIN Y,Y + 4 AT X + 3
530    HLIN X + 1,X + 2 AT Y + 2: RETURN

540    GOSUB 510: REM    A
550    HLIN X + 1,X + 2 AT Y: RETURN

560    VLIN Y,Y + 4 AT X: REM    N
570    VLIN Y + 1,Y + 2 AT X + 1
580    VLIN Y + 2,Y + 3 AT X + 2
590    VLIN Y,Y + 4 AT X + 3: RETURN

600    REM    INITIAL DISPLAY
605    COLOR= 1
610    Y = 0:X = 2: GOSUB 510: REM    H
615    X = 7: GOSUB 540: REM    A
620    X = 12: GOSUB 560: REM    N
630    VLIN 0,4 AT 17: HLIN 18,20 AT 0
635    HLIN 18,20 AT 4: VLIN 2,3 AT 20
640    PLOT 19,2: REM    G
650    VLIN 0,4 AT 22: VLIN 1,2 AT 23
655    VLIN 2,3 AT 24: VLIN 1,2 AT 25
660    VLIN 0,4 AT 26: REM    M
665    X = 28: GOSUB 540: REM    A
670    X = 33: GOSUB 560: REM    N
675    COLOR= 6
680    FOR Y = 7 TO 9: HLIN 10,34 AT Y: NEXT
685    FOR X = 30 TO 34: VLIN 10,39 AT X: NEXT
690    RETURN
```

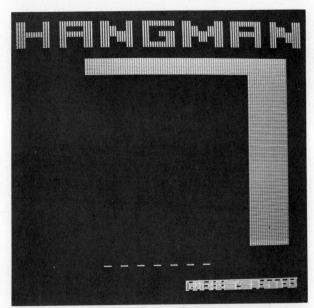

FIGURE 15.9   Result of running the Hangman program after adding the initial display subroutine.

```
LIST400-470
400    REM    GUESS A LETTER
410    VTAB 24: HTAB 23: INVERSE
420    PRINT "GUESS A LETTER";: NORMAL
       : PRINT " ";
430    GET G$
440    FOR J = 1 TO  LEN (S$)
450    IF G$ =  MID$ (S$,J,1) THEN
       430
460    NEXT J
470    S$ = S$ + G$: RETURN
```

FIGURE 15.10   The subroutine to guess a letter.

The "wrong guess" subroutine 900 is shown in Figure 15.11. Lines 910–930 print **NO** "letter" at the bottom of the screen for the first wrong guess. Subsequent wrong guesses are added to the list following a comma. Lines 935–995 add the appropriate part of the body to the hanging person. Line 935 is the ON . . . GOTO statement ON NH GOTO 940, 950, 960, 970, 980, 990. This statement will branch to line 940 if NH=1, to line 950 if NH=2, to line 960 if NH=3, and so on up to NH=6.* Lines 940–945 plot the head (first wrong guess); lines 950–955 plot the body (second wrong guess); lines 960–965 plot the right arm (on your left—third wrong guess); lines 970–975 plot the left arm (fourth wrong guess); line 980 plots the right leg (fifth wrong guess); line 990 plots the left leg (sixth and last wrong guess); line 995 plots the rope that does the hanging.

---

*The ON . . . GOSUB statement works in a similar fashion but uses GOSUB rather than GOTO.

```
LIST900-995
900    REM    WRONG GUESS
910    VTAB 24: HTAB 1
920    IF NH = 1 THEN  PRINT "NO ";
       G$;: GOTO 935
930    HTAB 2 * NH + 1: PRINT ",";G
       $;
935    ON NH GOTO 940,950,960,970,9
       80,990
940    COLOR= 11: HLIN 16,18 AT 13:
        HLIN 15,19 AT 14: HLIN 14,2
       0 AT 15: HLIN 15,19 AT 16: HLIN
       16,18 AT 17: HLIN 16,18 AT 1
       8
942    PLOT 17,19
945    COLOR= 2: PLOT 16,15: PLOT 1
       8,15: COLOR= 1: PLOT 17,17: RETURN
950    COLOR= 4: FOR Y = 20 TO 21: HLIN
       14,20 AT Y: NEXT
955    FOR X = 16 TO 18: VLIN 22,28
        AT X: NEXT : RETURN
960    COLOR= 8: FOR Y = 20 TO 21: HLIN
       10,13 AT Y: NEXT
965    FOR X = 10 TO 11: VLIN 22,27
        AT X: NEXT : RETURN
970    COLOR= 8: FOR Y = 20 TO 21: HLIN
       21,24 AT Y: NEXT
975    FOR X = 23 TO 24: VLIN 22,27
        AT X: NEXT : RETURN
980    COLOR= 3: FOR X = 14 TO 15: VLIN
       27,35 AT X: NEXT : RETURN
990    COLOR= 3: FOR X = 19 TO 20: VLIN
       27,35 AT X: NEXT
995    COLOR= 13: HLIN 16,21 AT 19:
        VLIN 12,18 AT 21: HLIN 17,2
       1 AT 11: PLOT 17,10: RETURN
```

FIGURE 15.11   The wrong guess subroutine prints NO "letter" and adds a part to the body.

Subroutine 300 shown in Figure 15.12 prints the correct word above the blanks when the person is hanged. Note the use of the function MID$ in line 330 to print each letter of the word W$ followed by a blank space.

FIGURE 15.12   This subroutine prints the correct word above the blanks.

```
LIST300-340
300    REM    PRINT CORRECT WORD
310    VTAB 21: HTAB 1
320    PRINT "WORD IS:";: HTAB (20 -
       L)
330    FOR I = 1 TO L: PRINT  MID$
       (W$,I,1);" ";: NEXT
340    RETURN
```

Subroutine 700 shown in Figure 15.13 blinks the word by using the **FLASH** statement in line 710 and then displaying the word in lines 730–740.

```
]LIST700-750
700   REM    BLINK WORD
710   FLASH
720   VTAB 22: HTAB 20 - L
730   FOR I = 1 TO L
740   PRINT  MID$ (W$,I,1);" ";: NEXT

750   RETURN
```

Figure 15.13   This subroutine blinks the word.

If all of the above subroutines are working properly, you can start adding some new random words in subroutine 1000. There are several ways to do this. One possibility is shown in Figure 15.14. Line 1010 sets a random seed for the random number generator. Line 1020 defines the number of words NW stored in the DATA statement starting at line 1100. You can add more words and increase the value of NW. In line 1030 X is assigned a random number between 1 and NW. Line 1040 moves the "pointer" to the beginning of the DATA statement. Line 1050 reads the first X

```
]LIST1000-
1000   REM    FIND A WORD
1020   NW = 10
1030   X =   INT ( RND (1) * NW + 1)

1040   RESTORE
1050   FOR I = 1 TO X: READ W$: NEXT

1060   RETURN
1100   DATA   HIPPOPOTAMUS,NURSE,FA
       MOUS,EMPIRE,ELK,DIGNITY
1110   DATA   CONDITIONAL,BRIBE,PAP
       ER,QUAIL
```

Figure 15.14   Subroutine that finds one of ten words at random.

words. Therefore word number X will end up in W$. Note that with this subroutine the same word can occur more than once. To avoid this you will have to keep track of the values of X that have been used and not use the same ones more than once (see Exercise 15-1). Of course, you will then be able to play only ten times before having to rerun the program.

A sample run of this program is shown in Figure 15.15.

(a)

(b)

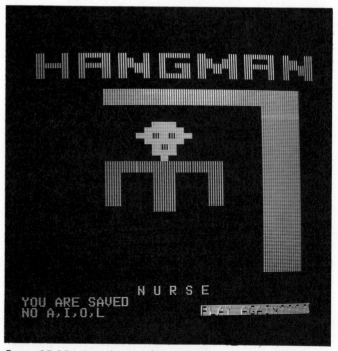

Figure 15.15   Sample run of Hangman program.

It is clear that to make this game really interesting, you need a good dictionary so that you will use different words each time you play. One way to do this is to store a large number of words on a diskette and read in a random group of words each time the game is played.

You may have been using diskettes to save and load your BASIC programs. It is also possible for you to include statements in your programs that will allow you to store *data* on a diskette and later read back this data. You do this with the DOS (Disk Operating System) commands WRITE and READ. However, in order to use these statements you must first use the OPEN statement and afterward, the CLOSE statement. In the following sections you will learn how to use the DOS commands OPEN, CLOSE, WRITE, READ, APPEND, and POSITION from within your BASIC program.

Storing Words in a Sequential File

The program shown in Figure 15.16 gives you the options to 1) write words to a new file, 2) add words to an existing file, or 3) read words from an existing file. Type in this program and add the four stubs

```
6500 RETURN
1000 RETURN
2000 RETURN
3000 RETURN
```

Executing this program will produce the menu shown in Figure 15.17.

```
]LIST-250
10   REM   STORING WORDS IN A
12   REM   SEQUENTIAL FILE
15   D$ =   CHR$ (4): REM   CTRL-D
17   GOSUB 6500: REM   STORE MACHIN
     E CODE FOR ERROR CHECKING
20   HOME : VTAB 3
30   HTAB 5: PRINT "1.   WRITE WORD
     S TO A NEW FILE": PRINT
40   HTAB 5: PRINT "2.   ADD WORDS
     TO AN EXISTING FILE": PRINT

50   HTAB 5: PRINT "3.   READ WORDS
     FROM EXISTING FILE": PRINT

60   HTAB 5: PRINT "4.   EXIT PROGR
     AM": PRINT : PRINT
70   GOSUB 200: REM   SELECT NUMBER

80   IF I = 4 THEN   HOME : END
85   ON I GOSUB 1000,2000,3000
90   GOTO 20
200  REM   PICK A NUMBER
210  INVERSE : PRINT "SELECT A NU
     MBER";: NORMAL : PRINT " ";
220  GET A$
230  I =   VAL (A$)
240  IF I < 1 OR I > 4 THEN 220
250  RETURN
```

FIGURE 15.16 BASIC listing of main program illustrating the use of sequential files.

FIGURE 15.17 Menu produced when the program in Fig. 15.16 is executed.

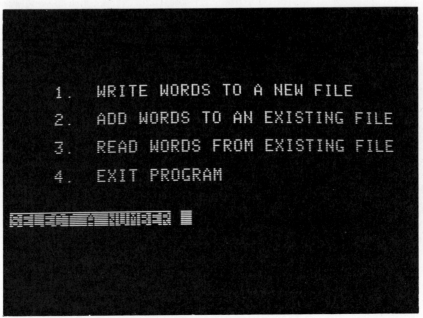

The subroutine at line 200 (which is called in line 70) waits for the user to press a key. If the key pressed is a number, I, between 1 and 4, then the subroutine is exited. If I=4 (key 4 was pressed), line 80 clears the screen and terminates the program.

The statement **ON I GOSUB 1000, 2000, 3000** in line 85 will branch to the subroutine at line 1000, 2000, or 3000 depending upon whether I is 1, 2, or 3. Thus, if key 1 was pressed, the value of I will be one, and the program will branch to the subroutine at line 1000. We only have the stub RETURN there now, so if you press key 1 the program will immediately return to line 90 and then branch back to line 20.

A subroutine at line 1000 that will allow you to write words into a new file is shown in Figure 15.18. Lines 1010–1030 cause the messages shown in Figure 15.19 to be displayed on the screen. Lines 1040–1050 allow the user to return to the main program (and the original menu) at this point by pressing any key other than "D". This is a good option to give a user who may not be prepared to actually write data on a diskette at this time.

If the user presses key "D", line 1060 asks the user to type in a file name. This file name will be stored in N\$ and will be the file in which the words will be written. The file must be opened before any words can be written to this file. This is done using the following statement given in line 1070: **PRINT D\$; "OPEN "; N\$.** The string variable D\$ contains the string character corresponding to CTRL-D. It was defined in line 15 of the main program (see Figure 15.16) by the statement **D\$ = CHR\$(4).** This means that D\$ is the character corresponding to the ASCII code 4. This is the code that

```
]LIST1000-1360
1000   REM   CREATE NEW FILE
1010   GOSUB 1200: REM   WRITE SET
UP
1020   PRINT "PRESS KEY 'D' TO STO
RE WORDS ON DISKETTE"
1030   PRINT "PRESS ANY OTHER KEY
TO EXIT"
1040   GET A$
1050   IF A$ <  > "D" THEN   RETURN

1060   PRINT : INPUT "WHAT FILE NA
ME? ";N$
1070   PRINT D$;"OPEN ";N$
1080   PRINT D$;"DELETE ";N$
1090   PRINT D$;"OPEN ";N$
1100   GOSUB 1300: REM   ENTER WORD
S
1110   PRINT D$;"CLOSE ";N$
1120   RETURN
1200   REM   WRITE SET UP
1210   HOME : VTAB 5
1220   PRINT "INSERT DISKETTE ON W
HICH WORDS"
1230   PRINT "ARE TO BE SAVED": PRINT

1240   RETURN
1300   REM   ENTER WORDS
1310   PRINT "ENTER WORDS; TYPE !
TO STOP"
1320   INPUT W$
1330   IF W$ = "!" THEN   RETURN
1340   PRINT D$;"WRITE ";N$
1350   PRINT W$
1355   PRINT D$
1360   GOTO 1320
```

FIGURE 15.18   Subroutine to write words into a new file.

FIGURE 15.19   Initial messages displayed when the subroutine in Fig. 15.18 is executed.

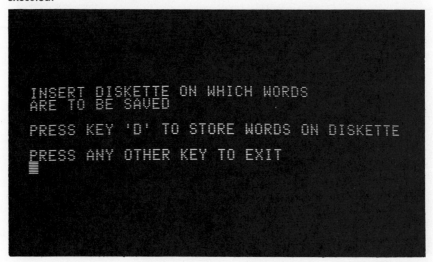

```
INSERT DISKETTE ON WHICH WORDS
ARE TO BE SAVED

PRESS KEY 'D' TO STORE WORDS ON DISKETTE

PRESS ANY OTHER KEY TO EXIT
```

the keyboard reads when you press the D key while holding down the CTRL key.

In order to use a DOS command from within a BASIC program, you must include the DOS command in a string that follows CTRL-D (D$) in a PRINT statement. For example, if you had typed HANGMAN WORDS when the program asked for a file name, N$ would contain HANGMAN WORDS. The statement **PRINT D$; "OPEN "; N$** is equivalent to **PRINT D$; "OPEN HANGMAN WORDS"**. This statement will open the file HANGMAN WORDS. It is important to remember that all DOS commands called from within a BASIC program must be of the general form **PRINT D$; "DOS Command"** where D$ is CTRL-D.

If you open a file that already exists and write words into the file, the words will be written starting at the beginning of the file. If you do not write over all of the words in the existing file, your new file may contain old words from a previous file so it is a good idea to delete a file before opening it for writing. (We will see how to *add* words to an existing file later.) However, a **FILE NOT FOUND** message will be displayed if you try to delete a file that does not exist. To avoid this problem you can write three statements like those shown in lines 1070–1090 in Figure 15.18. Line 1070 opens the file N$. Line 1080 then deletes this file, and line 1090 opens it again. The OPEN statement in line 1070 merely insures that the file N$ exists so that it can be deleted in line 1080.

Once the file N$ is opened, the subroutine at line 1300 is used to enter a list of words. This subroutine allows you to enter as many words as you wish. You type an exclamation point (!) to indicate the end of the list. Each word is stored in W$ using the INPUT statement in line 1320. Line 1340 is the WRITE DOS command which is equivalent to **PRINT D$; "WRITE HANGMAN WORDS"** if N$ contains "HANGMAN WORDS." After this WRITE command is executed, subsequent PRINT statements will send their output to the file HANGMAN WORDS (or, in general, N$) instead of to the TV screen. Thus, in line 1350 the statement **PRINT W$** will not print the word W$ on the TV screen, but rather will write this word into the diskette file N$.

Line 1360 branches back to the INPUT statement in line 1320. An INPUT statement will cancel a DOS WRITE statement. This is why the WRITE statement in line 1340 must be executed each time a new word is entered with the INPUT statement in line 1320, and could not have been inserted before line 1320.

Once the WRITE statement is executed, all output that would normally go to the TV screen is sent to the disk file instead. This will include even the question mark that the INPUT statement normally displays on the screen. To prevent this, it is necessary to cancel the WRITE command before the INPUT statement is executed. Printing any DOS command will cancel the WRITE command. The null DOS command D$ (CTRL-D) will suffice. Thus, the purpose of the statement **PRINT D$** in line 1355 is simply to cancel the WRITE command in line 1340 so that the question mark will be displayed on the screen when the INPUT statement in line 1320 is subsequently executed.

Type in the subroutine shown in Figure 15.18 and execute it by pressing key 1 after running the main program. An example of the screen output while this subroutine is being executed is shown in Figure 15.20.

If you enter an exclamation point in line 1320, line 1330 will cause the subroutine to return to line 1110.

FIGURE 15.20 Example of storing words on a diskette using the subroutine given in Fig. 15.18.

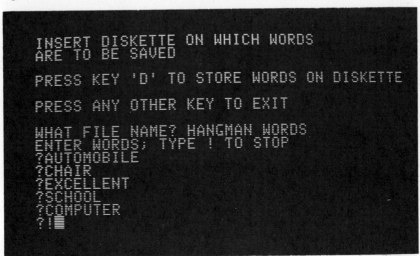

This line closes the file N$ using the DOS CLOSE command. All opened files must be closed using a statement of the form **PRINT D$; "CLOSE FILENAME"**. You may lose some data if you fail to close a file. If the DOS command CLOSE is used without a file name, all opened files will be closed.

Suppose that after writing some words into the file HANGMAN WORDS you want to *add* some more words at a later time. You cannot call the subroutine at line 1000 again because this will delete your old file and start a new one so you will lose all of your old words. Rather you must use the APPEND command instead of the OPEN command. This is illustrated in line 2070 of the subroutine shown in Figure 15.21.

FIGURE 15.21   Subroutine to add words to an existing file.

```
]LIST2000-2095
2000    REM   ADD WORDS TO FILE
2010    GOSUB 1200: REM   WRITE SET
        UP
2020    PRINT "PRESS KEY 'A' TO ADD
        WORDS"
2030    PRINT "PRESS ANY OTHER KEY
        TO EXIT"
2040    GET A$
2050    IF A$ <  > "A" THEN   RETURN

2060    PRINT : INPUT "WHAT FILE NA
        ME? ";N$
2070    PRINT D$;"APPEND ";N$
2080    GOSUB 1300: REM   ENTER WORD
        S
2090    PRINT D$;"CLOSE ";N$
2095    RETURN
```

This subroutine starts at line 2000 and is called in line 85 of the main program when key 2 is pressed.

Type in this subroutine and then add some more words to your existing word file. This will enable you to build up a large file of words to use in the Hangman program. However, before you can use these stored words in the Hangman program, you must learn how to *read* the words from the diskette.

Reading Words From a Sequential File

When key 3 is pressed in response to the menu in the main program in Figure 15.16, line 85 branches to the subroutine in line 3000. If at line 3000 we write the subroutine shown in Figure 15.22, this subroutine will produce a second menu shown in Figure 15.23.

FIGURE 15.22   Subroutine to read words.

```
]LIST3000-3090
3000    REM   READ WORDS
3010    HOME : VTAB 5
3020    PRINT "1.   READ ENTIRE FILE
        ": PRINT
3030    PRINT "2.   READ N WORDS STA
        RTING AT LOCATION L": PRINT
3040    PRINT "3.   READ N WORDS AT
        RANDOM": PRINT
3050    PRINT "4.   QUIT": PRINT : PRINT
3060    GOSUB 200: REM   PICK A NUMB
        ER
3070    IF I = 4 THEN   RETURN
3080    ON I GOSUB 3100,3200,3300
3090    GOTO 3010
```

FIGURE 15.23   Menu produced by the subroutine given in Fig. 15.22.

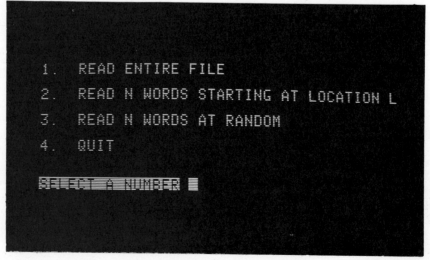

Note that this subroutine gives you three more choices other than returning to the main menu. This technique of using menus is a good way to steer a user through a large program. It is also a good way to keep the organization of your program under control.

To read the entire file the user presses key 1. This will cause line 3080 to branch to the subroutine at line 3100. This subroutine is shown in Figure 15.24. Line 3110 calls the subroutine at line 4000 that is shown in Figure 15.25. This subroutine displays the messages shown in Figure 15.26.

```
]LIST3100-3170
3100    REM   READ ENTIRE FILE
3105    HOME
3110    GOSUB 4000: REM   READ SET U
        P
3120    ONERR  GOTO 6000
3130    PRINT D$;"OPEN ";N$
3140    PRINT D$;"READ ";N$
3150    INPUT W$
3160    PRINT W$
3170    GOTO 3150
```
FIGURE 15.24   Subroutine to read entire file.

```
]LIST4000-4090
4000    REM   READ SET UP
4010    PRINT "INSERT DISKETTE CONT
        AINING"
4020    PRINT "WORDS TO BE READ": PRINT
4030    PRINT "PRESS KEY 'R' TO REA
        D FILE"
4040    PRINT "PRESS ANY OTHER KEY
        TO EXIT"
4050    GET A$
4060    IF A$ < > "R" THEN  RETURN
4070    PRINT : INPUT "WHAT FILE NA
        ME? ";N$
4080    IF N$ = "" THEN  RETURN
4090    RETURN
```
FIGURE 15.25   Subroutine to display initial messages for reading data.

FIGURE 15.26   Messages displayed by the subroutine shown in Fig. 15.25.

Line 3130 in Figure 15.24 opens file N$. Line 3140 executes the DOS READ command. If N$ contains the string HANGMAN WORDS, this statement is equivalent to the statement **PRINT D$; "READ HANGMAN WORDS"**. After the READ command subsequent input statements will accept their characters from the specified sequential disk file rather than from the keyboard. Thus, in line 3150 in Figure 15.24 the string that is stored in W$ will be the next word in the file N$. Line 3160 will print this word on the screen. Line 3170 branches back to line 3150 which will input the next word from the disk file. Note that there is *no exit* from this loop. When the program tries to read beyond the end of the file, an error condition will result.

It is possible for you to have your program branch to a specified line number when an error is detected. You do this by executing the ONERR GOTO statement before an error occurs. In line 3120 the statement **ONERR GOTO 6000** will cause the program to jump to line 6000 whenever an error is detected. In particular it will jump to line 6000 when it has read all of the words from the file N$ and tries to read beyond the end of the file. The error handling routine at line 6000 is shown in Figure 15.27.

```
]LIST6000-6070
6000    REM   ERROR HANDLING ROUTINE
6003    CALL 768: REM   FIX STACK PR
        OBLEM
6005 EC =  PEEK (222)
6010    IF EC = 5 THEN  PRINT "END
        OF DATA": GOTO 6050
6020    PRINT "ERROR NO. ";EC
6050    PRINT D$;"CLOSE ";N$
6060    PRINT : PRINT "PRESS ANY KE
        Y TO CONTINUE ";: GET A$
6070    RETURN
```
FIGURE 15.27   Error handling routine executed when an error occurs after the statement ONERR GOTO 6000.

It turns out that it is sometimes difficult to return from this error-handling routine when the error occurs from within a subroutine. After printing a proper error message, we would like to return to the part of the program that called the subroutine in which the error occurred. A portion of the computer memory called the *stack* is used to keep track of the point to which the program is supposed to return when a subroutine is completed. When an error occurs within a subroutine, the program can sometimes "lose its place." You can help it find its way again by executing a short machine language program that fixes up the stack. This program is stored at memory location 768 by executing the short subroutine shown in Figure 15.28. This subroutine is called in line 17 of the main program in Figure 15.16. The machine language program stored at location 768 is called in line 6003 in Figure 15.27.

```
]LIST6500-
6500    REM    STORE MACHINE LANGUAGE
        CODE
6510    DATA   104,168,104,166,223,1
        54,72,152,72,96
6520    FOR A = 768 TO 777
6530    READ C
6540    POKE A,C
6550    NEXT A
6560    RETURN
```

Figure 15.28   Subroutine that stores an error handling machine language program at location 768.

After an error occurs, an error code is stored in memory location 222. Line 6005 assigns this error code to the variable name EC. A list of all error codes is given in Appendix C. In particular, the error code 5 occurs when a program tries to read beyond the end of data in a disk file. This is what would happen eventually in line 3150 in Figure 15.24. When this occurs, line 6010 in Figure 15.27 will print the message **END OF DATA** and then close the file N$ in line 6050. Pressing any key will then return the program to line 3090 which will branch to line 3010 and re-display the read menu. An example of reading the entire file is shown in Figure 15.29.

Figure 15.29   Example of reading the entire file.

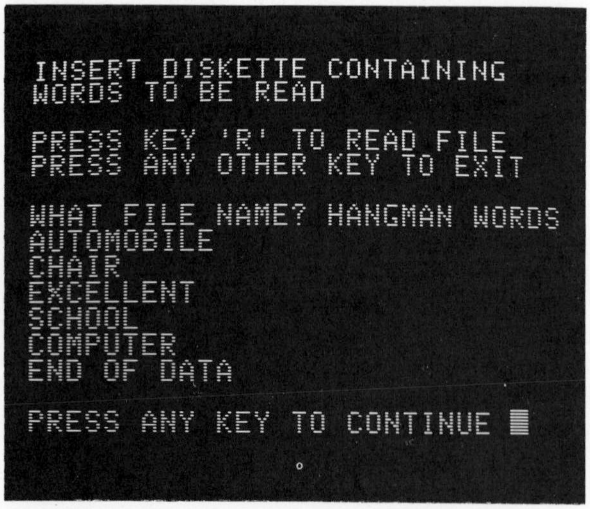

Suppose you have a data file containing a large number of words, and you want to read N of these words starting at location L. The subroutine shown in Figure 15.30 will do this. It is called from line 3080 in Figure 15.22 when key 2 is pressed.

```
]LIST3200-3290
3200    REM    READ N WORDS STARTING
        AT LOCATION L
3205    HOME
3210    INPUT "ENTER NUMBER OF WORD
        S TO BE READ ";N
3215    INPUT "ENTER STARTING LOCAT
        ION ";L
3217 L = L - 1
3220    PRINT : GOSUB 4000: REM   RE
        AD SET UP
3225    ONERR  GOTO 6000
3230    PRINT D$;"OPEN ";N$
3240    PRINT D$;"POSITION ";N$;",R
        ";L
3250    PRINT D$;"READ ";N$
3260    INPUT W$
3265    PRINT W$
3270 N = N - 1
3280    IF N < > 0 THEN 3260
3290    GOTO 6050
```

Figure 15.30   Subroutine to read N words from a data file starting at location N.

In lines 3210 and 3215 the user enters the number of words, N, and the starting location, L, from the keyboard. Line 3220 calls the set up subroutine at line 4000 shown in Figure 15.25. After opening the file N$ in line 3230 the statement **PRINT D$; "POSITION ";N$;",R";L** in line 3240 will move the position pointer ahead from its present position by L records. Each data field in a sequential file is terminated by a carriage return character. Since we generated the word file by executing the statement **PRINT W$** in line 1350 of Figure 15.18, each word will be followed by a carriage return character (because there is no punctuation at the end of the PRINT statement), and therefore each word will be a separate data field.

The general form of using the POSITION command in a BASIC statement is **PRINT D$; "POSITION FILENAME,Rn"** where n is the relative number of fields to move the position pointer ahead.

When a file is opened, the position pointer is placed at the beginning of the first data field. If the filename is N$, the statement in line 3240 will advance the pointer by L fields, or words. Since L was decremented by one in line 3217, line 3240 would not move the position pointer at all if L was set to 1 in line 3215, and the first word in the file would be the first word read.

Line 3250 executes the DOS READ command, and lines 3260–3280 will read the next N lines. The program will then branch (in line 3290) to line 6050 in Figure 15.27 which will close the file N$ and then wait for any key to be pressed before returning to line 3090 in Figure 15.22.

Note that if the subroutine in Figure 15.30 tries to read past the end of the file, line 3225 will cause a branch to the error-handling routine in Figure 15.27. An example of executing the subroutine in Figure 15.30 is shown in Figure 15.31.

FIGURE 15.31 Example of reading N words starting at location L.

(a)

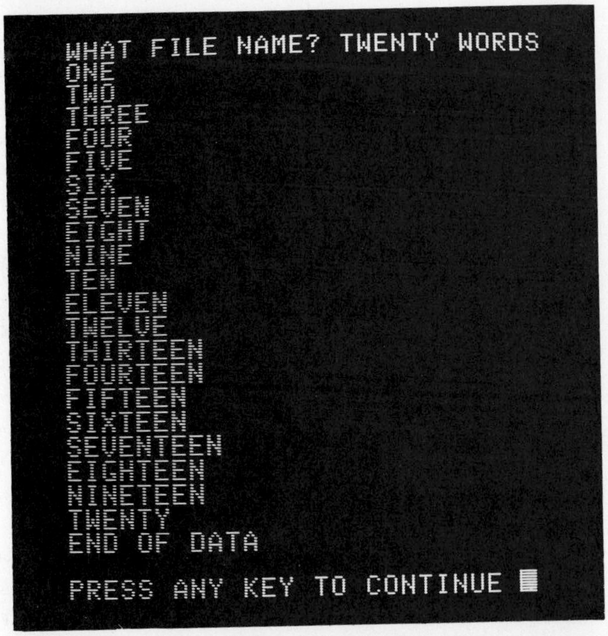

(b)

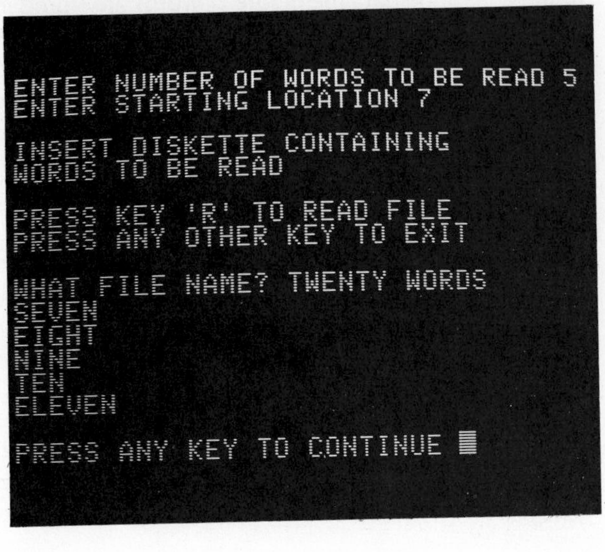

In order to read N words selected at random from the file N$, we might consider advancing the position pointer by P records each time we read a word, where P is some random integer. The subroutine shown in Figure 15.32 will do this. It is called in line 3080 in Figure 15.22 when key 3 is pressed. The user enters the number of words to be read in line 3310. The usual read set up subroutine in Figure 15.25 is called in line 3315.

```
]LIST3300-3450
3300   REM   READ N WORDS AT RANDOM

3305   HOME
3310   INPUT "ENTER NUMBER OF WORD
       S TO BE READ ";N
3315   GOSUB 4000: REM   READ SET U
       P
3320   ONERR   GOTO 6100
3325 R = 5
3330   X =  RND ( -  PEEK (78))
3340   PRINT D$;"OPEN ";N$
3350 P =  INT ( RND (1) * R)
3360   PRINT D$;"POSITION ";N$;",R
       ";P
3370   PRINT D$;"READ ";N$
3380   INPUT W$
3390   PRINT W$
3400 N = N - 1
3410   IF N <  > 0 THEN 3350
3420   PRINT D$;"CLOSE ";N$
3440   PRINT "PRESS ANY KEY TO CON
       TINUE";: GET A$
3450   RETURN
```

FIGURE 15.32 Subroutine to read N words at random.

Line 3330 sets a random seed for the random number generator. Line 3340 opens the file N$ which sets the position pointer at the beginning of the first word. Lines 3350–3410 form a loop that reads N words. Each time through the loop a random integer P between 0 and R is generated in line 3350. R is set to 5 in line 3325. You may change it to a larger value if you have a large data file. Line 3360 will advance the position pointer P words.

If the end of the data file is reached before N words are read, you don't want the END OF DATA message to be printed. Rather you would like to go back to the beginning of the file. This is accomplished with the new error-handling routine shown in Figure 15.33. This routine, located at line 6100, is called in the ONERR GOTO statement in line 3320, in Figure

```
JLIST6100-6140
6100    REM    RANDOM ERROR HANDLING
6105    CALL 768: REM    FIX STACK PR
        OBLEM
6110 EC =    PEEK (222)
6120    IF EC = 5 THEN 3340
6130    PRINT "ERROR NO. ";EC
6140    GOTO 3420
```

FIGURE 15.33 Error handling routine used with the random word reading subroutine in Fig. 15.32.

15.32. Note that if the INPUT statement in line 3380 tries to read past the end of the data file, the error code EC defined in line 6110 will be equal to 5 and line 6120 will branch back to the OPEN statement in line 3340. This will have the effect of moving the position pointer back to the beginning of the data file.

An example of reading N words at random using the subroutine in Figure 15.32 is shown in Figure 15.34.

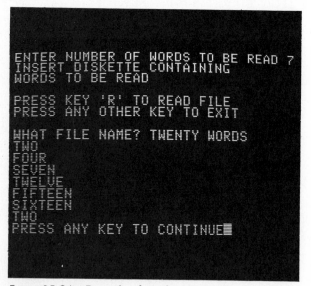

FIGURE 15.34 Example of reading N words at random.

Modified Hangman Program

Suppose you have created a data file called HANG-MAN WORDS that contains a large number of words (say 1000) using the program described earlier (see Figure 15.18). We saw in Figure 15.32 how to read N words at random from such a file. If the end of the file is reached in this subroutine before N words are read, the position pointer is moved to the beginning of the file again. This means that it would be possible to read the same word a second time. To avoid this we will try to read N words but will stop if the end of the file is reached. The position pointer will be moved by P records each time a word is read, where P is a random integer.

What range of values should the random integer P have? If you pick N words (say 50) equally spaced from a total of NT (say 1000) words, then you will pick one out of every NT/N words, and there will be NT/N-1 words between each one selected. If you picked a random number P between 0 and NT/N-1 you would seldom get much beyond the middle of the list before N words are selected. This is because the average of all the P values will be about (NT/N-1)/2. Therefore, in order to spread the N words out over all of the NT words, you can let P be a random number between 0 and 2*(NT/N-1).

To incorporate these ideas into the Hangman program, add the lines

15 N=0: I=RND(−PEEK(78)): DIM W$(50)
17 GOSUB 6500: REM STORE MACHINE CODE FOR ERROR CHECKING

to the main program shown in Figure 15.5. Then change the "find a word" subroutine given in Figure 15.14 to the subroutine shown in Figure 15.35. The first time this subroutine is called (or after N words have been used), the value of N will be 0 and lines 1020–1090 will be executed. These lines read another N random words from the disk file.

Line 1020 computes the value W=2*(NT/N−1) which will be the maximum value of the random integer P corresponding to the number of skipped words in the data file. The subroutine at line 1200, called in line 1025, reminds the user to load the data disk. Lines 1035–1040 open the data file HANGMAN WORDS.

The loop in lines 1045–1075 will read N words into the array W$(I) (line 1070). The position pointer is moved P words in line 1060 each time a word is read. A different random value of P between 0 and W is computed in line 1050 each time through the loop.

Inasmuch as P is "random," you cannot be sure that it will not have large enough values often enough to get to the end of the data file before N words are stored in W$(I). To test for this possibility the statement ONERR GOTO 1300 in line 1027 will cause the program to branch to line 1300 if it tries to read past the end of the data file. If this occurs, the number of words read to that point (I−1) is stored in N, and the program branches in line 1090, which closes the data file, and the subroutine continues at line 1100.

Once N words are read into the array W$(I), up to N Hangman games can be played before the disk has to be read again. If the value of N is not 0 when subroutine 1000 is entered, the program branches immediately to line 1100 where a random number I between 1 and N is computed. The new word W$ to be used in Hangman is the word stored in W$(I). Line 1110, after assigning W$(I) to W$, replaces the word in location I (which has just been used) by the word in

FIGURE 15.35 Modified Hangman subroutine that will find a word from a collection of words stored on a diskette.

```
]LIST1000-
1000   REM    FIND A WORD
1010   IF N < > 0 THEN 1100
1020 NT = 500:N = 50:W = 2 * (NT /
       N - 1)
1025   GOSUB 1200
1027   ONERR  GOTO 1300
1030 D$ =  CHR$ (13) +  CHR$ (4):
       REM  CTRL-D
1035   PRINT D$;"OPEN HANGMAN WORD
       S"
1045   FOR I = 1 TO N
1050 P =  INT (W * RND (1))
1060   PRINT D$;"POSITION HANGMAN
       WORDS,R";P
1067   PRINT D$;"READ HANGMAN WORD
       S"
1070   INPUT W$(I)
1075   NEXT I
1090   PRINT D$;"CLOSE HANGMAN WOR
       DS"
1100 I =  INT (N * RND (1) + 1)
1110 W$ = W$(I):W$(I) = W$(N)
1120 N = N - 1: RETURN
1130   RETURN
1200   REM  DISK MESSAGE
1210   VTAB 21: HTAB 3
1220   PRINT "INSERT DATA DISK"
1230   PRINT "PRESS ANY KEY TO CON
       TINUE";
1240   GET A$
1250   VTAB 21: HTAB 1: CALL  - 86
       8
1260   VTAB 22: HTAB 1: CALL  - 86
       8
1270   RETURN
1300   REM    ERROR HANDLING ROUTINE

1310   CALL 768: REM    FIX STACK
1320 EC =  PEEK (222)
1330   IF EC = 5 THEN N = I - 1: GOTO
       1090
1340   PRINT "ERROR NO. ";EC
1350   GOTO 1090
6500   REM   STORE MACHINE LANGUAGE
       CODE
6510   DATA  104,168,104,166,223,1
       54,72,152,72,96
6520   FOR A = 768 TO 777
6530   READ C
6540   POKE A,C
6550   NEXT A
6560   RETURN
```

location N. The value of N is then decremented by one in line 1120. This will insure that no word is used more than once, since each word is effectively removed from the list as it is used.

A sample run of the modified Hangman program using the subroutine in Figure 15.35 is shown in Figure 15.36.

FIGURE 15.36 Hangman program using words stored on disk.

(a)

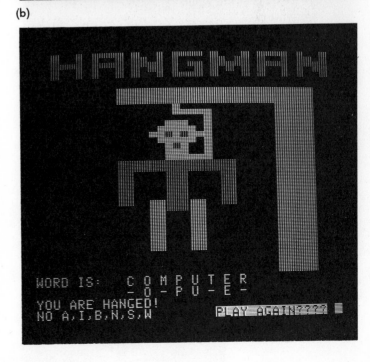

(b)

Storing Numbers in a Sequential File

The subroutine shown in Figure 15.18 stored words in a sequential file on a diskette. It is also possible to store numerical data on a diskette. To investigate this, substitute the line **1100 GOSUB 1400** in the subroutine in Figure 15.18 and then add the subroutine shown in Figure 15.37. This subroutine will store the numbers 1–10 on the disk. The important thing to remember when storing numerical data is that each numerical value must be followed by a carriage return character. This is why line 1430 is written as **PRINT I : PRINT I+1**. The form **PRINT I, I+1** will not work because the comma is not recognzied when writing to a disk file.

FIGURE 15.37   Subroutine to store numerical data on a diskette.

```
]LIST1400-1450
1400    REM   SAVE NUMERICAL DATA
1410    PRINT D$;"WRITE ";N$
1420    FOR I = 1 TO 10 STEP 2
1430    PRINT I: PRINT I + 1
1440    NEXT I
1450    RETURN
```

To read back the numerical data add the statements

3145 FOR I = 1 to 5
3150 INPUT X, Y
3160 PRINT X, Y
3165 NEXT I

to the subroutine in Figure 15.24. The resulting subroutine and its execution are shown in Figure 15.38. Note that the input statement **INPUT X,Y** will read two data fields and store the values in X and Y.

When writing programs that use disk files, you may find it useful to monitor the various DOS commands. You can do this by typing **MON C,I,O** in the immediate mode. When you then run the program, the computer will print all input, output, and DOS commands on the screen as they are executed. This can be very useful when debugging a program.

As an example, Figure 15.39 shows the screen display when the subroutine in Figure 15.37 is executed with MON C,I,O in effect. Figure 15.40 shows the screen display when the subroutine in Figure 15.38 is executed. To turn off this monitor mode, type **NOMON C,I,O**.

In the command MON C,I,O the letter C causes disk *commands* (such as OPEN, READ, and so on) to be monitored; the letter I causes *input* from the disk to be monitored; and the letter O causes *output* to the disk to be monitored. Any, or all, of these letters can be used with the MON command.

FIGURE 15.38   (a) Subroutine to read numerical data from a disk file.

```
]LIST3100-3170
3100    REM   READ ENTIRE FILE
3105    HOME
3110    GOSUB 4000: REM   READ SET U
     P
3120    ONERR  GOTO 6000
3130    PRINT D$;"OPEN ";N$
3140    PRINT D$;"READ ";N$
3145    FOR I = 1 TO 5
3150    INPUT X,Y
3160    PRINT X,Y
3165    NEXT I
3170    GOTO 3150
```

FIGURE 15.38   (b) Result of executing this subroutine.

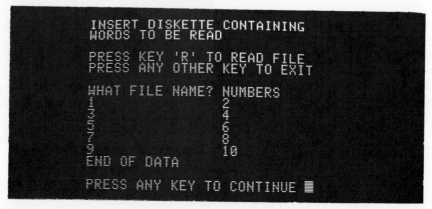

```
INSERT DISKETTE CONTAINING
WORDS TO BE READ

PRESS KEY 'R' TO READ FILE
PRESS ANY OTHER KEY TO EXIT

WHAT FILE NAME? NUMBERS
1              2
3              4
5              6
7              8
9              10
END OF DATA

PRESS ANY KEY TO CONTINUE ▊
```

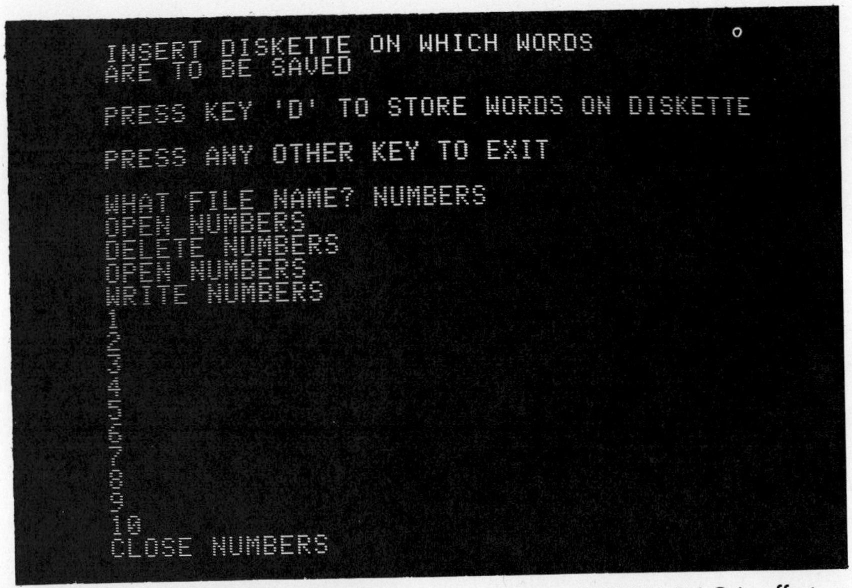

FIGURE 15.39 Executing the subroutine in Fig. 15.37 with MON C,I,O in effect.

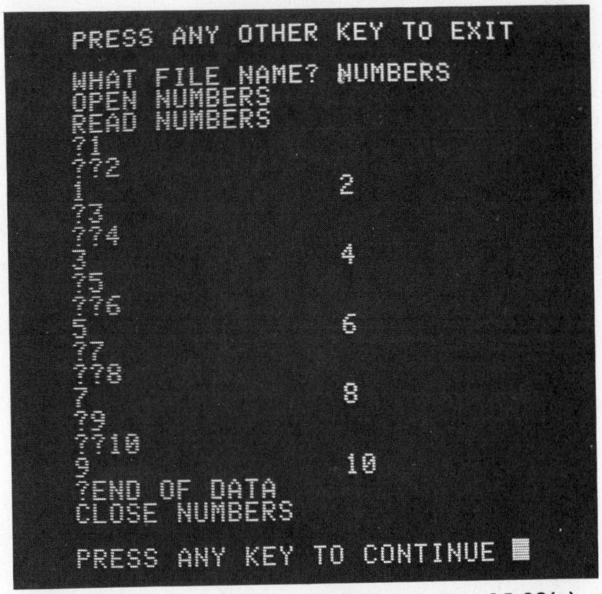

FIGURE 15.40 Executing the subroutine in Fig. 15.38(a) with MON C,I,O in effect.

In this chapter we have talked about *sequential* files. The Apple II computer can also store *random access* files on a diskette. For a discussion of random access files, see Appendix F.

APPLE II ORGAN

As another example of developing a BASIC program, we will turn the Apple II into a musical instrument. First we will learn how to play the notes of the scale by pressing keys on the keyboard, and then we will develop a complete program that will display the musical keys on the screen.

Playing a Tone When a Key is Pressed

You should review the section in Chapter 14 on making sounds with the Apple II. Recall that we must store a machine language speaker routine using the subroutine shown in Figure 15.41a, and then we can play a tone with pitch P and duration L by calling the subroutine at line 1000 shown in Figure 15.41b.

```
]LIST9000-
9000    REM    STORE SPEAKER ROUTINE
9010    DATA    160,0,174,0,3,173,48,
        192
9012    DATA    136,208,5,206,1,3,240
        ,5
9014    DATA    202,208,245,240,237,9
        6,256
9020 AD = 770
9030    READ X
9040    IF X = 256 THEN    RETURN
9050    POKE AD,X
9060 AD = AD + 1
9070    GOTO 9030
```

FIGURE 15.41 (a) Subroutine to store the machine language speaker routine and (b) subroutine to play a tone of pitch P and duration L.

```
]LIST1000-1020
1000    REM   PLAY NOTE WITH PITCH P
        AND DURATION L
1010    POKE 768,P: POKE 769,L
1020    CALL 770: RETURN
```

There is no easy way to tell when a key on the Apple II keyboard is released. This means that we will not be able to keep playing a note as long as a key is pressed. Rather, each note will be played for a fixed length of time L. A value of L=48 will correspond to an eighth note. Our organ will therefore play staccato music.

Add the following short main program to the subroutines given in Figure 15.41.

```
5 GOSUB 9000
10 P = 96 : L= 48
20 GET A$
30 GOSUB 1000 : GOTO 20
```

This program should play a short note each time any key is pressed. We must now make different keys play different notes.

Pitch Values for the Musical Scale

Before you can turn the Apple II into a musical instrument, you must know what pitch values P correspond to the notes of the musical scale. In Appendix E we show that the pitch P is related to the frequency F of the square wave going to the speaker by the equation $P = 50000/F$. Dividing a given value of P by 2 will double the frequency and result in a tone one octave higher. Dividing a value of P by 4 will result in a tone two octaves higher.

The frequencies and pitch values corresponding to the lowest octave on our Apple organ are given in Table 15.1. This table also lists the Apple II keys that we will use to correspond to the various notes. The keys along the middle row will be the "white" keys of the organ, and the keys in the row above will be used for sharps and flats (black keys).

TABLE 15.1 Frequencies and Pitch Values for the Musical Scale

Note	Frequency Hz	Pitch Value, P	Apple II key	
C	261.6	191	A	
$C^{\#}$ D^b	277.2	180		W
D	293.7	170	S	
$D^{\#}$ E^b	311.1	161		E
E	329.6	152	D	
F	349.2	143	F	
$F^{\#}$ G^b	370.0	135		T
G	392.0	128	G	
$G^{\#}$ A^b	415.3	120		Y
A	440.0	114	H	
$A^{\#}$ B^b	466.2	107		U
B	493.9	101	J	
C	523.3	96	K	
$C^{\#}$ D^b	554.4	90		O
D	587.3	85	L	
$D^{\#}$ E^b	622.3	80		P
E	659.3	76	;	

Screen Layout

The program we write will display 10 white keys and 7 black keys in high-resolution graphics according to the layout shown in Figure 15.42. The Apple II keys corresponding to each key on the screen will be printed on each key using a shape table for each letter. The words APPLE ORGAN will also be plotted using shape tables.

When a note is played, an eighth note will be displayed on the key being pressed for as long as the tone continues. As a song is played, this note will move from key to key. The shape of this note will be stored in a shape table.

The Apple organ will start out in octave 1. Pressing key 2 will change it to octave 2 (one octave higher), and pressing key 3 will change it to octave 3 (the next higher octave). Thus, the total range of the Apple organ will be over three octaves. For example, pressing key A on the Apple II keyboard when in the octave 2 mode will produce the same note as pressing key K when in the octave 1 mode. The octave number that is active at any time is displayed near the bottom of the screen.

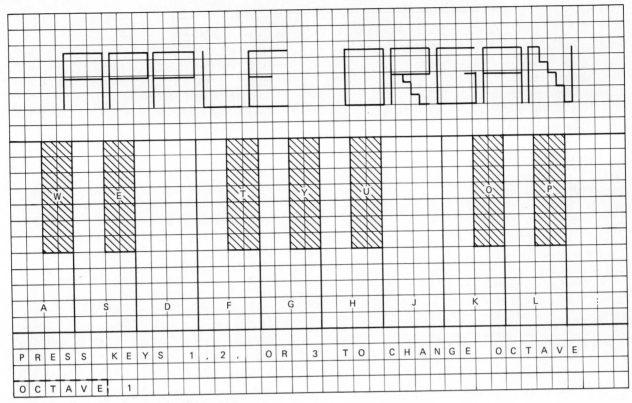

FIGURE 15.42 Screen layout for Apple organ.

Word-Description of Program

The program for the Apple organ can be understood from the pseudocode word-description given in Figure 15.43.

FIGURE 15.43 Pseudocode word-description for Apple II organ program.

Initialize variables; store shape tables; store speaker routine
Display keyboard
loop: Wait for key to be pressed
    Identify key
    if key is a note key
    then play note
    else if key is 1, 2, or 3
        then change octave number
repeat forever

Variable Definitions

The major variables used in the Apple organ program are defined in Figure 15.44. With these variables the pseudocode program shown in Figure 15.43 can be refined to that shown in Figure 15.45. Note how the *do until* loop is used to find the index I corresponding to

the key that was pressed. This value of I is then used to find the proper pitch which is stored in P%(I). If key 1, 2, or 3 is pressed, no match will occur in the *do until* loop, and I will equal 18. (Note that this is why K$(I) must be dimensioned to K$(18)). In this case I is changed to VAL(A$) (which will be 1, 2, or 3 for valid keys), and T is changed to 1, 2, or 4 corresponding to the new octave divisor.

We are now at the point where the BASIC program will practically write itself.

FIGURE 15.44 Major variables used in Apple II organ program.

K$(18)	—An array containing the Apple II key characters:
	—A,S,D,F,G,H,J,K,L,; for the white keys
	—W,E,T,Y,U,O,P for the black keys
P%(17)	—an integer array containing the pitch values for the corresponding keys in K$(I)
T	—octave divisor (equal to 1, 2, and 4 for octaves 1, 2, and 3)
P	—pitch value used in subroutine 1000
L	—duration of note used in subroutine 1000
A$	—character value corresponding to Apple II key pressed

FIGURE 15.45   Pseudocode description of Apple II organ program.

Fill arrays K$(I) and P%(I) with appropriate values
Store shape tables
Store speaker routine
Display keyboard
T = 1 : L = 48
loop: Wait for key A$ to be pressed
    I=1
    do until A$=K$(I) or I=18
        I=I+1
    enddo
    if I<18
    then P=P%(I)/T
      play note
    else I=VAL(A$)
      if I=0 or I>3
      then do nothing (invalid key)
      else if I=1 *then* T=1
          if I=2 *then* T=2
          if I=3 *then* T=4
repeat forever

The Main Program

The main program for the Apple organ is shown in Figure 15.46. It follows closely the pseudocode description shown in Figure 15.45. Lines 20–50 fill the arrays with the appropriate data. Note that all of the "white" keys are stored first in K$(I). Also note that the order of the pitch values stored in P%(I) is the same as the corresponding key values in K$(I) according to Table 15.1.

Lines 51–52 store tab data that will be used later (in subroutine 800) to plot the key labels. Line 53 stores the shape tables by calling subroutine 2000. For now simply type

2000 REM STORE SHAPE TABLE
2010 RETURN

Lines 70–170 are a direct implementation of the *loop . . . repeat forever* loop in Figure 15.45. Subroutine 1400 that is called in line 110 will play the note. Eventually this subroutine will display the eighth note on the screen keyboard before playing the note. However, for now you can test out the playing of the APPLE ogran by typing

1400 REM PLAY NOTE
1440 GOSUB 1000: REM PRODUCE TONE
1450 RETURN

```
]LIST-170
10   REM    APPLE II ORGAN
12   HIMEM: 36863
15   DIM K$(18),P%(17),TB%(7)
17   HOME : PRINT "STORING DATA --
     - BE PATIENT!!"
20   DATA  A,S,D,F,G,H,J,K,L,";",W
     ,E,T,Y,U,O,P
30   DATA  191,170,152,143,128,114
     ,101,96,85,76,180,161,135,12
     0,107,90,80
40   FOR I = 1 TO 17: READ K$(I): NEXT
50   FOR I = 1 TO 17: READ P%(I): NEXT
51   DATA  16,44,100,128,156,212,2
     40
52   FOR I = 1 TO 7: READ TB%(I): NEXT
53   GOSUB 2000: REM   STORE SHAPE
     TABLE
55   GOSUB 9000: REM   STORE SPEAKE
     R ROUTINE
60   GOSUB 600: REM   DISPLAY KEYBO
     ARD
65   T = 1:L = 48
70   VTAB 1: GET A$
75   IF A$ = "X" THEN   TEXT : HOME
     : END
80   I = 1
90   IF A$ = K$(I) OR I = 18 THEN
     110
100  I = I + 1: GOTO 90
110  IF I < 18 THEN P = P%(I) / T
     : GOSUB 1400: GOTO 70
120  I =   VAL (A$): IF I = 0 OR I >
     3 THEN 70
130  VTAB 24: HTAB 8: PRINT I;
140  IF I = 1 THEN T = 1: GOTO 70
150  IF I = 2 THEN T = 2: GOTO 70
160  IF I = 3 THEN T = 4
170  GOTO 70
```

FIGURE 15.46   Main program for Apple II organ.

which just calls the tone producing subroutine shown in Figure 15.41. You will also need to write the following stub for the keyboard display subroutine:

600 REM DISPLAY KEYBOARD
610 RETURN

Try running the program now.

Remaining Subroutines

Once you have the musical part of the Apple organ working, you can finish the Display Keyboard subroutine as shown in Figure 15.47. This subroutine will produce the keyboard shown in Figure 15.48 where the title and lettering on the keyboard are printed using subroutine 800 shown in Figure 15.49.

FIGURE 15.47 Subroutine to display the keyboard for the Apple organ.

```
]LIST600-730
600    REM    DISPLAY KEYBOARD
610    HOME : HGR : HCOLOR= 3
615    FOR Y = 63 TO 159
620    HPLOT 0,Y TO 278,Y: NEXT Y
625    HCOLOR= 0
630    FOR X = 27 TO 251 STEP 28
635    HPLOT X,64 TO X,159: NEXT X
640    Y = 64
650    FOR X = 14 TO 42 STEP 28
655    GOSUB 700: NEXT X
660    FOR X = 98 TO 154 STEP 28
665    GOSUB 700: NEXT X
670    FOR X = 210 TO 238 STEP 28
675    GOSUB 700: NEXT X
680    VTAB 22: HTAB 1
685    PRINT "PRESS KEYS 1,2, OR 3
       TO CHANGE OCTAVE"
690    PRINT : INVERSE : PRINT "OCT
       AVE";: NORMAL : PRINT " 1";
695    GOSUB 800: RETURN
700    REM  PLOT BLACK KEY AT X,Y
710    FOR I = 0 TO 12
720    HPLOT X + I,Y TO X + I,Y + 4
       8
730    NEXT I: RETURN
```

FIGURE 15.49 Subroutine to display the lettering on the organ keyboard.

```
]LIST800-910
800    REM   TITLE AND KEY LABELS
805    SCALE= 4: ROT= 0: HCOLOR= 3
810    X = 30:Y = 20:D = 20
815    DRAW 1 AT X,Y: REM  A
820    X = X + D: DRAW 17 AT X,Y: REM
       P
825    X = X + D: DRAW 17 AT X,Y: REM
       P
830    X = X + D: DRAW 9 AT X,Y: REM
       L
835    X = X + D: DRAW 12 AT X,Y: REM
       E
840    X = X + D * 2: DRAW 16 AT X,Y
       : REM  O
845    X = X + D: DRAW 18 AT X,Y: REM
       R
850    X = X + D: DRAW 5 AT X,Y: REM
       G
855    X = X + D: DRAW 1 AT X,Y: REM
       A
860    X = X + D: DRAW 19 AT X,Y: REM
       N
870    SCALE= 1:Y = 140
875    FOR I = 1 TO 10
880    X = 28 * I - 21
885    XDRAW I AT X,Y: NEXT I
890    Y = 100
895    FOR I = 1 TO 7
900    X = TB%(I)
905    XDRAW I + 10 AT X,Y: NEXT I
910    RETURN
```

FIGURE 15.48 The keyboard for the organ produced by the subroutine shown in Fig. 15.47.

TABLE 15.2   Shape Definitions used in the Apple organ program

SHAPE NO.

1	A:	2,2,2,2,2,2,4,4,4,4,4,4,5,5,5,5,6,6,6,2,2,2,4,4,4,7,7,7,7,8
2	S:	1,1,1,1,7,7,7,7,6,6,6,5,5,5,5,6,6,6,7,7,7,7,5,8
3	D:	6,6,6,6,6,6,5,5,5,4,5,4,4,4,4,7,4,7,7,7,8
4	F:	1,1,1,1,7,7,7,7,6,6,6,1,1,7,7,6,6,6,6,8
5	G:	1,1,1,1,7,7,7,7,6,6,6,6,6,6,5,5,5,5,4,4,4,7,7,8
6	H:	6,6,6,2,2,2,4,4,4,5,5,5,5,2,2,2,4,4,4,4,4,6,8
7	J:	1,1,1,1,6,6,6,6,6,6,7,7,7,7,4,6,8
8	K:	6,6,6,2,2,2,4,4,4,5,4,5,4,5,4,5,6,2,2,2,2,7,4,7,4,7,4,8
9	L:	6,6,6,6,6,6,5,5,5,5,7,8
10	; :	1,1,6,6,4,7,5,5,5,7,2,2,2,2,6,6,4,5,7,7,6,2,5,8
11	W:	6,6,6,6,6,6,5,5,4,4,4,5,2,2,5,5,4,4,4,4,4,6,8
12	E:	1,1,1,1,7,7,7,7,6,6,6,1,1,7,7,6,6,6,5,5,5,5,7,8
13	T:	5,5,1,1,7,7,6,6,6,6,6,6,4,8
14	Y:	6,5,6,5,2,2,2,2,4,4,4,4,5,4,5,4,6,8
15	U:	6,6,6,6,6,6,5,5,5,5,4,4,4,4,4,6,8
16	O:	6,6,6,6,6,6,5,5,5,5,4,4,4,4,4,7,7,7,7,8
17	P:	6,6,6,2,2,2,4,4,4,5,5,5,5,4,4,4,7,7,7,7,8
18	R:	6,6,6,2,2,2,4,4,4,5,5,5,5,4,4,4,7,7,7,7,2,2,2,2,1,6,5,6,5,6,5,7,8
19	N:	2,2,2,2,2,2,4,4,4,4,4,4,5,6,6,5,6,6,5,6,6,5,4,4,4,4,4,6,8
20	B:	5,5,5,6,5,6,7,6,3,3,5,5,6,5,5,6,7,6,7,7,7,4,4,4,4,4,8
21	C:	5,5,5,5,7,7,7,7,6,6,6,6,6,6,5,5,5,5,8
22	Eighth note:	6,5,2,4,4,4,5,4,2,6,6,6,6,6,5,4,4,4,4,4,6,1,6,6,6,4,1,4,
		4,4,4,4,4,4,4,4,4,4,4,6,1,6,5,6,5,6,6,8

The shape definitions used in this program are given in Table 15.2 and are stored in the Apple II memory using subroutine 1000 (called in line 53 of the main program) shown in Figure 15.50.

FIGURE 15.50   (a) Subroutine to store shape table.

```
]LIST2000-2125
2000   REM   STORE SHAPE TABLE
2005 S = 36864
2010 S1 =   INT (S / 256):S2 = S -
       S1 * 256
2015   POKE 232,S2: POKE 233,S1
2020   READ N:K = N
2025   POKE S,N: POKE S + 1,0
2030 M = S + 2 * (N + 1):S2 = S +
       2
2035 D = M - S
2040   IF D > 255 THEN 2055
2045   POKE S2,D: POKE S2 + 1,0
2050   GOTO 2065
2055 D1 =   INT (D / 256):D2 = D -
       D1 * 256
2060   POKE S2,D2: POKE S2 + 1,D1
2065 S2 = S2 + 2
2068   READ A
2070   IF A = 8 THEN 2110
2075   READ B
2080   IF B = 8 THEN 2100
2085 X = B * 8 + A
2090   POKE M,X:M = M + 1
2095   GOTO 2068
2100   POKE M,A:M = M + 1
2110   POKE M,0:M = M + 1
2115 K = K - 1
2120   IF K = 0 THEN   RETURN
2125   GOTO 2035
```

FIGURE 15.50   (b) Continuation of subroutine to store shape tables given in Table 15.4.

```
]LIST2130-2250
2130   DATA   22
2140   DATA   2,2,2,2,2,2,4,4,4,4,4
       ,4,5,5,5,5,6,6,6,2,2,2,4,4,4
       ,7,7,7,7,8: REM   A
2145   DATA   1,1,1,1,7,7,7,7,6,6,6
       ,5,5,5,5,6,6,6,7,7,7,7,5,8: REM
       S
2150   DATA   6,6,6,6,6,6,5,5,5,4,5
       ,4,4,4,4,7,4,7,7,7,8: REM   D
2155   DATA   1,1,1,1,7,7,7,7,6,6,6
       ,1,1,7,7,6,6,6,6,8: REM   F
2160   DATA   1,1,1,1,7,7,7,7,6,6,6
       ,6,6,6,5,5,5,5,4,4,4,7,7,8: REM
       G
2165   DATA   6,6,6,2,2,2,4,4,4,5,5
       ,5,5,2,2,2,4,4,4,4,4,6,8: REM
       H
2170   DATA   1,1,1,1,6,6,6,6,6,6,7
       ,7,7,7,4,6,8
2175   DATA   6,6,6,2,2,2,4,4,4,5,4
       ,5,4,5,4,5,6,2,2,2,2,2,7,4,7
       ,4,7,4,8: REM   K
2180   DATA   6,6,6,6,6,6,5,5,5,5,7
       ,8
2185   DATA   1,1,6,6,4,7,5,5,7,2,2
       ,2,2,6,6,4,5,7,7,6,2,5,8
2190   DATA   6,6,6,6,6,6,5,5,4,4,4
       ,6,2,2,5,5,4,4,4,4,4,6,8: REM
       W
2195   DATA   1,1,1,1,7,7,7,7,6,6,6
       ,1,1,7,7,6,6,6,5,5,5,5,7,8: REM
       E
```

```
2200   DATA  5,5,1,1,7,7,6,6,6,6,6
       ,6,4,8: REM   T
2205   DATA  6,5,6,5,2,2,2,2,4,4,4
       ,4,5,4,5,4,6,8: REM   Y
2210   DATA  6,6,6,6,6,6,5,5,5,5,4
       ,4,4,4,4,4,6,8
2215   DATA  6,6,6,6,6,6,5,5,5,5,4
       ,4,4,4,4,7,7,7,7,8
2220   DATA  6,6,6,2,2,2,4,4,4,5,5
       ,5,5,4,4,4,7,7,7,7,8: REM   R

2225   DATA  6,6,6,2,2,2,4,4,4,5,5
       ,5,5,4,4,4,7,7,7,7,2,2,2,1,6
       ,5,6,5,6,5,7,8: REM   R
2230   DATA  2,2,2,2,2,2,4,4,4,4,4
       ,4,5,6,6,5,6,6,5,6,6,5,4,4,4
       ,4,4,4,6,8: REM   N
2235   DATA  5,5,5,6,5,6,7,6,3,3,,
       5,5,6,7,6,7,7,7,4,4,4,4,4,4,
       8: REM   B
2240   DATA  5,5,5,5,7,7,7,7,6,6,6
       ,6,6,6,5,5,5,5,8
2250   DATA  6,5,2,4,4,4,5,4,2,6,6
       ,6,6,6,5,4,4,4,4,4,6,1,6,6,6
       ,4,1,4,4,4,4,4,4,4,4,4,4,4,4
       ,6,1,6,5,6,5,6,6,8: REM   NOT
     E
```

FIGURE 15.50   (b) (cont.)

The eighth note shape is displayed when a note is played using subroutine 1400 shown in Figure 15.51. The value of I in line 1410 is the value found in the "do until" loop in lines 90–100 of the main program. If this value is greater than 10, a "black" key was pressed, and the coordinates XN,YN at which the note will be plotted are determined in line 1420. The X position at which the note is XDRAWn in line 1430 is determined by the value in the tab array TB%(I–10) (line 1420) that was initialized in lines 51–52 in Figure 15.46. After displaying the eighth note in line 1430, the note is played in line 1440. The eighth note is then erased in line 1450.

FIGURE 15.51   Subroutine to display the eighth note and produce the tone.

```
]LIST1400-1460
1400   REM  PLAY NOTE
1410   IF I < 11 THEN YN = 135:XN =
       28 * I - 12: GOTO 1430
1420   YN = 90:XN = TB%(I - 10)
1430   XDRAW 22 AT XN,YN
1440   GOSUB 1000
1450   XDRAW 22 AT XN,YN
1460   RETURN
```

The coordinates XN,YN for plotting the note on the white keys are given in the THEN clause in line 1410. Since the spacing of the white keys is uniform, the position of the note on the line can be calculated by the equation XN=28*I–12 as given in line 1410. Examples of the eighth note that is displayed when the Apple organ is played are shown in Figure 15.52.

FIGURE 15.52   (a) Apple organ when playing a white note (key F). (b) apple organ when playing a black note (key T).

(a)

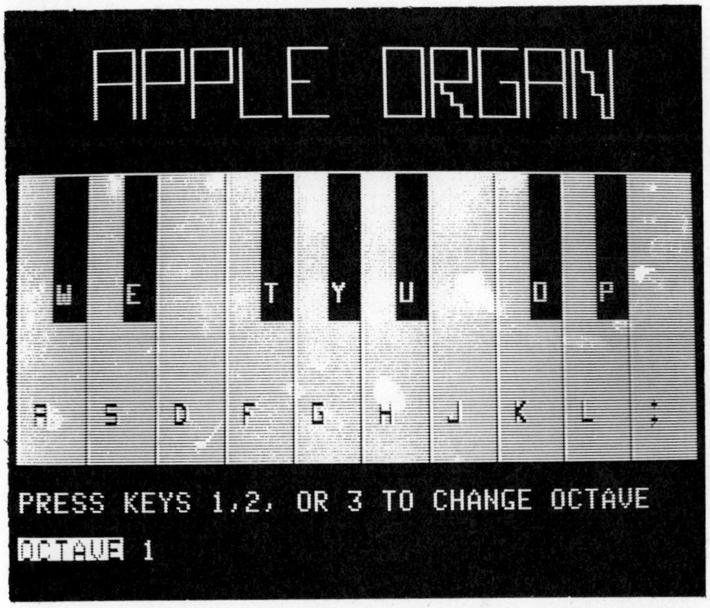

(b)

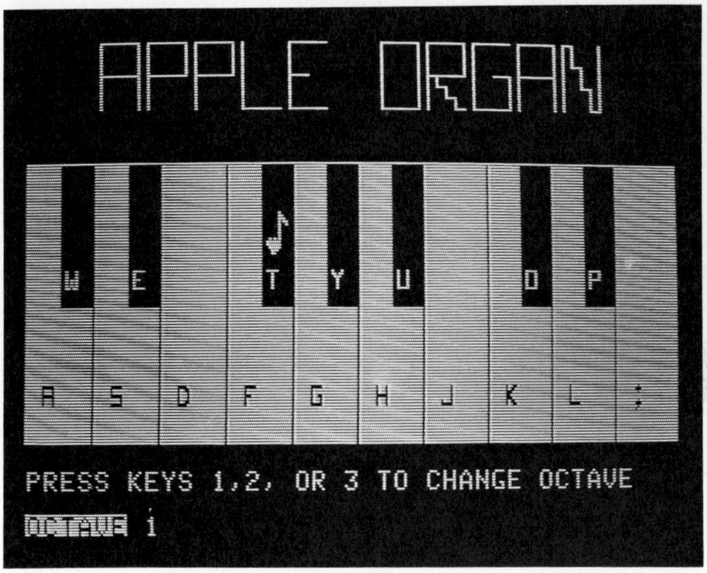

The Hangman and the APPLE organ programs were developed using the six steps outlined at the beginning of this chapter. This is not the only way to develop a program, and these steps may not always be appropriate for all the programs you write. However, they are a good guide to use when you get stuck and do not know how to proceed. In the last analysis you will have to develop your own approach to writing computer programs. Programming is a skill that still requires insight, creativity, a knack for problem solving, and *practice*.

If you have read this entire book, typed in all the examples on your Apple II, and worked a good number of exercises, you will have a fundamental understanding of how to write BASIC programs on an Apple II. It is now time for you to start writing your own. Many useful programs can be written for the Apple II. Pick an area in which you are an expert. How can the Apple II help you in this area? Start by writing a short program, and then expand it into a longer, more complex program. You will find that writing computer programs is challenging, rewarding, and fun. Good luck.

EXERCISE 15-1

Modify the subroutine for finding a word in Figure 15.14 so that no word is selected more than once.

EXERCISE 15-2

Write a program to play the game MASTERMIND®. The computer thinks of an N digit number where each digit can be in the range 1–M. The player is allowed to select N and M at the beginning of the game. The player guesses a number (all N digits), and the computer responds with two numbers P and W. P is the number of digits that were correctly guessed that are in the correct position in the number, and W is the number of digits guessed that are in the number but were guessed in the wrong position. The player continues to guess numbers until the number is guessed (or the player gives up and asks for the answer). When the number is guessed, the computer displays the number of tries that it took to guess the number.

EXERCISE 15-3

Write a program to play the card game Blackjack against the computer. The player first places a bet. Two cards are dealt to the player, and two cards are dealt to the computer (one face up and one face down). The player can ask for a hit (another card) as many times as he or she wants. The player's goal is to have a higher count than the computer without going over 21. Face cards count 10, and an ace can count either 1 or 11. Being dealt an ace and a face card is a blackjack and is an automatic winner. If the player's count goes over 21, it is a bust, and the player loses. After the player stops taking hits (with the card count less than or equal to 21), the computer turns over its face-down card and can then take additional cards to try to beat the player. The computer will always take a hit if its card count is less than 17. The computer will always stand for a card count of 17 or greater. No money is won or lost on a tie. Have the program continue playing and keep a running total of the player's winnings.

EXERCISE 15-4

Write a program to play tic-tac-toe (see Exercise 8-6). The player should have the option to play against a second player or the computer.

EXERCISE 15-5

Write a program that will store a song in a sequential file on a disk in the form P1, L1, P2, L2, P3, L3 . . . where P1 is the pitch of the first note, L1 is the length of the first note, and so on. Store several songs in different files. Write a separate program that will allow the user to select a song from a menu and will then read in the song from the disk and play it.

APPENDICES

APPENDIX A

Reserved Words

None of the following *reserved words* can be used as part of a variable name in an APPLESOFT BASIC program.

				LEN	PDL	RND	STR$
				LET	PEEK	ROT=	TAB(
				LIST	PLOT	RUN	TAN
				LOAD	POKE	SAVE	TEXT
				LOG	POP	SCALE=	THEN
ABS	COS	FOR	HLIN	LOMEN:	POS	SCRN(	TO
AND	DATA	FRE	HOME	MID$	PRINT	SGN	TRACE
ASC	DEF	GET	HPLOT	NEW	PR#	SHLOAD	USR
AT	DEL	GOSUB	HTAB	NEXT	READ	SIN	VAL
ATN	DIM	GOTO	IF	NORMAL	RECALL	SPC(	VLIN
CALL	DRAW	GR	IN#	NOT	REM	SPEED=	VTAB
CHR$	END	HCOLOR	INPUT	NOTRACE	RESTORE	SQR	WAIT
CLEAR	EXP	HGR	INT	ON	RESUME	STEP	XPLOT
COLOR=	FLASH	HGR2	INVERSE	ONERR	RETURN	STOP	XDRAW
CONT	FN	HIMEM:	LEFT$	OR	RIGHT$	STORE	

ASCII Codes

Character, C$ or Keystroke	ASC(C$)	Keystroke PEEK (−16384)	CTRL −	SA = Screen address POKE SA, A Inverse A	Flashing A	Normal A
Blank (space)	32	160		32	96	160
!	33	161		33	97	161
"	34	162		34	98	162
#	35	163		35	99	163
$	36	164		36	100	164
%	37	165		37	101	165
&	38	166		38	102	166
'	39	167		39	103	167
(	40	168		40	104	168
)	41	169		41	105	169
*	42	170		42	106	170
+	43	171		43	107	171
,	44	172		44	108	172
-	45	173		45	109	173
.	46	174		46	110	174
/	47	175		47	111	175
0	48	176		48	112	176
1	49	177		49	113	177
2	50	178		50	114	178
3	51	179		51	115	179
4	52	180		52	116	180
5	53	181		53	117	181
6	54	182		54	118	182
7	55	183		55	119	183
8	56	184		56	120	184
9	57	185		57	121	185
:	58	186		58	122	186
;	59	187		59	123	187
	60	188		60	124	188
=	61	189		61	125	189
	62	190		62	126	190
?	63	191		63	127	191
@	64	192	128	0	64	192
A	65	193	129	1	65	193
B	66	194	130	2	66	194
C	67	195	131	3	67	195
D	68	196	132	4	68	196
E	69	197	133	5	69	197
F	70	198	134	6	70	198
G	71	199	135	7	71	199
H	72	200	136	8	72	200
I	73	201	137	9	73	201
J	74	202	138	10	74	202
K	75	203	139	11	75	203
L	76	204	140	12	76	204
M	77	205	141	13	77	205
N	78	206	142	14	78	206
O	79	207	143	15	79	207
P	80	208	144	16	80	208
Q	81	209	145	17	81	209
R	82	210	146	18	82	210
S	83	211	147	19	83	211
T	84	212	148	20	84	212
U	85	213	149	21	85	213

Character, C$ or Keystroke	ASC(C$)	Keystroke PEEK (−16384)	CTRL −	SA = Screen address POKE SA, A Inverse A	Flashing A	Normal A
V	86	214	150	22	86	214
W	87	215	151	23	87	215
X	88	216	152	24	88	216
Y	89	217	153	25	89	217
Z	90	218	154	26	90	218
[	91			27	91	219
	92			28	92	220
] (shift-m)	93	221		29	93	221
	94	222		30	94	222
−	95			31	95	223
		136				
		149				
ESC		155				
RETURN		141				

APPENDIX C

ONERR GOTO Codes

Error code is stored in memory location 222.

EC = PEEK(222)

EC	ERROR
0	NEXT without FOR
1	LANGUAGE NOT AVAILABLE
2,3	RANGE ERROR
4	WRITE PROTECTED
5	END OF DATA
6	FILE NOT FOUND
7	VOLUME MISMATCH
8	I/O ERROR
9	DISK FULL
10	FILE LOCKED
11	SYNTAX ERROR
12	NO BUFFERS AVAILABLE
13	FILE TYPE MISMATCH
14	PROGRAM TOO LARGE
15	NOT DIRECT COMMAND
16	SYNTAX
22	RETURN without GOSUB
42	OUT OF DATA
53	ILLEGAL QUANTITY
69	OVERFLOW
77	OUT OF MEMORY
90	UNDEFINED STATEMENT
107	BAD SUBSCRIPT
120	REDIMENSIONED ARRAY
133	DIVISION BY ZERO
163	TYPE MISMATCH
176	STRING TOO LONG
191	FORMULA TOO COMPLEX
224	UNDEFINED FUNCTION
254	BAD RESPONSE TO INPUT STATEMENT
255	CTRL C INTERRUPT ATTEMPTED

APPENDIX D

Hexadecimal Numbers

Consider a box containing one marble. If the marble is in the box, we will say that the box is *full* and associate the digit 1 with the box. If we take the marble out of the box, the box will be empty, and we will then associate the digit 0 with the box. The two binary digits 0 and 1 are called *bits,* and with one bit we can count from zero (box empty) to one (box full) as shown in Figure D.1.

0 = empty box   1 = full box
Number of marbles = 0   Number of marbles = 1

FIGURE D.1   You can count from 0 to 1 with one bit.

Consider now a second box that can also be only full (1) or empty (0). However, when this box is full, it will contain *2* marbles as shown in Figure D.2. With these two boxes (two bits) we can now count from zero to three as shown in Figure D.3.

0 = empty box   1 = full box

FIGURE D.2   This box can contain either two marbles (full) or no marbles.

Total number of marbles

0

1

2

3

FIGURE D.3   You can count from 0 to 3 with two bits.

Note that the value of each two-bit binary number shown in Figure D.3 is equal to the total number of marbles in the two boxes.

We can add a third bit to the binary number by adding a third box that is full (bit=1) when it contains 4 marbles and is empty (bit=0) when it contains no marbles. It must be either full (bit=1) or empty (bit=0). With this third box (3 bits) we can count from 0 to 7 as shown in Figure D.4.

FIGURE D.4   You can count from 0 to 7 with three bits.

0

1

2

3

4

5

6

7

If you want to count beyond 7, you must add another box. How many marbles should this fourth box contain when it is full (bit=1)? It should be clear that this box must contain 8 marbles. The binary number 8 would then be written as **1000**. Remember that a 1 in a binary number means that the corresponding box is full of marbles, and the number of marbles that constitutes a full box varies as 1,2,4,8 starting at the right. This means that with four bits we can count from 0 to 15 as shown in Figure D.5.

FIGURE D.5   You can count from 0 to 15 with four bits.

| No. of Marbles in each box | | | | Total no. of marbles | Hex Digit |
8	4	2	1		
0	0	0	0	0	0
0	0	0	1	1	1
0	0	1	0	2	2
0	0	1	1	3	3
0	1	0	0	4	4
0	1	0	1	5	5
0	1	1	0	6	6
0	1	1	1	7	7
1	0	0	0	8	8
1	0	0	1	9	9
1	0	1	0	10	A
1	0	1	1	11	B
1	1	0	0	12	C
1	1	0	1	13	D
1	1	1	0	14	E
1	1	1	1	15	F

It is convenient to represent the total number of marbles in the four boxes represented by the four bit binary numbers shown in Figure D.5 by a single digit. We call this a *hexadecimal* digit, and the sixteen hexadecimal digits are shown in the right-hand column of Figure D.5. The hexadecimal digits 0–9 are the same as the decimal digits 0–9. However, the decimal numbers 10–15 are represented by the hexadecimal digits A–F. Thus, for example, the hexadecimal digit D is equivalent to the decimal number 13.

To count beyond 15 in binary you must add more boxes. Each full box you add must contain twice as many marbles as the previous full box. With eight bits you can count from 0 to 255. A few examples are shown in Figure D.6. Given a binary number, the corresponding decimal number is equal to the total number of marbles in all of the boxes. To find this number just add up all of the marbles in the full boxes (the ones with binary digits = 1).

FIGURE D.6   You can count from 0 to 255 with eight bits.

| No. of marbles in each box | | | | | | | | Total no. of marbles |
128	64	32	16	8	4	2	1	
0	0	1	1	0	1	0	0	52
1	0	1	0	0	0	1	1	163
1	1	1	1	1	1	1	1	255

As the length of a binary number increases, it becomes more cumbersome. We then use the corresponding *hexadecimal number* as a shorthand method of representing the binary number. This is very easy to do. You just divide the binary number into groups of four bits starting at the right and then represent each four-bit group by its corresponding hexadecimal digit given in Figure D.5. For example, the binary number

$$\underline{1001}\,\underline{1010}$$

$$9 \qquad A$$

is equivalent to the hexadecimal number 9A. You should verify that the total number of marbles represented by this binary number is 154. However, instead of counting the marbles in the "binary boxes" you can count the marbles in "hexadecimal" boxes where the first box contains A*1=10 marbles and the second box contains 9×16=144 marbles. Therefore, the total number of marbles is equal to 144+10=154.

A third hexadecimal box would contain a multiple of 16^2=256 marbles, and a fourth hexadecimal number would contain a multiple of 16^3=4,096 marbles. As an example of the 16 bit binary number

$$\underline{1000}\,\underline{0111}\,\underline{1100}\,\underline{1001}$$

$$8 \qquad 7 \qquad C \qquad 9$$

is equivalent to the decimal number 34,761, that is, it represents 34,761 marbles. This can be seen by expanding the hexadecimal number as follows:

$$
\begin{aligned}
8 \times 16^3 &= 8 \times 4{,}096 = 32{,}768 \\
7 \times 16^2 &= 7 \times 256 = 1{,}792 \\
C \times 16^1 &= 12 \times 16 = 192 \\
9 \times 16^0 &= 9 \times 1 = \underline{\quad 9} \\
& 34{,}761
\end{aligned}
$$

You can see that by working with hexadecimal numbers you can reduce by a factor of 4 the number of digits that you have to work with.

The following table will allow you to conveniently convert up to four digit hexadecimal numbers to their decimal equivalent. Note, for example, how the four terms in the conversion of 87C9 given above can be read directly from the table.

HEXADECIMAL AND DECIMAL CONVERSION

15	BYTE		8	7	BYTE		0
15	CHAR	12	11	CHAR	8	7	CHAR	4	3	CHAR	0

HEX	DEC	HEX	DEC	HEX	DEC	HEX	DEC
0	0	0	0	0	0	0	0
1	4,096	1	256	1	16	1	1
2	8,192	2	512	2	32	2	2
3	12,288	3	768	3	48	3	3
4	16,384	4	1,024	4	64	4	4
5	20,480	5	1,280	5	80	5	5
6	24,576	6	1,536	6	96	6	6
7	28,672	7	1,792	7	112	7	7
8	32,768	8	2,048	8	128	8	8
9	36,864	9	2,304	9	144	9	9
A	40,960	A	2,560	A	160	A	10
B	45,056	B	2,816	B	176	B	11
C	49,152	C	3,072	C	192	C	12
D	53,248	D	3,328	D	208	D	13
E	57,344	E	3,584	E	224	E	14
F	61,440	F	3,840	F	240	F	15

APPENDIX E

Machine Language Subroutine to Produce a Tone on the Apple II Speaker

The assembly language subroutine shown in Figure E.1 will produce a tone of pitch P and duration L on the Apple II speaker. A hex value of P between 00 and FF is stored in location 300 (hex). A hex value of L is stored in location 301. The subroutine begins at hex address 302.

Index register Y counts continually from FF to 00 at address 30A. Index register X counts down from P to 0 at address 312. When X decrements to zero, a half-cycle is complete, and the program branches back to

```
                        ;          MUSIC TONE
                        ;
                        P      EQU 300
                        L      EQU 301
                               ORG 302
0302-   A0 00      NOTE  LDY # $00
0304-   AE 00 03   N1    LDX P           ;X=PITCH
0307-   AD 30 C0         LDA $C030       ;TOGGLE SPEAKER
030A-   88         N2    DEY             ;COUNT TO 256
030B-   D0 05            BNE N3
030D-   CE 01 03         DEC L           ;IF TONE DONE
0310-   F0 05            BEQ N4          ;THEN EXIT
0312-   CA         N3    DEX             ;ELSE COUNT PITCH TIME
0313-   D0 F5            BNE N2
0315-   F0 ED            BEQ N1          ;END OF HALF-CYCLE
0317-   60         N4    RTS
```

N1 where P is reloaded with the pitch value, and the speaker is toggled again. After Y is decremented 256 times the value of L (location 301) is decremented once. When L goes to zero the subroutine is exited, and the tone stops.

When Y is non-zero the loop from 30A to 313 takes 10 clock cycles. For a 1 MHz clock the period of a half-cycle of the sound wave will then be $10 \times P$ microseconds. The period of a full cycle will be $20 \times P$ microseconds, and the frequency of the sound wave will then be

$$\text{freq.} = \frac{1}{\text{period}}$$

$$= \frac{1}{20*P \text{ microseconds}}$$

$$= \frac{10^6}{20*P}$$

$$\text{from which } P = \frac{50,000}{\text{freq}}$$

Every time Y decrements to zero the statements at addresses 30D and 310 take 9 microseconds to execute. Therefore, the total time required for Y to decrement 256 times is (neglecting the extra 11 microseconds that occur every time the speaker toggles)

256*10 microseconds + 9 microseconds = 2.569 milliseconds

The duration of the tone will therefore be approximately 2.569*L milliseconds.

APPENDIX F

Random Access Files

The use of sequential files was described in Chapter 15. A sequential file consists of a series of data fields, each of which ends with a RETURN character. The length of the data field varies from one field to the next. Storage space is used efficiently in sequential files, but one needs to search through the file sequentially to find a particular data field. When fast access to a particular data entry is required, random access files can be used.

Random access files store data in *fixed length records* within the file. You must specify the length of the record in bytes when you open the file. You do this by adding a length parameter, L, to the OPEN statement in the form **PRINT D$; "OPEN FILENAME, L150"**. This OPEN statement specifies a random access file named FILENAME containing 150-byte long records.

Within each record of a random access file you can store a sequence of data entries, each ending with the RETURN character, as in a sequential file. You can store data in a particular record within a random access file by adding a record number parameter, R, to the DOS WRITE statement. For example, to store data in record number 5 you would use the statement **PRINT D$; "WRITE FILENAME, R5"**. Subsequent PRINT statements would store data in the random access file named FILENAME beginning with the first byte of record number 5. The first record in a file is assigned record number 0.

You can read data from a particular record in a random access file by adding the R parameter to the

DOS READ command. For example, the statement **PRINT D$; "READ FILENAME, R7"** will cause subsequent INPUT statements to read data starting with the first byte of record number 7.

Random access files do not use disk storage space very efficiently because each record is assigned the same number of bytes specified by the L parameter in the OPEN statement. As long as you never write more than this specified number of bytes into any record, you will not have any problems. If you do write too many bytes into a record, you will overwrite the next record and cause some of your data to be lost.

APPENDIX G

Initializing Your Diskette

To initialize a new diskette you must create a HELLO file that will be executed each time you turn on the Apple II with your diskette in the disk drive. To do this type

```
NEW
10 PRINT "your name"
20 PRINT "date"
```

Use your name and today's date in the above PRINT statements. If you RUN this program it will just print your name and today's date. You can include additional PRINT statements if you wish.

Now type **INIT HELLO**. The disk drive will whir for a minute or two while it is initializing your disk. When the blinking cursor returns to the screen, you can type **CATALOG**. The file HELLO should be listed in your directory. If you turn off the Apple II and then turn it back on with your new disk in the disk drive, it should boot up and display your HELLO message (your name and date) on the screen.

APPENDIX H

Using Machine Language Subroutines with BASIC

This appendix assumes that you know how to write 6502 assembly language programs. If you have a machine language subroutine there are two ways that you can access this subroutine from a BASIC program. The first is to use the **CALL** command, discussed in Chapter 14, and the second is to use the **USR** function.

The BASIC command **CALL Addr** will transfer control to a machine language program starting at the decimal address **Addr**. This command can be used in either the immediate mode or the deferred mode. When the machine language subroutine executes an RTS instruction, control will return to the calling BASIC program.

Data values can be passed to and from a machine language subroutine by using the **USR** function. When the BASIC statement **X=USR(A)** is executed the value of A is placed in the floating point accumulator in the hex locations $9D–$A3, and control is then transferred to location $000A where a JMP instruction to your machine language program must be executed. Thus, $4C (JMP) must be placed in location $000A and the starting address of your machine language subroutine must be placed in locations $000B (LSB) and $000C (MSB).

Within the machine language subroutine the floating point value of A can be converted to a 16-bit integer value by executing a built-in floating-to-integer subroutine at location $E10C using **JSR $E10C**. After executing this subroutine the high order byte of A is in location $00A0 and the low order byte is in location $00A1. This integer value can then be used in your machine language subroutine.

When your machine language subroutine executes an RTS instruction, the floating point number currently stored in the floating point accumulator will be assigned to the function **USR**. That is, it will become the value of X in the statement X=USR(A). In order to pass a 16-bit integer value, V, back to the BASIC program, store the most significant byte in accumulator A, the least significant byte in index register Y, and execute **JSR $E2F2** which is a built-in interger-to-floating subroutine. Then execute an RTS instruction which will return control to the BASIC program with the value of **USR** equal to the original 16-bit integer value V.

Appendices 179

APPENDIX I

Summary of BASIC Statements

The following summary gives examples of using various statements in Applesoft BASIC. For a more detailed discussion of each statement refer to the pages cited.

Data Transfer Statements	Page
PRINT A$; B, C	27
INPUT "ENTER VALUE"; C	39
GET A$	46
READ A, B, C$	84
DATA 5, 10, JOE	84
RESTORE	85
PRINT D$; "OPEN FILENAME"	156
PRINT D$; "WRITE FILENAME"	157
PRINT D$; "READ FILENAME"	159
PRINT D$; "CLOSE FILENAME"	158
PRINT D$; "APPEND FILENAME"	158
PRINT D$; "POSITION FILENAME, R5"	160
POKE 768, 75	133
X = PEEK(1024)	132

Branching and Looping Statements	Page
GOTO 40	18
IF M1>M2 THEN PRINT "TOO SMALL": GOTO 20	47
FOR I=1 TO 10: PRINT I: NEXT I	69
GOSUB 500	77
RETURN	77
ON I GOSUB 100,200,300	156
ON NH GOTO 960,965,970,975,980,985	153
ONERR GOTO 9000	159
CALL -936	142

String Related Statements	Page
B$ = LEFT$(A$, I)	101
B$ = RIGHT$(A$, I)	101
B$ = MID$(A$, I, J)	102
B$ = MID$(A$, I)	102
N = LEN(A$)	102
N = VAL(A$)	102
A$ = STR$(A)	103
N = ASC(A$)	104
A$ = CHR$(A)	105

BASIC Functions		Page
Z = SQR(X)	square root	33
Z = ABS(X)	absolute value	34
Z = INT(X)	integer value	34
Z = SGN(X)	sign	34
Z = PDL(1)	paddle function	34
X = RND(1)	random number	35

		Page
Z = SIN(X)	sine	36
Z = COS(X)	cosine	36
Z = TAN(X)	tangent	36
Z = ATN(X)	arctangent	36
Z = LOG(X)	natural logarithm	36
Z = EXP(X)	exponential function	36
DEF FNA(R) = π*R 2	define user function	38

Low Resolution Graphics Statements	Page
GR	9
COLOR = 15	9
PLOT X,Y	10
HLIN X1, X2 AT Y	12
VLIN Y1, Y2 AT X	12
TEXT	12

High Resolution Graphics Statements	Page
HGR	114
HGR2	138
HCOLOR = 3	114
HPLOT X1, Y1 TO X2, Y2	115
ROT = 0	125
SCALE = 1	125
DRAW 1 AT X, Y	125
XDRAW 1 AT X, Y	127

Other Statements and Commands	Page
DIM A(20, B$(3,15)	94
? FRE(1)	95
NEW	17
SAVE	17
LOAD	17
RUN	18
CONT	18
STOP	19
END	19
LIST	21
REM REMARK	20
CLEAR	95
FLASH	32
INVERSE	32
NORMAL	32
HIMEN: 30399	141
LOMEN: 16384	140
VTAB 12	29
HTAB 23	30
SPC	28
TAB	29
HOME	4

INDEX